The Umbilical Cord Blood Controversies in Medical Law

Since the therapeutic value of umbilical cord blood (UCB) stem cells was first recognised in the late 1980s, there has been a proliferation of both public and private UCB banks worldwide. However, the ability to utilise such a potentially valuable resource has provoked a number of controversies. In a distinctly accessible style, this book unpacks the socio-legal implications of the UCB collection process and constructs a detailed analysis of the law and ethics that surrounds UCB banking in the UK, including ownership of the cells. Its enquiry is located within the theoretical framework of altruism versus self-interest and explores the notions of risk and choice associated with this distinctive blend of public/private healthcare provision. The book evaluates the impact of the Human Tissue Act 2004 and the European Union Tissues and Cells Directive (2004/23/EC) on the UCB industry and provides a unique insight into the effect that the law may have on the NHS whose maternity staff and premises are used to collect UCB. This book would be of interest primarily to a UK readership in addition to expectant families, health professionals, students, academics, practitioners and the UCB industry elsewhere in the world.

Dr Karen Devine is a senior lecturer at the University of Kent teaching on the Medical Law and Ethics and Obligations modules. Her research interests lie in the legal and ethical aspects of bio-banking, clinical negligence and the relationship between legal obligations, autonomy, choice and consent.

Biomedical Law and Ethics Library

Series Editor: Sheila A.M. McLean

Scientific and clinical advances, social and political developments and the impact of healthcare on our lives raise profound ethical and legal questions. Medical law and ethics have become central to our understanding of these problems, and are important tools for the analysis and resolution of problems – real or imagined.

In this series, scholars at the forefront of biomedical law and ethics contribute to the debates in this area, with accessible, thought-provoking, and sometimes controversial, ideas. Each book in the series develops an independent hypothesis and argues cogently for a particular position. One of the major contributions of this series is the extent to which both law and ethics are utilised in the content of the books, and the shape of the series itself.

The books in this series are analytical, with a key target audience of lawyers, doctors, nurses, and the intelligent lay public.

Available titles:

The Legitimacy of Medical Treatment
What role for the medical exception?
Sara Fovargue and Alexandra Mullock

Pregnancy, Property and Personhood
Mary Neal

Revisiting the Regulation of Human Fertilisation and Embryology
Kirsty Horsey

Pioneering Healthcare Law
Essays in honour of Margaret Brazier
Catherine Stanton, Sarah Devaney, Anne-Marree Farrell and Alexandra Mullock

End of Life Decision Making for Critically Impaired Infants
Resource allocation and difficult decisions
Neera Bhatia

Autonomy and Pregnancy
A comparative analysis of compelled obstetric intervention
Samantha Halliday

The Ethical and Legal Consequences of Posthumous Reproduction
Arrogance, avarice and anguish
Browne Lewis

The Umbilical Cord Blood Controversies in Medical Law

Karen Devine

Routledge
Taylor & Francis Group
LONDON AND NEW YORK

First published 2017
by Routledge

2 Park Square, Milton Park, Abingdon, Oxfordshire OX14 4RN
52 Vanderbilt Avenue, New York, NY 10017

Routledge is an imprint of the Taylor & Francis Group, an informa business

First issued in paperback 2020

British Library Cataloguing in Publication Data
A catalogue record for this book is available from the British Library

Library of Congress Cataloging in Publication Data
Names: Devine, Karen, author.
Title: The umbilical cord blood : controversies in medical law / Karen Devine.
Description: Abingdon, Oxon [UK] ; New York : Routledge, 2017. |
Series: Biomedical law and ethics library
Identifiers: LCCN 2016029647 | ISBN 978-1-138-84088-1 (hbk) |
ISBN 978-1-315-73259-6 (ebk)
Subjects: LCSH: Biomedical engineering—Law and legislation. | Genetic engineering—Law and legislation. | Human experimentation in medicine—Law and legislation. | Human experimentation in medicine—Moral and ethical aspects. | Fetal blood—Transplantation—Moral and ethical aspects. | Stem cells—Transplantation—Moral and ethical aspects. | Blood banks—Law and legislation. | Fetal blood—Therapeutic use. | Hematopoietic stem cells. | Informed consent (Medical law)
Classification: LCC K3611.G46 D48 2017 | DDC 344.04/196—dc23
LC record available at https://lccn.loc.gov/2016029647

ISBN: 978-1-138-84088-1 (hbk)
ISBN: 978-0-367-59547-0 (pbk)

Typeset in Galliard
by FiSH Books Ltd, Enfield

For Molly and Nancy

Contents

List of abbreviations ix
Table of cases xi
Acknowledgements xvi

Introduction 1
Premise of the book 5
Chapter outlines – the umbilical cord blood controversies 6

1 **Background to the controversies** 11
Cord blood use – setting the scene 11
The benefits of cord blood over bone marrow 15
Using PGD and TT techniques to procure specific cord blood 19
Cord blood as a resource and the problem of its availability within the NHS 24
Unravelling the (dis)cord: private cord blood use and the sceptics 31
Conclusion 35

2 **The risks of cord blood collection** 37
Scientific risks 38
Practical risks 43
Legal risks – an overview 51
Conclusion 61

3 **The rise of the cord blood industry** 63
Public banks 64
Private banks 66
Public versus private banks 72
Altruism, self-interest and UCB donor motivations 73
'Mixed banking' – the Virgin Health Bank 81

UCB collection, the EUTCD and the Human Tissue Regulations 2007 *87*
Third party liability *94*
Vicarious liability *97*
Conclusion *98*

4 Cord blood and the role of informed consent in law in the UK 100
Cord blood collection and the role of informed consent *103*
Consent and the Human Tissue Act 2004 *104*
Information provision, knowledge and understanding *108*
Cord blood collection, consent and the competent minor *115*
Conclusion *118*

5 Cord blood and the standards of care in negligence in the UK 120
The standard of care in negligence – Bolam *examined* *120*
Sidaway *and the 'significance' of risk disclosure in cord blood collection* *125*
The long road to Chester *128*
Causation, public policy and the 'fairness' of Fairchild *132*
The Montgomery *milestone* *134*
Conclusion *140*

6 Cord blood ownership 142
The property law model and rights over cord blood *145*
The curious case of John Moore's spleen *151*
'Application of work and skill' and the use of cord blood *153*
Yearworth, *'the right to use' and the generation of cord blood* *157*
Disputed cord blood rights and 'best interests' *162*
Contract and bailment – an alternative course of action for damaged UCB? *166*
'Loss of chance' claims in property-based cord blood claims *168*
Conclusion *170*

Concluding remarks 175

Bibliography 179
Index 201

List of abbreviations

AAP	American Academy of Pediatrics
ACA	Affordable Care Act
ACOG	American Congress of Obstetricians and Gynecologists
ANC	Absolute neutrophil count
ART	Assisted reproductive technologies
ASA	Advertising Standards Authority
BAME	Black, Asian and Minority Ethnic
BBMR	British Bone Marrow Registry
BCBB	Belfast Cord Blood Bank
BMJ	*British Medical Journal*
CA	Court of Appeal
CNST	Clinical Negligence Scheme for Trusts
DH	Department of Health
DHSS	Department of Health and Social Security
DI	Designated Individual
EBMT	European Society for Blood and Marrow Transplantation
ECHR	European Convention on Human Rights
EGE	European Group on Ethics in Science and New Technologies
ES cells	Embryonic stem cells
EUTCD	European Union Tissues and Cells Directive
FACT	Foundation for the Accreditation of Cellular Therapy
GMC	General Medical Council
GVHD	Graft-versus-host disease
HA	Health Authority
HFEA	Human Fertilisation and Embryology Authority
HIE	Hypoxic-ischemic encephalopathy
HLA	Human leukocyte antigens
HRA	Human Rights Act
HSCs	Haematopoietic stem cells
HTA	Human Tissue Authority
IOM	Institute of Medicine
iPSCs	Induced pluripotent stem cells
ISCT	International Society for Cellular Therapy

IVF	In-vitro fertilisation
IVH	Intraventricular haemorrhage
JACIE	Joint Accreditation Committee of the ISCT and EBMT
LH	Licence Holder
ME	Myalgic encephalomyelitis
MRC	Medical Research Council
MSCs	Mesenchymal stem cells
NHS	National Health Service
NHSBT	NHS Blood and Transplant
NHSCBB	NHS Cord Blood Bank
NHSLA	NHS Litigation Authority
NIBTS	Northern Ireland Blood Transfusion Service
NICE	National Institute for Health and Care Excellence
NIH	National Institutes of Health
NMC	Nursing and Midwifery Council
OFT	Office of Fair Trading
PGD	Pre-implantation genetic diagnosis
PTSD	Post-traumatic stress disorder
QALY	Quality Adjusted Life Year
PPACA	Patient Protection and Affordable Care Act
PPH	Post-partum haemorrhage
RCM	Royal College of Midwives
RCOG	Royal College of Obstetricians and Gynaecologists
REC	Research Ethics Committee
SCI	Spinal cord injury
SNBTS	Scottish National Blood Transfusion Service
SNCBB	Scottish National Cord Blood Bank
TNC	Total nuclear cell
TT	Tissue Typing
UCB	Umbilical cord blood
VHB	Virgin Health Bank

Table of cases

A (a child) v Ministry of Defence [2004] EWCA Civ 641.
A (a minor) and B (a minor) by C (their mother and next friend) v A Health and Social Services Trust [2010] NIQB 108.
A v East Kent Hospitals University NHS Foundation Trust [2015] EWHC 1038 (QB).
A v Hoare [2008] UKHL 6.
AB v Leeds Teaching Hospital NHS Trust [2004] EWHC 644.
Adams v Bracknell Forest BC [2004] UKHL 29.
Al Hamwi v Johnson and Another [2005] EWHC 206.
Allied Maples Group v Simmons and Simmons [1995] 1 WLR 1602.
Attia v British Gas [1998] 1 QB 304.

Bailey (by her father and litigant friend) v MOD and another [2008] EWCA Civ 883.
Bannerman v White (1861) 10 CB NS 844.
Bentley (Dick) Productions Ltd v Harold Smith (Motors) [1965] 1 WLR 932, HL.
Birch v University London College Hospital NHS Foundation Trust [2008] EWHC 2237 (QB).
Bisset v Wilkinson (1927) AC 177.
Blyth v Bloomsbury Health Authority [1993] 4 Med LR 151.
Bolam v Friern Hospital Management Committee [1957] 2 All ER 118.
Bolitho v City and Hackney Health Authority [1998] AC 232.
Bonnington Castings v Wardlaw [1956] AC 613.
Bull v Devon Area Health Authority [1993] 4 Med LR 117.

Canterbury v Spence (1972) 464 F 2d 772.
Caparo Industries v Dickman [1990] 2 AC 605.
Carlill v Carbolic Smoke Ball Company [1893] 1 QB 256, 57 JP 325, CA.
Cassidy v Ministry of Health [1951] 2 KB 343.
Catalona v Washington University 128 S Ct 1122, 169 L Ed 2d 949 (2008).
Chaplin v Hicks [1911] 2 KB 786.
Chatterton v Gerson [1981] QB 432.

Chester v Afshar [2000] WL 33201379.
Chester v Afshar [2004] UKHL 41.
Coggs v Bernard (1703) 92 E.R. 107.

Director of Public Prosecutions v Smith [2006] EWHC 94 (Admin).
Dixon v Clement Jones Solicitors [2004] EWCA Civ 1005.
Dobson v North Tyneside Health Authority [1996] 4 All ER 479.
Donoghue v Stevenson [1932] AC 562 15.
Doodeward v Spence (1908) 6 CLR 406.

Ecay v Godfrey (1947) 80 Lloyd's Rep 286.
Evans v Amicus Healthcare [2004] EWCA Civ 727.
Evans v United Kingdom (2006) 43 EHRR 21 Application 6339/05.
Esso Petroleum v Mardon [1976] 2 All ER 5.

Fairchild v Glenhaven Funeral Services Ltd [2003] 1 AC 32.
Farley v Skinner [2001] UKHL 49.

Gillick v West Norfolk and Wisbech Area Health Authority [1984] QB 581.
Gillick v West Norfolk and Wisbech Area Health Authority [1985] 2 WLR 413.
Gillick v West Norfolk and Wisbech Area Health Authority [1986] AC 112.
Gold v Haringey Health Authority [1988] QB 481.
Graham v Voigt (1989) 95 FLR 146.
Gregg v Scott [2005] 2 AC 176.
Gwilliam v West Hertfordshire Hospitals NHS Trust [2002] EWCA Civ 1041.

Hecht v Superior Court of Los Angeles County (1993) 20 Cal. Rptr. 2d 275.
Helibut, Symons and Co v Buckleton [1913] AC 30, HL.
Hills v Potter [1984] 1 WLR 641.
Home Office v Dorset Yacht Co. Ltd [1970] AC 1004.
Hotson v East Berkshire Area Health Authority [1985] 3 All ER 167.
Hunter v Hamley 1955 SC 200, 206.

Jarvis v Swan Tours Ltd [1973] 1 QB 233.
Johnson v Unisys Ltd [2001] UKHL 13.
Jones v Royal Wolverhampton Hospitals NHS Trust [2015] EWHC 2154 (QB).

Kitchen v Royal Air Force Association [1958] 2 All ER 241.

Leigh and Sillavan Ltd v Aliakmon Shipping Co Ltd [1996] AC 785.
Lister v Helsey Hall [2001] UKHL 22.

M v Calderdale Kirkless Health Authority [1998] Lloyd's Rep Med 157.
Market Investigations Ltd v Minister of Social Security [1969] 2 QB 173.

Mason v Westside Cemeteries Ltd (1996) 135 DLR (4th) 361.
Maynard v West Midlands Regional Health Authority [1985] 1 All ER 635.
McGhee v National Coal Board [1972] 3 All ER 1008.
Ministry of Defence v AB and others [2012] UKSC 89.
Montgomery v Lanarkshire Health Board [2015] UKSC 11.
Moore v Regents of the University of California 793 P 2d 479 (Cal, 1990).

NA v Nottingham County Council [2015] EWCA Civ 1139.

Overseas Tankship (UK) v Morts Dock & Engineering Co; The Wagon Mound 1 [1961] AC 388.

Page v Smith [1996] AC 155.
Pearce v United Bristol Healthcare NHS Trust [1999] PIQR 53.
Peekay Intermark v Australia and ANZ Banking Group (2006) 2 Lloyds Rep 511.

R v Bentham [2005] 1 UKHL 18.
R (Burke) v GMC [2005] EWCA Civ 1003.
R v Cambridge HA ex parte B (1995) 25 BMLR 5.
R v Herbert (1961) 25 JCL 163.
R (Quintavalle) v HFEA [2002] EWHC 2785 (Admin).
R (Quintavalle) v Human Fertilisation and Embryology Authority (Secretary of State for Health Intervening) [2003] EWCA Civ 667.
R (Quintavalle) v Human Fertilisation and Embryology Authority [2005] UKHL 28.
R v Kelly [1998] 3 All ER 714.
R v Rothery [1976] RTR 550 (CA).
R v Welsh [1974] RTR 478.
Re MB (An adult: Medical Treatment) [1997] 2 FLR 426.
Re R (a minor) (wardship: medical treatment) [1992] Fam 11.
Re Y (Adult Patient) transplant: Bone Marrow [1997] Fam 110.
Redgrave v Hurd (1881) 20 Ch D 1, CA.
Rees v Darlington Memorial Hospital NHS Trust [2002] EWCA Civ 88.
Reibl v Hughes (1980) 114 DLR (3d) 1.
Roche v Douglas (2000) 22 WAR 331 (WA SC).
Roe v Minister of Health [1954] 2 QB 66.
Rogers v Whitaker (1992) HCA 58 (1992)175 CLR 470.
Rothwell v Chemical and Insulating Co Ltd [2007] UKHL 39.

Schawel v Reade [1913] 2 IR 64, HL.
Sidaway v Board of Governors of the Bethlem Royal Hospital [1985] 1 All ER 643.
Smith v Barking, Havering and Brentwood Health Authority [1994] 5 Med LR 285.

Smith v Littlewoods Organisation Ltd [1987] 1 AC 241.
Smith v Tunbridge Wells Health Authority [1994] 5 Med LR 334.
Spencer v Hillingdon [2015] 1058 (QB).
St George's Healthcare NHS Trust v S [1998] 3 All ER 673.
Strunk v Strunk 445 SW 2d 145 (1969).

Thompson v Smiths Shiprepairers (North Shields) Ltd [1984] 1 All ER 1.
TRM Copy Centres v Lanwall Services [2008] EWCA Civ 382.

Various Claimants v Catholic Child Welfare Society and Others [2012] UKSC 56.

Walkin v South Manchester Health Authority [1995] 1 WLR 1543.
Washington University v Catalona 437 F Supp 2d 985 (US Dist 2006).
Watts v Marrow [1991] 1 WLR 1421.
Wells v Cooper [1958] 2 QB 265.
Whiston v London Strategic Health Authority [2010] EWCA Civ.
Whitehouse v Jordan [1981] 1 WLR 246.
Wilsher v Area Essex Health Authority [1988] AC 1074.
Wootton v J Docter Ltd & Anor [2008] EWCA Civ 136.
Wright (a Child) v Cambridge Medical Group [2011] EWCA Civ 669.
Wyatt v Curtis [2003] EWCA Civ 1779.

Yearworth v North Bristol NHS Trust [2009] EWCA Civ 37.
York v Jones (1989) 717 F. Supp. 421 (E.D. Va. 1989).

Statutes, Regulations and Orders

Abolition of Slavery Act 1833
Occupiers' Liability Act 1957
Human Tissue (Northern Ireland) Act 1962
Misrepresentation Act 1967
Theft Act 1968
Family Reform Act 1969
Limitation Act 1980
Surrogacy Agreements Act 1985
Children Act 1989
Data Protection Act 1998
Human Rights Act 1998
Human Tissue Act 2004
Mental Capacity Act 2005
Human Tissue (Scotland) Act 2006
Human Fertilisation and Embryology Act 1990, as amended 2008
Protection and Affordable Care Act 2010
Health and Social Care Act 2012

Human Transplantation (Wales) Act 2013

Medicines for Human Use (Clinical Regulations) 2004 SI 2004/1031
Human Tissue (Quality and Safety for Human Application) Regulations 2007 SI 2007/1523
The HFEA (Disclosure of Donor Information) Regulations 2004 SI 2004/1511
Human Organ Transplant (Northern Ireland) Order 1989
Anatomy (Northern Ireland) Order 1992

Acknowledgements

Since my interest in umbilical cord blood (UCB) stem cells was first sparked by a BBC *Horizon* documentary back in 2001,[1] I think it is safe to say that what began as a curiosity in the science of stem cells and the burgeoning industry that surrounded UCB use, quickly evolved into a passion that has never really abated. This book's origins are founded in my doctoral thesis, 'Unravelling the (dis)cord: examining the social, ethical and legal implications of umbilical cord blood collection', examined in 2009. I am very grateful to the viva examiners, Sally Sheldon and Jonathan Herring, for their helpful feedback on the original thesis and for their continued interest in my work. I am particularly thankful to Sally for encouraging me towards publications, not only of this monograph, but also of the published articles that preceded it.

This book contains revised material from my earlier work: (2010) 'Risky business? The risks and benefits of umbilical cord blood collection' 18 *Medical Law Review* 330–362 (with permission from Oxford University Press); (2010) 'Tying the cord around the midwife's neck: the problem with umbilical cord blood collection' 26 *Professional Negligence* 2, 83–95 (with permission from Bloomsbury Professional Ltd) and (2013) 'Ethics and choice in healthcare: the case of public v private cord blood banking' in Nicky Priaulx and Anthony Wrigley (eds) *Ethics, Law and Society* Volume V, Surrey: Ashgate (with permission from Ashgate Publishing Ltd), pp 55–68.

There are several colleagues to whom I owe special thanks: to Nicky Priaulx and Robin Mackenzie for nurturing my initial interest in cord blood as a law undergraduate; to my PhD supervisor, Hazel Biggs and my tort law 'partner-in crime', Kirsty Horsey, for their support and advice, which ultimately shaped my early academic career. Thanks also to Helen Strotton for her comments on early draft chapters of the book and guidance in areas of law that were unfamiliar to me; and to the series editor, Sheila McLean and the anonymous reviewers of the original monograph proposal, whose suggestions have been extremely helpful in formulating the internal chapters.

1 BBC Science & Nature Documentary, 'Lifeblood' *Horizon* BBC Two 9pm, 11 October 2001.

Extra special thanks must go to my husband, Dave, and daughters, Molly and Nancy, for their unconditional support throughout my legal studies and academic career and for their unequivocal faith in me as an academic, a mum – and now, as an author.

I would like to dedicate this book to my ex-employers, the Kent Fire and Rescue Service, without whom I would never have known that I had a brain in my head.

Introduction

> It may be that, some ages hence … the restoration of grey hairs to juvenility and the renewing of the exhausted marrow may at length be elicited without a miracle.
>
> (Joseph Glanvill 1661 AD. Founder member of the Royal Society)[1]

It must have been impossible for fifteenth-century physicians to have envisaged the vast array of medical possibilities available to their modern day counterparts; with the knowledge and techniques that we have at our disposal today being nothing more than their musings of unimaginable realities. Miracles, however, are no longer a prerequisite in the quest for the restoration of health – rather, advancements in medicine, science and biotechnology have equipped us with the scientific and technical knowledge necessary to drive substantial improvements in health outcomes. Arguably, stem cell technology has been a key player in the renewal of sick bodies, with the UK placing itself at the forefront of stem cell research. Indeed, it is able to cite the first isolation of mouse embryonic stem (ES) cells at Cambridge University in 1981;[2] the first cloning of a mammal through the use of cell nuclear transfer techniques at the Roslin Institute, Edinburgh University in 1997;[3] and the generation of the UK's first human ES cell lines in 2003 by researchers at King's College London[4] as amongst its landmark achievements. In May 2004, the UK Stem Cell Bank, operated by the Medical Research Council (MRC), was launched and acts as a repository for all types

1 J Glanville, as quoted in: The UK Stem Cell Initiative – Report and Recommendations (November 2005) at 1 http://webarchive.nationalarchives.gov.uk/20130107105354/http://www.dh.gov.uk/prod_consum_dh/groups/dh_digitalassets/@dh/@en/documents/digitalasset/dh_4124088.pdf accessed 8 April 2016.

2 M J Evans and M H Kaufman, 'Establishment in culture of pluripotent stem cells from mouse embryos' (1981) 292 *Nature* 154–156.

3 I Wilmut and others, 'Viable offspring derived from fetal and adult mammalian cells' (27 February 1997) 385 *Nature* (Letters) 810–813.

4 S J Pickering and others, 'Pre-implantation genetic diagnosis as a novel source of embryos for stem cell research' (2003) 7 *Reproductive Biomedicine Online* 3, 353–364.

of stem cells from embryonic, fetal and adult tissues available to researchers – the first bank of its kind in the world.[5]

Haematopoietic stem cells (HSCs) – or blood-forming stem cells – are routinely used to treat patients with cancers and other disorders of the blood and immune systems. It is reported that the number of patients who benefit from unrelated HSC transplants has tripled over the last decade; and with survival rates improving each year, its popularity as a curative therapy shows no sign of abating.[6] Notably, stem cells derived from umbilical cord blood (UCB) – stem cells procured from the umbilical cord and placenta of newborn babies – have been increasingly utilised in the treatment of blood-borne diseases and disorders following continued investment in this ethical alternative source of stem cell provision since the NHS Cord Blood Bank was established in 1996.

In March 2005, the UK Stem Cell Initiative was set up at the request of the then Chancellor of the Exchequer, the Right Honourable Gordon Brown, and reported in the same year on the current state of stem cell provision. One of the key problems identified was to the National Health Service (NHS). In terms of its health economics, the report highlighted a real need to capitalise on our strengths and maintain a strong position within stem cell research.[7] It reported that failure to continue to produce home-grown cell therapies and treatments would result in an over-reliance on extremely expensive imported stem cell products and expertise from overseas for treatment and research purposes, placing an unnecessary financial burden on the public purse. It was envisaged that continued growth in this sector of healthcare would not only be more cost effective but would secure the UK's leading role in stem cell research on a global stage.

It was against this backdrop that the UK heightened its efforts in maintaining a prominent position and in January 2010, the UK Stem Cell Strategic Forum was established to report specifically upon best practice in the provision of stem cells derived from adult unrelated donors and cord blood. Following an intensive collaboration between scientists, clinicians, economists and patient representatives, a report was produced in July 2010.[8] It recommended that in the current economic climate, our focus should be centred upon 'efficiency, effectiveness, quality and patient outcomes', which could be better achieved by streamlining efforts and reducing waste in terms

5 The UK Stem Cell Initiative 2005, at 44.

6 NHS Blood and Transplant (NHSBT), 'Unrelated donor stem cell transplantation in the UK: effective, affordable, sustainable. A report from the UK Stem Cell Strategic Oversight Committee' (November 2014) www.nhsbt.nhs.uk/download/unrelated_donor_stem_cell_transplantation_in_the_uk.pdf accessed 11 April 2016.

7 The UK Stem Cell Initiative 2005, at 1.

8 NHSBT, 'The future of unrelated donor stem cell transplantation in the UK: a report from the UK stem cell strategic forum' (July 2010) www.nhsbt.nhs.uk/download/uk_stem_cell_strategic_forum_report.pdf accessed 11 April 2016.

of both finances and poor quality resources. It called for a more formalised infrastructure across the four countries of the UK supported by continued investment and an expansion of the number of available stem cell deposits that have been subject to stringent selection criteria to ensure its maximum potential for utilisation.

In terms of UCB provision, it recommended that the UK should work towards an optimal inventory of 50,000 available cord blood units to ensure equity of access to all NHS patients and that all newly banked units should be of a high cell dose quality.[9] Given that the UK has a unique, rich, ethnically diverse population, the Forum also warned that the UK could not rely upon imports of cord blood from international registries, particularly in the treatment of Black and ethnic minority communities, and that greater efforts to encourage recruitment of cord blood from these groups would ensure a more sustainable UK inventory, ideally an increase of between 30–50 per cent of current available stocks, which could potentially save up to 200 more lives per year.

The Forum's recommendations for introducing an improved framework for stem cell provision across the UK were officially approved; and in 2011 the health minister, Andrew Lansley, established the UK Stem Cell Strategic Oversight Committee to co-ordinate and supervise the implementation of its recommendations. In its review in 2014, the Committee reported that the majority of the proposed aims and objectives had been actualised and that the implemented strategies had proven effective. Indeed, the commitment of a cash injection of £4 million per year from the Department of Health (DH) has been a major influential factor in ensuring best practice is carried out to safeguard efficient use of funds, equity of access and to maximise clinical benefits to meet the needs of UK patients.

Such investment and planning is also supported by a robust national regulatory framework, which is overseen by the Human Tissue Authority (HTA). The Human Tissue Act 2004 sets out the legal framework in England, Wales and Northern Ireland for the storage and use of human tissue from the living and for the removal, storage and use of human tissue and organs from the dead. In addition to its regulatory function, the HTA produces as part of its statutory provisions a variety of Codes of Practice, such as best practice with regards to consent and the import and export of human bodies, body parts and tissue. In Scotland, the Human Tissue (Scotland) Act largely mirrors the 2004 Act.

The implementation in 2008 of the European Union Tissues and Cells Directive (EUTCD) and its associated Regulations – the Human Tissue (Quality and Safety for Human Application) 2007 Regulations – saw the UK

9 It recommended that a total nuclear cell (TNC) dose threshold of over 9 × 108 from ethnic minority donors and 12 × 108 from Caucasian donors should be the requisite cell quality. TNC dosage is explained in more detail in Chapter 2.

cord blood industry regulated for the first time. Since its introduction, the procurement and storage of all UCB units must adhere to strict guidelines which dictate that only suitably qualified personnel can procure the cells on premises approved by the HTA licensing committee to ensure the safety of the donor and the quality and traceability of the preserved UCB unit. Since 2010, all UK centres performing stem cell transplants are accredited by JACIE – the Joint Accreditation Committee of the International Society for Cellular Therapy (ISCT) and the European Society for Blood and Marrow Transplantation (EBMT) to ensure high-quality patient care and laboratory performance through the development of global standards.

Internationally, cord blood banks are accredited by the Netcord-FACT organisation. FACT (Foundation for the Accreditation of Cellular Therapy) was set up in 1996 to drive excellence in operating standards by assessing all clinical and laboratory aspects of stem cell transplantation; and Netcord, founded in 1998, was established to promote high-quality cord blood banks and to improve the screening and selection of suitable donors. The collaboration of Netcord-FACT in 2000 saw the unification of international standards for cord blood collection, processing, banking selection and release of cord blood for transplantation.[10]

The regulation and promotion of cord blood use is of course good news for the many sufferers of life-threatening illnesses desperate to secure a donor for treatment purposes. The first successful UCB transplant took place in 1988 on Matthew Farrow,[11] a boy from North Carolina, USA who suffered from a potentially fatal genetic disorder, Fanconi's anaemia. Since then, a great deal of interest has been generated around UCB's use and future potential.[12] UCB can be collected and stored for personal use with a commercial cord blood company or donated for communal access to a public bank. The ability to capitalise on what could be a life-saving resource has made private UCB banking an increasingly popular storage option, which can be purchased for a fee. Celebrities such as prima ballerina Darcey Bussell,[13] premiership footballer Thierry Henry,[14] *Sky Sports'* Natalie Pinkham,[15] Indian

10 For example, see: Netcord-FACT, 'Sixth edition of Netcord-FACT international standards for cord blood collection, banking and release for administration' (2016) www.factweb.org/forms/store/ProductFormPublic/sixth-edition-netcord-fact-international-standards-for-cord-blood-collection-banking-and-release-for-administration-free-download accessed 30 September 2016.

11 Matthew was only five years old when he became the first recipient of this innovative procedure, which was carried out on 25 February 1988 at a hospital in Paris.

12 C P McGuckin and others, 'Production of stem cells with embryonic characteristics from human umbilical cord blood' (2005) 38 *Cell Proliferation* 245.

13 Editorial, 'The 2-minute treatment that could save my baby's life (20 years from now!)' *The Daily Mail* (London 25 May 2004).

14 Editorial, 'Pa-pa voom!' *FQ Magazine* (Nov–Dec 2005).

15 Biovault Family, 'Sky Sports F1's Natalie Pinkham chooses Biovault Family' http://biovaultfamily.com/news/sky-sports-f1s-natalie-pinkham-chooses-biovault-family/ accessed 8 April 2016.

international cricketer Ajit Agarkar,[16] Ana Ortiz of *Ugly Betty* fame,[17] actress Tori Spelling,[18] and New Zealand newsreader Giuliana Rancic[19] have all publicly endorsed private UCB banking. Even one of the Kardashians[20] has reportedly got in on the act by purchasing the latest 'must-have' service.

Premise of the book

The knowledge that UCB contains powerful stem cells capable of providing curative or enhanced health treatment, combined with the ability to collect and preserve those cells for either private or public use, has paved the way for an expansion in UCB banking over the last 25 years, with the public UCB banking system supported by the recent substantial governmental funding. However, the ability to harness such a potentially 'valuable' biological resource in itself raises a number of controversial issues. The premise of this book is to explore those controversies – in particular the social, legal and ethical implications involved in stem cell use as a therapeutic treatment option; the personal risks as well as the benefits of preserving the cells; equitable access to, and funding issues that arise from, financing an effective UCB infrastructure; the interplay between public and private healthcare; the legal obligations that arise from the collection process, particularly for those who procure the cells; and the potential ownership claims or inter-familial disputes over privately stored cells that such a service can foster.

Thankfully, there have been no reported cases of personal harms or inter-familial disputes arising from cord blood anywhere in the world, yet. However, with the number of collections increasing it may only be a matter of time before we see a cord blood-related claim grace our courts. In the absence of any legal precedent, this book provides an academic enquiry into how potential legal issues could be resolved should the need arise. The book's focus is on the law of tort as it applies in the UK and it provides a detailed doctrinal analysis of how this might play out in a claim involving cord blood. It is anticipated that the observations made may also be of use

16 Editorial, 'Need a heart – bank a cell' *The Telegraph* (Calcutta 7 January 2007) www.telegraphindia.com/1070107/asp/insight/story_7215292.asp accessed 8 April 2016.

17 Cordbank, 'Celeb mums who have banked cord blood – Ana Ortiz' www.cordbank.co.nz/celeb-mums-ana-ortiz-cord-blood/ accessed 8 April 2016.

18 Insception Lifebank, 'Celebrities banking cord blood' www.insception.com/blog/celebrities-banking-cord-blood/ accessed 8 April 2016.

19 Editorial, 'After our own health scares, it was a no-brainer: Guiliana and Bill Rancic have banked newborn Edward's cord blood' *The Mail Online* (26 September 2012) www.dailymail.co.uk/tvshowbiz/article-2208980/Giuliana-Bill-Rancic-banked-newborn-Edwards-cord-blood.html accessed 8 April 2016.

20 Editorial, 'Why is Kourtney Kardashian carrying around umbilical cord blood?' *Hollywood Life* (9 December 2009) http://hollywoodlife.com/2009/12/09/would-you-save-your-babys-umbilical-chord-blood-like-kourtney-kardashian-intends-to-do/ accessed 8 April 2016.

to other countries with common law jurisdictions. This enquiry is further located within the theoretical framework of altruism versus self-interests and explores the notion of risk and choice within maternity care.

We live in an era where choice in healthcare is plentiful. We have the ability to choose a preferred GP practice and to make choices about our NHS care; we are offered an array of therapeutic and non-therapeutic treatments by the public and private healthcare sectors and via health tourism; we have the ability to overcome childlessness by tapping into one or more of a plethora of assisted reproductive techniques; and we have seen an emergence of 'personalised medicine' in the form of direct-to-customer genetic testing and individual tailored drug regimes.[21] Whether or not to privately bank UCB (and if so, which collection method to adopt) or to donate or discard what could be a potentially valuable biological cell resource is now one more choice available. However, this type of decision-making can present as either a blessing or a burden for expectant families. Indeed, the ability to bank for private or public use may not be a choice that is open to all, and to those that are afforded the opportunity, the choice may not be as easy to make as you might at first think.

Chapter outlines – the umbilical cord blood controversies

The first chapter of this book traces the origins of UCB stem cell use and maps its rise as an alternative resource to bone marrow stem cells in the treatment of patients with certain blood-borne disorders and diseases, particularly where no suitable bone marrow donor exists; and locates this potentially valuable biological material within the context of the allocation of NHS healthcare resources. It questions why, in spite of its resourcefulness[22] and the public perception that more should be done to preserve UCB, its collection is not routine.[23] It seeks to address the concerns raised by proponents of the Umbilical Cord Blood (Donation) Bill (2008),[24] which calls upon the government to actively promote UCB donation. In doing so, the chapter outlines the fears raised by the UCB sceptics, the criticism meted out towards the commercial cord blood industry and unravels the (dis)cord that surrounds cord blood use.

Chapter 2 focuses upon the risks associated with UCB collection. It identifies these risks as threefold – scientific, practical, and legal – all of which may

21 D Dickenson, *Me Medicine vs We Medicine: Reclaiming Biotechnology for the Common Good* (New York: Columbia University Press, 2013) p 1.
22 E Marshall, 'Clinical promise, ethical quandary' (1996) 271 *Science* 5249, 586.
23 The Royal College of Obstetricians and Gynaecologists (RCOG), the Royal College of Midwives (RCM), the American Congress of Obstetricians and Gynecologists (ACOG), the European Group on Ethics in Science and New Technologies (EGE) and the American Academy of Pediatrics (AAP) do not support the routine collection of UCB.
24 Umbilical Cord Blood (Donation) Bill 2008 [50] www.publications.parliament.uk/pa/cm200708/cmbills/050/08050.i-i.html accessed 14 April 2016.

present personal implications for the birthing mother and child. In particular, the chapter examines the risk to the mother from participating in an additional birth procedure that takes places during the third stage of labour, which is a time when maternal haemorrhage is at its greatest. Moreover, maternity staff may be distracted by facilitating the collection process themselves or by others performing the procedure under a third party agreement on the mother's behalf. Should this occur, vital maternal observations during the third stage of labour may be overlooked, resulting in possible harm to the mother or child. Furthermore, the procured unit itself may be 'damaged' by negligent procurement, processing or storage. Perhaps more worryingly, as early as 1995, concerns have been raised about the potential health implications to the baby by removing blood from the umbilical cord during the process of it transferring from the placenta to the child. Rather than procuring it as a 'biological insurance' for the future, there is evidence – albeit conflicting evidence – that the baby may need all of its blood from birth.

The chapter continues by examining the potential legal liabilities that may arise for those who facilitate the collection process, with a particular focus on midwives and the NHS. While private banks supply the collection kit and storage facilities, they rely on NHS midwifery staff to collect the cells and/or the goodwill of the NHS to allow a UCB collector supplied by the private bank to facilitate the process under the guidance and control of the midwife via a third party agreement. However, in permitting such a practice, midwives may be at risk of being held personally liable for any negligent execution of the collection process and the NHS Trusts vicariously liable for any torts either the midwife or third party may commit on NHS premises. This places the NHS in a peculiarly vulnerable position. Although commercial UCB banks are profit-making enterprises, in the UK it is the NHS and its staff that bear the risks associated with UCB collection on their behalf. Although later chapters discuss the legal risks in more detail, a brief overview is provided at the end of Chapter 2 in order to emphasise their importance and relevance to the overall arguments.

Chapter 3 explores the rise of the cord blood industry and the different types of banking systems before examining the impact of recent regulation. Before the turn of the twenty-first century there were no private UCB banks operating in the UK, but following the proliferation of international private UCB banks and the industry's infiltration of the UK market, the first UK private banking facility, Cells4Life, was set up in 2002. Recognising that international companies were fulfilling a consumer need, the UK soon witnessed an expansion of banking facilities within the private sector. In a previously unregulated area, the implementation of the European Union Tissues and Cells Directive (2004/23/EC),[25] which was transposed into UK

25 Council Directive (EC) 2004/23 on setting standards of quality for the donation, procurement, testing, processing, preservation, storage and distribution of human tissues and cells [2004] OJ L102.

law via the Human Tissue (Quality and Safety for Human Application) Regulations in 2007, imposes strict rules with regard to the licensing of premises that procure UCB for either public or private use. This has had an impact on the procurement of UCB because under the new regulations, only specialist personnel who are trained to procure units of the highest quality on premises that meet essential standards are permitted to collect UCB. This requirement places a ban on unqualified parties such as fathers or birth partners from collecting the cells, which had previously been used as an option by some private banks. While the new regulations offer protection to midwifery staff who procure the cells on behalf of the pregnant woman, I shall argue that they do not go far enough – rather, the introduction of UCB collections made under a third party agreement leaves midwives and the NHS vicariously at risk of litigation despite the new rules.

Further, the chapter explores the motivations behind UCB donation and why those who choose to store privately consider it a worthwhile exercise. Indeed, as the opportunity to preserve a potentially valuable resource exists, then those that can afford to do so may simply say 'Why not?' The exclusivity of private storage, however, provokes a dichotomy between altruism and self-interest and these conflicting ideologies are examined in the context of private banking in its denial of public access to the stored cells and considers whether they may be better placed in a public UCB bank for equal access to all.

Chapters 4 and 5 analyse the law of negligence in greater detail and consider how this tort could be applied to the UCB collection process. Chapter 4 traces the law of informed consent in the UK post the tragic events of organ retention at the Bristol and Alder Hey hospitals in the late 1980s and explores its current statutory provisions. Further, the chapter examines the type of information available to those considering both public and private UCB banking, and whether such information is sufficient enough for pregnant women to make an informed choice. It also considers the role of *Gillick*[26] competency for competent under 16s (the so-called 'Baby Mums') and how they might be affected by the UCB industry. Although pregnant women cannot *demand* that UCB collection takes place, there is evidence to suggest that NHS midwifery staff go out of their way to facilitate the decision by pregnant women to undergo UCB collection and it is therefore of concern that they may also be tempted to permit riskier collection methods, such as the use of early cord clamping and in-utero collection, which procure a greater quantity of UCB, if requested to do so. But as it is imperative to gain valid consent before any medical procedure is carried out, the nature and content of that consent can be the subject of judicial scrutiny if a claim should come before the courts.

26 *Gillick v West Norfolk and Wisbech Area Health Authority* [1986] AC 112.

Chapter 5 continues this enquiry and explores via relevant case law the standards of care in negligence, including the law on risk disclosure and the duty to warn, before analysing the complex rules relating to causation. Modern day jurisprudence has placed the patient at the centre of the medical decision-making process and the 'doctor–patient relationship' has been recast as a 'doctor–patient partnership' by rejecting medical paternalism in favour of what the reasonably prudent patient in the patient's position wants to know about their own treatment. Of particular focus are the risk disclosure cases in the House of Lords decisions in *Sidaway v Board of Governors of the Bethlem Royal Hospital* [1985][27] and *Chester v Afshar* [2004];[28] and more recently, the landmark ruling of the Supreme Court in *Montgomery v Lanarkshire* [2015].[29] These cases demonstrate that following the recent judicial shift from medical paternalism[30] towards patient autonomy,[31] it is imperative that a clear communication process takes places between the pregnant woman undergoing UCB collection and their UCB collector to ensure that the choice she makes is an informed one and her consent is valid.

In the final chapter we explore whether UCB is capable of being owned, and if so, by whom. Although this issue has yet to be considered by the courts anywhere in the world, this is an important question because outside of a claim for personal injury or loss of autonomy derived from a lack of consent, damage to the UCB itself can only be compensated for in the law of tort if it is regarded as a property giving rise to a remedy for its interference. In order to address this question, Chapter 6 explores Anthony Honoré's definition of property before applying the elements of 'a bundle of rights' to UCB. By its physical nature and ability to be controlled by the mother for an intended purpose and her ability to restrict access to its use, I shall argue that a property-based model can encompass UCB and that a procured UCB unit for private use demonstrates the nuances of property capable of being owned. This line of enquiry is continued by analysing the common law using cases that relate to property in the body with particular reference to *Yearworth v North Bristol NHS Trust* [2009],[32] a case involving the negligent destruction of frozen sperm, which was held to be property by the Court of Appeal in 2009. Through the prism of *Yearworth* I map out the arguments in favour of treating UCB as analogous to sperm and why there

27 *Sidaway v Board of Governors of the Bethlem Royal Hospital* [1985] 1 All ER 643.

28 *Chester v Afshar* [2004] UKHL 41.

29 *Montgomery v Lanarkshire Health Board* [2015] UKSC 11.

30 As seen in the early risk disclosure cases of *Sidaway v Board of Governors of the Bethlem Royal Hospital* [1985] 1 All ER 643, *Gold v Haringey Health Authority* [1988] QB 481 and *Blyth v Bloomsbury Health Authority* [1993] 4 Med LR 151.

31 As evidenced later in *Smith v Tunbridge Wells Health Authority* [1994] 5 Med LR, *Pearce v United Bristol Healthcare NHS Trust* [1999] PIQR 53; *Chester v Afshar* [2004] UKHL 41 and *Birch v University London College Hospital NHS Foundation Trust* [2008] EWHC 2237 (QB).

32 *Yearworth v North Bristol NHS Trust* [2009] EWCA Civ 37.

should therefore be no bar to viewing UCB as property for the purposes of a civil claim, and that a basis for a claim may be possible in either negligence, contract, or bailment; or even potential for a claim from the negligent 'loss of a chance' to utilise the cells. In addition, I question who, if anyone, has greater 'rights' over the stored UCB unit in the case of an inter-familial dispute.

1 Background to the controversies

Whoever said you enter the world with nothing didn't know about stem cells.[1]

Cord blood use – setting the scene

Prior to the late 1980s the conventional treatment for blood cancers and serious genetic blood disorders was bone marrow transplantation.[2] Although this type of procedure provided successful life-saving treatment for many, its use also proved problematic. For example, to secure a realistic chance of success, compatibility between patient and donor is crucial, otherwise the transplanted cells can attack the host's body, with potentially fatal consequences, typically graft-versus-host disease (GVHD). This is a common and serious complication of transplants where there is a reaction between the donated cells and the recipients' own tissue, often leading to organ damage and death.[3]

Bone marrow is a jelly-like substance located in the pelvis and other large bones. To secure a realistic chance of a successful transplant, patients rely on finding a bone marrow donor with a high number of human leukocyte antigens (HLA), or a matching HLA-type, each of which reduces the likelihood of rejection by the recipient. Antigens assist the body's immune system to recognise foreign bodies and are found on the surface of nearly all cells within the body. HLA contains eight groups of antigens, each performing a function for transplant purposes. These are known as groups HLA-A, HLA-B, HLA-C and HLA-DR with each group comprised of two antigens, one from each parent. HLA-typing is the term given to the process of recognising antigen types.[4] Ideally an 8/8 high resolution HLA match (known as a

1 Virgin Health Bank (VHB) Marketing Brochure (2007), www.virginhealth.co.uk.

2 G Burgio and F Locatelli (1997) 'Transplant of bone marrow and cord blood hematopoietic stem cells in pediatric practice, revisited according to the fundamental principles of bioethics' 19 *Bone Marrow Transplant* 12, 1163–1168.

3 E Meyer, K Hanna and K Gebbie, *Cord Blood* (Washington, DC: National Academies Press, 2005) p 2.

4 A Berger, 'Science commentary: HLA typing' (2001) 322 *British Medical Journal* 218.

'perfect' or 'Grade A' match) is preferable for transplants, although bone marrow transplants can be carried out with 7/8 match with a reduction in the five-year overall survival rate by 8 per cent.[5]

The greatest chance of finding a 'perfect' match is from a related donor – more often than not from a sibling – with suitable donors for 30 per cent of those in need within the UK found from within the familial group.[6] The remaining 70 per cent, however, are reliant upon accessing unrelated donations from bone marrow registries, the vagaries of which dictate that the odds of finding a reliable match are considerably lower. The UK developed the world's first bone marrow registry, established by the Antony Nolan Trust in 1974. Although the British Bone Marrow Registry (BBMR) and the Antony Nolan Registry have a combined total of 770,000 willing donors on its registers,[7] and a reported international database of over 22 million adult donors across 73 international registries,[8] it was reported in 2012 that only half of those searching for an unrelated donor will be successful,[9] with Blacks and ethnic minority groups facing extremely low odds of finding a suitable donor. Similarly, in the US, data collected following an in-depth study from the National Marrow Donor Program and the Cord Blood Unit Registry revealed that the odds of finding a 8/8 HLA bone marrow match were at 75 per cent for white patients of European descent but only 46 per cent for white patients of Middle Eastern or North African descent. For black Americans of all ethnic backgrounds, the probabilities were lower at 16–19 per cent and Hispanics, Asians and Native Americans ranging between 27–52 per cent.[10]

Yet following the UK's more recent efforts to address the shortfall in donor stocks, availability of donor stem cells has begun to improve. In 2013 the UK's three registries were aligned to produce one single searchable point for NHS transplant centres, thus decreasing the search time amongst its inventory; and

5 S Lee and others (2007) 'High-resolution donor-recipient HLA matching contributes to the success of unrelated donor marrow transplantation' 110 *Blood* 13, 4576–4583.

6 NHS Blood and Transplant (NHSBT), 'Q&A' (Undated), www.nhsbt.nhs.uk/bonemarrow/qa/ accessed 20 October 2015.

7 NHSBT, 'The future of unrelated donor stem cell transplantation in the UK: a report from the UK stem cell strategic forum' (July 2010) at 5 www.nhsbt.nhs.uk/download/uk_stem_cell_strategic_forum_report.pdf accessed 14 April 2016.

8 G Parkes, 'Improving the UK stem cell supply chain to ensure better stem cell transplant patient outcomes' (2014) 43 *Blood and Transplant Matters* 5–6.

9 Antony Nolan, '365 days. 1,000 chances of life' (28 September 2012) www.anthonynolan.org/news/2012/09/28/365-days-1000-chances-life accessed 20 October 2015. Similarly, general blood stocks for ethnic minority groups remains low. See: L Eleftheriou-Smith, 'NHS calls for rare blood donors as O and B negative stocks hit four-year low' *The Independent* (15 March 2014) www.independent.co.uk/life-style/health-and-families/health-news/nhs-calls-for-rare-blood-group-donors-at-o-and-b-negative-stocks-hit-four-year-low-9194378.html accessed 25 November 2015.

10 L Gragert and others, 'HLA match likelihoods for hematopoietic stem-cell grafts in the U.S. Registry' (2014) 371 *New England Journal of Medicine* 4, 339–348.

by 2014, the UK Stem Cell Strategy Oversight Committee reported that over 60 per cent of black, Asian and minority ethnic (BAME) patients are now able to find a suitable mis-matched donor. However, they were keen to point out that, 'there is clearly much still to be done to ensure equity of patient access regardless of ethnic group'.[11] Despite expanding recruitment efforts amongst the BAME communities, shortage of donors remains, as the plight of Birmingham teenager, Aneesa Hussain, clearly demonstrates. Pakistan-born Aneesa failed to find a suitable bone marrow match following a ten-month worldwide search, falling victim to the global problem of a lack of BAME donors. Against all the odds, she survived – but only after a low mis-matched bone marrow transplant from her father, which was used as a last resort.[12]

Frustrated at the lack of available and compatible bone marrow for use in bone marrow transplants, scientists and medical experts of the 1970s embarked upon radical new research to devise an alternative method of stem cell production. Pioneering work in the US carried out in the early 1980s revealed that in fact another part of the human anatomy also houses valuable stem cells – a part of the body that had been previously discarded – the umbilical cord blood of a newborn baby.

The blood system of a foetus in-utero is very different from that of children and adults. Before birth, the stem cells are not in the bone marrow but begin in the liver and it is not until the onset of birth that the stem cells start their journey to the bone marrow. As a result, both the placenta and umbilical cord are full of umbilical cord blood (UCB) stem cells at the moment of delivery. As stem cells decrease in quality overtime, these cells are believed by some[13] to be of higher value than adult stem cells, and this value is further exemplified by the fact that, unlike their bone marrow counterpart, matching requirements for cord blood are less stringent, with current standards requiring matching from antigens at levels of only HLA-A, HLA-B and high resolution HLA-DR with a 6/6 HLA as optimal. Furthermore, a UCB transplant does not necessarily require a 'perfect match' to be successful at transplantation. Rather, UCB transplants can be commenced at the much lower rate of a 4/6 HLA match, further demonstrating its utility.[14]

11 NHSBT, 'Unrelated donor stem cell transplantation in the UK: effective, affordable, sustainable. A report from the UK Stem Cell Strategic Oversight Committee' (November 2014) www.nhsbt.nhs.uk/download/unrelated_donor_stem_cell_transplantation_in_the_uk.pdf accessed 25 November 2015.

12 A Hoyle, 'Bone marrow transplant teenager: "I feel angry that my community let me down"' *Telegraph Online* (London 20 October 2014) www.telegraph.co.uk/news/health/11172662/Bone-marrow-transplant-teenager-I-feel-angry-that-my-community-let-me-down.html accessed 7 October 2015.

13 European Commission, 'Stem cells: therapies for the future?' *European Commission Research DG/Life Sciences Directorates Projects Catalogue* (Brussels 18–19 December 2001) http://ec.europa.eu/research/quality-of-life/stemcells/pdf/projects_en.pdf accessed 20 October 2015.

14 N J Chao, S G Emerson and K I Weinberg, 'Stem cell transplants (cord blood transplantation)' (2004) 1 *Hematology* 354.

The viability of UCB transplantation, however, could only be proven by its successful use. After years of research and dedication by a committed team of stem cell experts desperate to prove cord blood's worth, a major breakthrough occurred in 1988. Set against a medical world dominated by bone marrow transplant as the preferred choice in the treatment of blood cancers and genetic blood disorders, UCB came into its own. On 25 February 1988, Matthew Farrow, a five-year-old boy from North Carolina, US, who suffered a rare and potentially fatal genetic blood disease known as Fanconi's anaemia, became the first recipient of this innovative procedure. His UCB transplant, led by Fanconi's anaemia expert, Dr Eliane Gluckman, was carried out at a hospital in Paris and Matthew's entire blood system was completely rebuilt by stem cells from the cord blood of his newborn sister, Alison. This proved to be the first successful UCB transplant carried out in the world, signalling a major boost for the advocates of cord blood use, with initial hopes and aspirations for its long-term efficacy kept alive by Matthew's continued health today. He is now in his thirties, a husband and father; and has continued to champion cord blood's use, currently acting as a spokesperson for the US-based CORD:USE Foundation.[15]

Transplants using UCB can take two different forms – autologous and allogeneic. An autologous UCB transplant refers to the re-infusement of a patient's own UCB collected and cryopreserved at birth. In contrast, an allogeneic UCB transplant is carried out using UCB from a donor, including blood-related donors such as occurred in the case of Matthew Farrow. This type of transplant is also known as an allogeneic 'directed donation' and is typically carried out using a sibling donor to treat disorders such as thalassaemia, immunodeficiency, inherited metabolic diseases, aplastic anaemia and acute leukaemia.[16] Siblings demonstrate a high rate of HLA compatibility and identical twins are almost always compatible.[17]

To date, UCB has been used in 35,000 transplants worldwide.[18] In 2007, a one-year survival rate was estimated to be in the region of 75–90 per cent after a sibling HLA-matched UCB transplant and 40–80 per cent for an unrelated mis-matched UCB transplant.[19] By 2014, the UK Stem Cell Strategic Oversight Committee had reported that the five-year survival rate

15 CORD:USE Foundation (28 February 2015) www.zoominfo.com/CachedPage/?archive_id=0&page_id=5097744653&page_url=//www.cordusefoundation.org/index.php&page_last_updated=2015-02-28T01:55:05&firstName=Matthew&lastName=Farrow accessed 20 October 2015.

16 H Blacklock and others, 'Volunteer cord blood banking and transplantation' (2005) 118 *New Zealand Medical Journal* 1208.

17 C T Scott, *Stem Cell Now – From the Experiment that Shook the World to the New Politics of Life* (New York: PI Press, 2006) p 218.

18 K K Ballen, F Verter and J Kurtzberg, 'Umbilical cord blood donation: public or private?' (2015) 50 *Bone Marrow Transplantation* 10, 1271–1278.

19 B H Lubin and others, 'Cord blood banking for potential future transplantation' (2007) 119 *Pediatrics* 1.

in children following an unrelated UCB transplant was in the region of 70 per cent.[20]

The benefits of cord blood over bone marrow

As indicated above, one of the distinct advantages of UCB over bone marrow is that it does not require an HLA 'perfect match' and therefore offers a greater flexibility for HLA matching purposes. As early as 2001, the *British Medical Journal* (*BMJ*) reported on a study[21] carried out at the Royal Victoria Infirmary, Newcastle, involving 50 patients with acute leukaemia. The study showed that 15 out of 50 patients were able to obtain a 6/6 HLA match from the 630 cord blood donations then stored in its bank, with a further 22 patients obtaining a 5/6 match. Furthermore, research published in 2007 has revealed that the five-year leukaemia-free survival rate in 503 children with acute lymphoblastic leukaemia who received an HLA mis-matched UCB transplant was similar to the survival rate of 282 children who received bone marrow transplants. Although this demonstrates comparable outcomes, for a number of reasons, UCB is much easier to obtain than bone marrow.

First, UCB is more easily accessed because the units are harvested and stored in anticipation of being needed for transplantation, whereas bone marrow donors' details are held on a register until they are contacted to donate. In the meantime, however, those on the registry may have become sick themselves, changed addresses or simply changed their mind, especially as donating bone marrow involves a particularly invasive and aggressive procedure; and their voluntary services may therefore be lost.

Second, results of the 2001 study showed that the median time of locating a bone marrow match was 49 days, compared to 13.5 days for a suitable UCB match. Yet today, the waiting time has been vastly improved for both bone marrow and UCB recipients due to the introduction of advanced computerised systems, allowing matching, tracing and communicating with donors and recipients much easier. In addition, a pioneering technique known as New Generation Sequence DNA-Testing, developed over three years by the NHS Blood and Transplant's Histocompatability and Immunogenetics Team, has shown to halve the time spent in matching a donor with a recipient by producing large amounts of HLA-typing data quickly and cheaply. This 'recent revolution in DNA sequencing technology'[22] is currently being used for all bone marrow donors and UCB units registered at NHS Blood and Transplant and it is anticipated that 10,000

20 NHSBT, November 2014.

21 S J Proctor and others, 'Umbilical cord blood banks in the UK have proved their worth and now deserve a firmer foundation' (2001) 323 *British Medical Journal* 60.

22 S Davey, 'Next generation sequencing – tissue (HLA) typing adult and cord blood stem cell donors for transplantation' (January 2015) 44 *Blood and Transplant Matters* 18–19.

UCB units subjected to this technique will be held by the end of 2015, and will be seven times more likely to be selected for transplant after being HLA-typed using this method.[23]

One of the key advantages of UCB use over bone marrow is its relationship with graft-versus-host disease. Early research carried out in 1998 by the Eurocord-Cord Blood Transplant Group, Paris, concluded that recipients of related UCB transplant showed a lower incidence of acute and chronic graft-versus-host disease than did those of bone marrow transplant.[24] The world's first unrelated donor UCB transplant was performed on a three-year-old child at the Duke University Hospital, North Carolina, in 1993, with the outcome of this and 24 subsequent unrelated donor UCB transplants revealing that incidence and severity of graft-versus-host disease in unrelated donors were lower and milder than those seen in recipients of bone marrow from unrelated donors.[25] Later studies have not only confirmed this finding,[26,27] but have also reported that whilst there is no evidence to suggest that UCB transplants increase the risk of chronic GVHD,[28] using alternative sources such as peripheral blood cells in transplants produces even higher incidences of the condition than bone marrow.[29]

UCB's resourcefulness can be attributed to its biological makeup. One of its key features is that it contains pluripotent[30] stem cells – cells that have the ability to become most other cell types found in the embryo, foetus, or a developed organism, which in turn have the potential to develop into

23 NHSBT, 'NHS blood and transplant first in UK to use new generation sequencing for HLA tying bone marrow donors for the British Bone Marrow Registry' (16 February 2015) *NHS Blood and Transplant News* www.nhsbt.nhs.uk/news-and-media/news-articles/news_2015_02_16.asp accessed 25 November 2015.

24 V Rocha and others, 'Graft-versus-host disease in children who have received a cord blood or bone marrow transplant from an HLA-identical sibling' (2000) 342 *The New England Journal of Medicine* 25.

25 J Wagner and others, 'Successful transplantation of HLA-matched and HLA-mismatched umbilical cord blood from unrelated donors: analysis of engraftment and acute graft-versus-host disease' (1996) 88 *Blood* 3, 795.

26 M J Laughlin and others, 'Hematopoietic engraftment and survival in adult recipients of umbilical-cord blood from unrelated donors' (2001) 344 *The New England Journal of Medicine* 24, 1815.

27 K Sugimoto and others, 'Clinical characteristics of chronic graft-versus-host disease following umbilical cord blood transplantation for adults (2008) 41 *Bone Marrow Transplant*, 729–736.

28 R C Wadlow and D L Porter 'Umbilical cord blood transplantation: where do we stand? (2002) 8 *Biology of Blood and Marrow Transplantation* 637–647.

29 H Screzenmeier and others, 'Worse outcome and more chronic GVHD with peripheral blood progenitor cells than bone marrow in HLA-matched sibling donor transplants for young patients with severe acquired aplastic anemia' (2007) 110 *Blood* 1397–1400.

30 However, it is noted here that due to the advancements made in medical technology, induced pluripotent stem cells (iPS cells) can now be created from adult somatic cells and provide an alternative source of cells. See: S Holm, 'Time to reconsider stem cell ethics – the importance of induced pluripotent stem cells' (2008) 34 *Journal of Medical Ethics* 63.

neuronal, muscle and bone-forming cells.[31] More specifically, studies using animal models have shown that UCB stem cells have the potential to improve cardiac function,[32] treat diseases of the central nervous system,[33] and brain injury, including stroke.[34] They may also be valuable in the treatment of children brain damaged due to hypoxic incidents during birth,[35] and in gene therapy.[36]

By 2007, scientists had become excited by UCB's regenerative qualities and its potential use in regenerative medicine following a review that showed UCB contained multiple populations of pluripotent stem cells capable of giving rise to a vast range of different tissues both in vitro and ex vivo. The review concluded that:

> Cumulatively, the identification and isolation of these populations of pluripotent stem cells within cord blood represents a scientific breakthrough that could potentially impact every field of medicine, via their use in regenerative medicine. Thus, UCB stem cells are amenable to the treatment of a wide variety of diseases including cardiovascular, hepatic, ophthalmic, orthopaedic, neurological and endocrine diseases.[37]

Not only does this view continue to be held today[38] but the results of more recent studies have endorsed this earlier excitement. Through continued UCB research, advancements have been made in the development of stem cell therapies for diabetes,[39] hearing restoration,[40] optical

31 J Kurtzberg and others, 'Placental blood as a source of haematopoietic stem cells for transplantation to unrelated recipients' (1996) 335 *New England Journal of Medicine* 157.

32 P Vanelli and others, 'Cardiac precursors in human bone marrow and cord blood: in vitro cell cardiogenesis' (2004) 5 *Italian Heart Journal* 5, 384.

33 M D Newman and others, 'Transplantation of human umbilical cord blood cells in the repair of CNS diseases' (2004) 4 *Expert Opinion on Biological Therapy* 2, 121.

34 A Taguchi and others, 'Administration of CD34 cells after stroke enhances neurogenesis via angiogenesis in a mouse model' (2004) 114 *Journal of Clinical Investigation* 3, 330.

35 T Verina and others, 'Pluripotent possibilities: human umbilical cord blood cell treatment after neonatal brain injury' (2013) 48 *Pediatric Neurology* 5, 346–354.

36 S M Kim and others, 'Gene therapy using TRAIL-secreting human umbilical cord blood-derived mesenchymal stem cells against intracranial glioma' (2008) 68 *Cancer Research* 23.

37 D T Harris and I Rogers, 'Umbilical cord blood: a unique source of pluripotent stem cells for regenerative medicine' (2007) 2 *Current Stem Cell Research and Therapy* 4, 301–309.

38 T H Jaing, 'Umbilical cord blood: a trustworthy source of multipotent stem cells for regenerative medicine' (2014) 23 *Cell Transplant* 4, 493–496.

39 B Sun and others, 'Mechanism study for hypoxia induced differentiation insulin-producing cells from umbilical-cord blood-derived mesenchymal stem cells' (2015) *Biomedical and Biophysical Research Communications* http://dx.doi.org/10.1016/ j.bbrc.2015.09.047 (in press).

40 M Young Choi, S Wong Yeo and K Ho Park, 'Hearing restoration in a deaf animal model with intravenous transplantation of mesenchymal stem cells derived from human umbilical cord blood' (2012) 427 *Biomedical and Biophysical Research Communications* 629–636.

nerve recovery[41] and in the treatment of HIV.[42]

In addition to pluripotent stem cells, UCB has been shown to contain another type of resourceful cell type. Despite initial scepticism,[43] a team from Taiwan conclusively proved in 2004 that UCB also contained the multipotent (specialized) mesenchymal stem cells (MSCs) found in the bone marrow – cells that possess the lineage of connective and skeletal tissue and can differentiate into such as connective tissues, bone, cartilage and fat, presenting enormous potential for regenerative medicine.[44] Mesenchymal cells are of multipotent potency – that is, like pluripotent cells, they have the ability to differentiate into other cells – but multipotent cells are specialised cells that have already been 'committed' to a particular cell line and are therefore perfect for use in regenerative medicine involving connective tissue. The discovery is of huge importance because although MSCs can be harvested from bone marrow, obtaining them is both painful for the donor and yields a low number of cells.[45] The main reason as to why there have been fewer studies using pluripotent stem cells to generate bone, cartilage and fat cells is that MSCs are an excellent source for this purpose. In fact, technically, it would be more difficult to differentiate other sources of MSCs, such as from induced pluripotent stem cells (iPSCs),[46] into mesodermal lineage progenies compared to MSCs from the prospective of efficiency.[47]

Given that there are only 0.01–0.001 per cent of mesenchymal cells housed within the bone marrow[48] and to isolate them requires a particularly

41 Z J Zhang and others, 'Human umbilical cord blood stem cells and brain-derived neurotrophic factor for optic nerve injury: a biomechanical evaluation' (2015) 10 *Neural Regeneration Research* 7, 1134–1138.

42 L Petz, 'Cord blood transplantation for cure of HIV infections' (2013) 2 *Stem Cells Translational Medicine* 9, 635–637.

43 K Mareschi and others, 'Isolation of mesenchymal stem cells: bone marrow versus umbilical cord blood' (2001) 86 *Haematologica* 1099–1100.

44 O K Lee and others, 'Isolation of multipotent mesenchymal stem cell from umbilical cord blood' (2004) 103 *Blood* 5, 1669–1675.

45 M Secco and others, 'Mesenchymal stem cells from umbilical cord: do not discard the cord!' (2008) 18 *Neuromuscular Disorders* 17–18.

46 Induced pluripotent stem cells (iPSCs) were first reported in mouse models in 2006 and human iPSCs in late 2007. iPSCs are adult stem cells that are reprogrammed to become embryonic-like and demonstrate the all-important pluripotent stem cell characteristics. For further information on iPSCs see: National Institutes of Health (NIH), 'What are induced pluripotent stem cells?' http://stemcells.nih.gov/info/basics/pages/basics10.aspx accessed 29 September 2015.

47 I am very grateful to Professor Oscar K Lee, Director of Stem Cell Research Centre, Taiwan for his extremely helpful explanation of the properties and uses of UCB-derived MSCs.

48 E A Jones and others, 'Isolation and characterization of bone marrow multipotential mesenchymal progenitor cells' (2002) 46 *Arthritis Rheumatology* 3349–3360. See also: EuroStemCell, Factsheet (20 June 2012) 'Mesenchymal stem cells: the "other" bone marrow stem cells' www.eurostemcell.org/factsheet/mesenchymal-stem-cells-other-bone-marrow-stem-cells accessed 29 September 2015.

aggressive procedure, the discovery of an additional source of these cells and the relative ease with which they can be procured is certainly advantageous for those working and researching within the field of regenerative medicine – and for those that they treat. As Bianco *et al.* suggest, 'MSCs truly are the newcomers to the club, or maybe the founders of a new one'.[49]

Indeed, scientists claim to have made huge inroads into treating patients suffering from spinal injuries by utilising UCB's powerful mesenchymal cell properties. Following a succession of studies using dog[50] and rat[51] models, the results of research involving human subjects were published in 2013.[52] During the study, a total of 22 patients (six with complete spinal cord injury (SCI) and 16 with incomplete SCI) were treated with cord blood derived mesenchymal cells, administered via intrathecal injection. Whilst there was no improvement from any of the participants suffering complete SCI, 81.25 per cent of those with incomplete SCI reported improved bowel and bladder control and improved motor and/or sensory functions. These results suggest that the use of UCB has the potential to improve neurologic function and the quality of life of most patients with incomplete SCI. Although it is not yet clear whether MSCs derived from UCB or bone marrow are the most superior, what is clear is that through their discovery and isolation, UCB continues to demonstrate its usefulness as a medical resource, particularly as UCB is readily available.

Using PGD and TT techniques to procure specific cord blood

The use of assisted reproductive techniques has further enhanced UCB's potential. The combined techniques of Pre-implantation Genetic Diagnosis (PGD) and Tissue Typing (TT) can ensure that an embryo created by in-vitro fertilisation (IVF) has the exact biological makeup to act as a future UCB donor for an identified recipient,[53] typically a sibling.[54] PGD screens

49 P Bianco and others, 'The meaning, the sense and the significance: translating the science of mesenchymal stem cells into medicine' (2013) 13 *Nature Medicine* 1, 35–42.

50 J H Lee and others, 'Percutaneous transplantation of human umbilical cord blood-derived multipotent stem cells in a canine model of spinal cord injury' (2009) 11 *Journal of Neurosurgery: Spine* 6, 749–757.

51 Z Zhilai and others, 'A combination of taxol infusion and human umbilical cord mesenchymal stem cells transplantation for the treatment of rat spinal cord injury' (2012) 24 *Brain Research* 1481, 79–89.

52 J Liu and others, 'Clinical analysis of the treatment of spinal cord injury with umbilical cord mesenchymal stem cells' (2013) 15 *Cytotherapy* 2, 185–191.

53 Y Verlinsky and others, 'Preimplantation diagnosis for Fanconi anemia combined with HLA matching' (2001) 285 *Journal of the American Medical Association* 3130.

54 A Browne, 'Six couples seek "ethical" designer babies' *The Guardian Online* (London 24 February 2002) www.theguardian.com/uk/2002/feb/24/medicalscience.genetics accessed 29 September 2015.

embryos created by assisted reproduction for defects, disorders and disease,[55] and acts as a type of 'selection process' for embryos suitable for implantation and subsequent provision of UCB at birth. This procedure is performed by the removal of a single cell three to five days after fertilisation when the embryo is at the six-to-ten cell stage. The process of TT enhances the selection process further in that it detects the presence of HLA, ensuring that only embryos with the requisite HLA match are selected for implantation, maximising the chances of a successful outcome. When used together, the techniques greatly enhance cord blood's resourcefulness in that PGD prevents an identified disease from materialising whilst TT provides a perfect blood match for transplantation purposes.

The combination of PGD and TT techniques was first used in 2000 by a couple from the US. Their six-year-old daughter, Molly Nash, suffered from the same blood disorder as Matthew Farrow – Fanconi's anaemia. Because both parents carried the gene for the condition, they had a 25 per cent chance of conceiving another affected child.[56] PGD and TT were carried out at a clinic in the US during a series of four IVF attempts between 1999 and 2000, and five embryos out of 30 tested were found to be both free from the disease and HLA-compatible.[57] The final embryo to be implanted during the third cycle of treatment resulted in the birth of an unaffected child, Adam Nash, who became a UCB donor for Molly. This case is believed to have been the first in the world to use pre-implantation diagnostic genetics to benefit a relative.[58] The first successful 'saviour sibling' treatment to be performed in the UK was reported in 2010.[59]

In the UK, this kind of treatment is governed by the Human Fertilisation and Embryology Act 1990 as amended by the Human Fertilisation and Embryology (HFE) Act 2008. It is overseen by the Human Fertilisation and Embryology Authority (HFEA), which was set up to license and police assisted reproductive practices and which considers applications for PGD and TT on a case-by-case basis. Current legal provision allows PGD to be carried out in very limited circumstances, such as where the couple is at risk of conceiving and ultimately delivering a child with a serious inherited genetic, mitochondrial or chromosomal condition.[60] Following a ruling by the Court of Appeal[61] in

55 This process has been used to detect conditions such as Duchenne muscular dystrophy, cystic fibrosis, haemophilia, and other rare genetic disorders since 1990.

56 D Josefson, 'Couple select healthy embryo to provide stems cells for sister' (2000) 321 *British Medical Journal* 917.

57 Verlinsky and others, 2001.

58 Z Kmietowicz, 'Couple seeks permission to select an embryo to save a son's life' (2001) 323 *British Medical Journal* 767.

59 F Walsh, 'The first successful saviour sibling treatment in the UK' *BBC News Online* (21 December 2010) www.bbc.co.uk/news/health-12055034 accessed 29 September 2015.

60 Human Fertilisation and Embryology Act 1990 (as amended) sch 2 para 1ZA.

61 *R (Quintavalle) v Human Fertilisation and Embryology Authority (Secretary of State for Health Intervening)* [2003] EWCA Civ 667.

2003, later confirmed in the House of Lords,[62] the HFEA was given permission to grant licences for TT in cases where PGD is already permissible to avoid serious medical conditions. Since the introduction of the HFE Act 2008, section 10 of the HFEA's Code of Practice (eighth edition) permits the tissue typing of embryos whether or not this is in conjunction with PGD.[63] The Hashmi family, whose terminally ill son suffered from Beta-Thalassaemia, was the first to be approved for the combined treatment in the UK on the basis that a potential sibling had a realistic chance of inheriting the disease they wished to avoid.[64]

Although a successful ruling was achieved for the Hashmi family, it was not without some form of backlash. No sooner had the original permission in 2001 been granted, than a chorus of protests began to emerge, presenting one of the first controversies surrounding cord blood:

> Within hours, the relieved sighs of the parents of dying children were drowned out by protest. The language was as mindless as it was predictable, from 'spare-part babies' to 'designer baby laboratories'. There were 'principles at stake'.[65]

The possibilities behind this new medical advancement have sparked a number of ethical concerns.[66] First, the use of any form of research, engineering or destruction of embryos may be regarded as morally questionable, regardless of the 'greater good' in offering hope for new therapies. While the resultant UCB stem cells are ethically harvested, it is their creation via the specific PGD/TT 'selection' procedure that raises the issue of humans being treated as a commodity and that the techniques pave the way for the creation of spare parts and baby-farming.[67] Second, there are concerns about the future psychological impact this treatment may have on those directly involved. One argument is that the recipient may experience a life of indebtedness to its sibling for saving their life[68] and, like bone marrow sibling

62 *R (Quintavalle) v Human Fertilisation and Embryology Authority* [2005] UKHL 28.

63 Human Fertilisation and Embryology Authority (HFEA), Code of Practice (8th edition) (2009) s 10 'Embryo testing and sex selection' www.hfea.gov.uk/docs/HFEA_Code_of_Practice_8th_Edtion_(Apr_2015).pdf accessed 29 September 2015.

64 An immediate High Court action by the ProLife Alliance originally secured a bar upon the procedure. See: *R (Quintavalle) v HFEA* [2002] EWHC 2785 (Admin). This bar, however, was lifted by the Court of Appeal later in 2003, and confirmed by the House of Lords in April 2005.

65 C Scarler, 'Trust the science and save a child' *The Guardian Online* (London 16 December 2001) www.theguardian.com/education/2001/dec/16/research.highereducation last accessed 29 September 2015.

66 R J Boyle and J Savulescu, 'Ethics of using pre-implantation genetic diagnosis to select a stem cell donor for an existing person' (2001) 323 *British Medical Journal* 1240.

67 Editorial, 'Designer baby ruling condemned' *BBC News Online* (London 21 July 2002) http://news.bbc.co.uk/1/hi/health/2134314.stm accessed 29 September 2015.

68 L M Terry, 'The child that might be born' (2002) 32 *Hastings Centre Report* 11.

donors, those created specifically to provide UCB might experience psychological problems later in life as a result of enforced altruism.[69]

However, these claims have often been rebutted by reference to the well-publicised case of the Ayala family.[70] Marissa Ayala was conceived naturally, but with the specific aim of acting as a bone marrow and UCB donor for her sister Anissa; and fears that both children would suffer adverse psychological effects have proven to be unfounded.[71] Marissa's own account of her personal contribution towards her sister's survival can only be described as heart-warming. But whilst this particular story culminates in a fairy tale ending, no in-depth studies have been conducted to confirm whether the long-term psycho-social implications of being a 'saviour sibling' have a lasting impact on the donor. Indeed, a qualitative study involving 15 bone marrow sibling donors[72] from a Canadian children's hospital has shown that although many feelings of positivity were experienced by bone marrow donors of successful transplants, anger, guilt and blame were common emotions felt by some of the donors with unsuccessful transplants.[73] If such negative reactions can be evoked in bone marrow sibling donors, it is arguable that those who are specially selected and born for their UCB may suffer similar consequences if their sibling's UCB transplant fails.

In addition to the potential long-term effects on the emotional state of the donor, it has also been proposed that it is better to have been born to be a donor than not at all (unless it transpires that the donor endures a life that 'is not worth living') and that the benefits of existence outweigh any negative effects that the donor may experience.[74] Such assertions have often been premised on Derek Parfit's 'non-identity principle'.[75] This is the moral dilemma of whether to bring a person into existence in the knowledge that that existence would be flawed in some way, but still worth having, with the alternative being to deny that existence at all. If applied here, the principle questions whether the 'saviour sibling' would want to exist within the life to which it was born, as opposed to non-existence; but that is to assert that a

69 Editorial, 'Preimplantation donor selection' (2001) 358 *The Lancet* 9289, 1195.

70 J Rachels, 'When philosophers shoot from the hip' (1991) 5 *Bioethics* 66.

71 J Dulaney, 'Born to save her sister's life, Marissa Ayala, now 23, will graduate from CSULB' *Press-Telegram News* (London 21 May 2013) www.presstelegram.com/general-news/20130521/born-to-save-her-sisters-life-marissa-ayala-now-23-will-graduate-from-csulb accessed 29 September 2015.

72 The sibling bone marrow donors were aged between 7 and 20 years at the time of transplant and 12 to 28 years at the time of interview, respectively.

73 K MacLeod and others, 'Pediatric sibling donors of successful and unsuccessful hematopoietic stem cell transplants: a qualitative study of their psychosocial experience' (2003) 28 *Journal of Pediatric Psychology* 4, 223–231.

74 Boyle and Savulescu, 2001. Also see: S Sheldon and S Wilkinson, 'Should selecting saviour siblings be banned?' (2004) 30 *Journal of Medical Ethics* 6, 533–537.

75 D Parfit, *Reasons and Persons* (Oxford: Clarendon Press, 1984) Chapter 16 'The non-identity problem'.

hypothetical, non-existent being not only has an interest in being born, but that it would benefit in real terms from a life not yet played out. As Taylor-Sands points out: '[a]rguments in support of PGD and TT based on individual benefit to the child to be born look more like rationalisations for a procedure that is primarily motivated by the interests of the parents and the existing sibling'.[76] She certainly has a point.

That said, Taylor-Sands advocates for a re-conceptualisation of the problem. Rather than focusing on whether or not the donor would be harmed by being brought into the world for the benefit of the sibling and therefore requires protection, she argues that the welfare of the child is intrinsically associated with the 'collective interests of the family' and to be a part of that enterprise enhances human flourishing. As the collective interest is to save the sick child, the donor child benefits by being an integral part of the family experience. Put another way, 'Although [PGD and TT] may not promote the individual interests of the child to be born, the child's welfare may ultimately be enhanced by virtue of his/her involvement in the shared family journey to save the life of the existing sibling'.[77] Moreover, treating and caring for a sick child can have serious knock-on effects to the family as a whole, placing a strain on relationships and diverting care and attention away from other siblings. In that respect, providing effective treatment for a sick child can have the cumulative effect of 'treating' the entire family.

Conversely, the destruction of human life already brought into existence also courts controversy. Embryo screening and selection for 'saviour sibling' purposes ultimately infers that embryos failing to meet the required specification will be discarded; and whilst surplus embryos created in vitro for reproductive purposes may be frozen for later use, those screened by PGD and found to be diseased are likely to be destroyed, unless donated for research purposes. Such disposal of potential life can be ethically objectionable to pro-life groups and some religious sects – whose objections are often underpinned by the principles of sanctity of life and human dignity – and by those who crave the ability to naturally procreate but lack the physiology to do so.[78] Clearly, the use of PGD and TT in the pursuit of UCB as a treatment option is far from unproblematic.

In contrast, the collection and use of stem cells from naturally created UCB fails to raise the same concerns associated with the aborted foetuses and embryos created via assisted reproductive technology because it is a blood product without reproductive quality. In fact, UCB for public use has been

76 M Taylor-Sands, 'Saviour siblings and collective family interests' (2010) 29 *Monash Bioethics Review* 2, 12.1–12.15.

77 Ibid.

78 D Marian, 'Ethical implications of a new application of pre-implantation diagnosis' (2001) 285 *The Journal of the American Medical Association* 24.

endorsed by the Catholic, Anglican, Islamic, Hindu and Buddhist religious communities.[79]

The *British Medical Journal* (*BMJ*) declared in 2001 that UCB had 'proven its worth'[80] and promptly called for a more comprehensive system of UCB collection with greater co-ordination and a more secure financial infrastructure.[81] The Royal College of Obstetricians and Gynaecologists (RCOG) also supported this view in its report on public and private UCB banking, published June 2006[82] and was reiterated in a statement in 2011.[83] Together with the Royal College of Midwives (RCM), they have recently endorsed the UK Stem Cell Strategic Forum's recommendation for an optimal bank of 50,000 UCB units within the UK to meet transplant demand.[84] Given the promise that UCB has shown, the RCOG has argued for the NHS to consider greater financial provision in support of public UCB banking and has welcomed the funding for an increase in the UK cord blood inventory. However, with the budgetary restraints imposed on the NHS and the problems associated with resource allocation, this has proven to be anything but straightforward.

Cord blood as a resource and the problem of its availability within the NHS

Since its inception in 1948, it is apparent that the NHS has fought a losing battle in upholding the ideals upon which it had originally been based.[85] The founding principle of community responsibility in direct response to individual need rather than the ability to pay appears to be at odds with the realities of a modern working state health service. It seems that hardly a day goes by without a plethora of popular press articles and media news items that highlight the plight of yet another unfortunate patient being denied treatment;

79 C F C Jordens and others, 'Religious perspectives on umbilical cord blood banking' (2012) 19 *Journal of Law, Medicine and Ethics* 497–511.

80 Proctor and others, 2001.

81 Ibid.

82 Royal College of Obstetricians and Gynaecologists (RCOG), Scientific Impact Paper No. 2, 'Umbilical cord blood banking' (2006) www.rcog.org.uk/globalassets/documents/guidelines/scientific-impact-papers/sip_2.pdf accessed 6 October 2015. This replaces their previous opinion paper of 2001.

83 RCOG and Royal College of Midwives (RCM), 'RCOG/RCM statement on umbilical cord blood collection and banking' (2011) www.rcm.org.uk/sites/default/files/Joint%20Statement%20-%20UCB%20-%20aug%2011%20(6)%20v2.pdf accessed 20 October 2015.

84 NHSBT, UK Stem Cell Strategic Forum,'The future of unrelated donor stem cell transplantation in the UK: a report from the UK stem cell strategic forum' (July 2010) www.nhsbt.nhs.uk/download/uk_stem_cell_strategic_forum_report.pdf, accessed 20 October 2015.

85 C Newdick, *Who Should We Treat?* (2nd edn, Oxford: Oxford University Press, 2005) p 5.

from the obese[86] to the hepatitis sufferer,[87] the infertile,[88] the elderly[89] and those seeking life-saving cancer treatments.[90] Those in need of a bone marrow or UCB transplant have also found themselves at the mercy of available resources,[91] the lack of which has led desperate parents of sufferers such as Antony Nolan, in whose memory the Antony Nolan Trust was set up, to launch appeals for a donor through the media. More recently, the search for suitable donors has been conducted through the use of social networking mediums, for example Twitter[92] and Facebook.[93]

Such tales of despair and conflict within the NHS are undoubtedly a world away from the original hopes and aspirations of those who set up the state system almost 70 years ago. So what is to blame? Perhaps the answer lies somewhere within the costs involved in modern medicine and research, an ever increasing and diverse population, combined with a greater life expectancy in general. Furthermore, the public may be more aware of available treatments as technological advancements are more widely publicised and better understood, especially since the birth of the Internet. Certainly UCB's potential and the ability to either store this valuable resource solely for private use in a commercial bank or donate to a public bank has become more widely known in the last five to ten years thanks to online advertising.

But the range of NHS treatments available may serve only to exacerbate the situation in that just because we possess the knowledge and technology

86 Editorial, 'Obese people in Wales "denied" lifesaving treatment' *BBC News Online* (London 25 February 2014) www.bbc.co.uk/news/uk-wales-26334460 accessed 20 October 2015.

87 J Doward, 'Hepatitis C patients in England denied lifesaving liver drug' *The Guardian Online* (London 16 August 2015) www.theguardian.com/society/2015/aug/16/hepatitis-c-patients-england-denied-liver-drug-regulator accessed 20 October 2015.

88 K Dutta and K Grant, 'Cuts mean more women denied IVF on the NHS' *The Independent* (London 15 September 2015) www.independent.co.uk/life-style/health-and-families/health-news/cuts-mean-more-women-are-denied-ivf-on-the-nhs-9733538.html accessed 20 October 2015.

89 D Campbell, 'Age UK sounds alarm over cuts to care for older people' *The Guardian* (London 6 March 2014) www.theguardian.com/society/2014/mar/06/age-uk-cuts-to-elderly-care accessed 20 October 2015.

90 Editorial, 'Cancer patients denied "too expensive" drugs' *Sky News Online* (London 15 August 2014) http://news.sky.com/story/1319051/cancer-patients-denied-too-expensive-drug accessed 20 October 2015.

91 Editorial, 'Bone marrow appeal' *BBC News Online* (London 10 March 2004) http://news.bbc.co.uk/1/hi/programmes/breakfast/3497042.stm accessed 20 October 2015.

92 Editorial, 'London siblings' bone marrow Twitter plea boosts Jewish donors' *BBC News Online* (London 19 January 2013) www.bbc.co.uk/news/uk-england-london-21089305 accessed 20 October 2015.

93 M Pyrnne, 'Bone marrow donor found for girl, 8, after #pantsonyourhead social media campaign' *The Telegraph Online* (London 14 July 2014) www.guardian.co.uk/technology/2008/dec/15/facebook-transplant-donor-campaign accessed 20 October 2015.

to provide advanced medical techniques, limited available funding means that not every available treatment can be offered to all who seek or need it. Furthermore, a changing political will, imposed austerity measures and the continued growth of the institution itself appears to have added to the system's financial troubles. Whether money should be spent on medicine (and which facet of medicine), acute or chronic care, estates, or research – and which type of research, or whether or not to prioritise innovative projects – continues to put pressure on finite reserves. In spite of a major overhaul of the NHS orchestrated by the Coalition government, culminating in the NHS Health and Social Care Act 2012, which came into force on 1 April 2013, spiralling costs of treatment and administrative burdens have led to 66 per cent of NHS trusts forecasting a deficit by the end of the fiscal year 2015/16, and NHS providers indicating an overspend by all trusts totalling in excess of £2 billion by April 2016.[94]

If UCB availability and use are contextualised within the issue of NHS funding, there appear to be two main (albeit related) areas of controversy. The first concerns the availability of publicly-held UCB units for transplantation purposes and the other relates to the cost of banking and utilising the cells. Despite the acceptance of UCB's use by the medico-scientific community in recent years and the shedding of its 'experimental status',[95] there are currently only two fully operational public banks in the UK. These are the NHS Cord Blood Bank (NHSCBB) and the charity-based Antony Nolan Cord Blood Bank, both of which collect from only a small number of hospitals.[96] The Antony Nolan Cord Blood Bank is incorporated within the Antony Nolan Cell Therapy Centre, and is now known simply as 'the Antony Nolan'. The NHSCBB was set up in 1996 and is orchestrated by NHS Blood and Transport (NHSBT). It currently has in the region of 20,000 units stored[97] and it is hoped that by expanding collection at the Antony Nolan, the banks will have a combined total of 30,000 by 2018.[98] However, given that there are more than 710,000 live births in the UK each year,[99] it is perhaps a little surprising that our total publicly banked UCB unit count is not considerably more, especially when compared to the 600,000 units that

94 The King's Fund, 'Quarterly Monitoring Report' (July 2015) www.gov.uk/government/publications/nhs-foundation-trusts-quarterly-performance-report-quarter-3-201415 accessed 20 October 2015.

95 Proctor and others, 2001.

96 Discussed further in Chapter 3.

97 P Pushpanathan and J James, 'NHS Blood and Transplant Cord Blood Bank: an update for 2013' (2013) 18 *Blood and Transplant Matters* 17 www.blood.co.uk/pdf/publications/blood_matters_38.pdf accessed 20 October 2015.

98 Anthony Nolan, 'Frequently asked questions' www.anthonynolan.org/8-ways-you-could-save-life/donate-your-umbilical-cord-blood/frequently-asked-questions accessed 20 October 2015.

99 Statistics from the Office of National Statistics show that the total number of lives births in 2014/15 was 695,233 in England and Wales and 2,871 in Northern Ireland with the National Records for Scotland recording 14,930 for the same period.

are banked worldwide.[100] Internationally, the UK has the lowest number of public banks when compared to neighbouring France who have five, Spain seven, Canada three, China ten, Japan 11; and there are 21 public banks across the US.[101] In terms of public bank availability, the UK are certainly the poor relations.

Akin to the so-called NHS resources 'postcode lottery', those who wish to publicly donate UCB in the UK face further restrictions because the Anthony Nolan only collects from four hospitals across Manchester, London and Leicester; and the NHSCBB from a further six across London. That said, the pregnant woman's 'choice' to donate UCB is severely restricted as only those who reside in the 'right' location can be considered. In an attempt to raise awareness of the benefits of UCB use, a private members' bill was introduced by David Burrowes, the Conservative MP for Enfield, Southgate in 2008. The Umbilical Cord Blood (Donation) Bill 2008 aimed to educate parents and the wider public of the value and benefits of UCB and to encourage pregnant women to consider UCB donation.[102] However, following its second reading in the House of Commons, the bill failed to make any further ground – although it certainly fed into the wider aspects of the stem cell debate. Following a Parliamentary speech on 31 January 2011 by Mr Burrowes, who is now the Chair of the All-Party Parliamentary Group on Umbilical Cord Blood, the issues raised by the debate were responded to in a very positive and constructive manner, contributing significantly to the current financial commitment from the government.

In spite of this commitment, collection of UCB is not routine and the ability to donate remains limited. A cursory search for the topic of cord blood donation across online parenting websites uncovers an array of disgruntled would-be donors whose description of being denied the ability to donate ranges from: 'It's such a shame – I would have loved to have donated [UCB], and I'm sure others would too', to 'What a dreadful waste of such a helpful material!' In addition, others have offered to start a campaign to *demand* that the ability to donate is made more widespread,[103] culminating in an e-petition to government in early 2014, which attracted over 30,000 signatures.[104] The Republic of Ireland has met with a similar

100 K K Ballen, E Gluckman and H E Broxmeyer, 'Umbilical cord blood transplantation: the first 25 years and beyond' (2013) 122 *Blood* 4, 491–498.

101 Technopolis Group, 'Cord blood banking in the UK: an international comparison of policy and practice' (2009) www.hematos.com/docs/952_final_090114.pdf accessed 20 October 2015.

102 Mr David Burrowes (Enfield, Southgate) (Cons) Hansard HC Vol 1480 Cols 1101–1109 (17 October 2008).

103 Mumsnet, www.mumsnet.com/Talk/pregnancy/2173940-Cord-blood-donation accessed 20 October 2015.

104 Government and Parliament, 'Petition to increase awareness and availability of umbilical cord donation' (February 2014) https://petition.parliament.uk/archived/petitions/45622 accessed 20 October 2015.

response. In the absence of a public bank and many hospitals refusing to allow collections for private storage, Professor Colin McGuckin, then president of Novus Sanguis, an international consortium on cord blood and stem cell research, warned in 2009 that parents of babies born in Ireland may sue Irish health authorities for preventing the collection of UCB at birth.[105]

Whilst expanding the number of banks and collection sites may therefore seem the logical thing to do, it would appear that funding the existing framework has played a major factor in enforcing a streamlined service. In 2008, the UK government commissioned an international review of UCB policies and practices, including a cost-analysis of UCB collection, storage and use. It revealed that in addition to the original start-up costs, the annual estimated costs of maintaining a bank of approximately 20,000 units would be in the region of £3.5 million and would cost in excess of £140 million if the original figure (as suggested by the Anthony Nolan) of 44,000 optimal UCB units were obtained.[106] By 2014, this optimal number had increased to a suggested 50,000.[107]

The high administrative costs have also impacted on the scope of the charity-funded Anthony Nolan Cord Blood Bank. In an online Q&A session with parental support group Mumsnet, a representative from the Antony Nolan communications team spoke of the dilemma:

> Q: If cord blood is so good, why is collecting it so restricted? I bet it's a cost issue.
> A: We are working closely with the NHS and the government to open more collection centres, but unfortunately the costs involved in running a collection centre are very high.[108]

So, is it possible to attribute the perceived low collection rate within the UK solely on the rising costs involved and logistical demands of its infrastructure? If we look to the experiences of public cord blood banking in both Scotland and Northern Ireland, it is apparent that the recent raising of standards and an additional genomic factor have also played a significant role in its restriction.

Scotland

Blood services in Scotland are co-ordinated by the Scottish National Blood Transfusion Service (SNBTS), the specialist provider of transfusion medicine in Scotland. In 2010 the SNBTS launched the long-awaited Scottish National Cord Blood Bank (SNCBB), collecting from the Princess Royal

105 H Colleran, 'Irish parents urged to sue HSE over right to cord blood harvesting' (15 June 2009) *Bionews* www.bionews.org.uk/page_46203.asp accessed 20 October 2015.
106 Technopolis Group, 2009.
107 NHSBT, UK stem cell strategy oversight committee, November 2014.
108 Mumsnet, www.mumsnet.com/qanda/anthony-nolan accessed 20 October 2015.

Maternity Hospital in Glasgow. The SNBTS's long-term aim was to consolidate all of its blood and tissue resources and infrastructure into the new National Centre in Edinburgh, due to be completed by the Spring of 2017. However, by January 2015, the SNCBB had ceased to operate. Whilst costs were a factor in its closure, the primary concerns focused upon the significant changes in the regulatory and quality requirements for cord blood use and the limitations of the Scottish demographic.

With the requirement to improve processing standards and the need to store units of sufficient quality and HLA diversity for transplantation purposes, UCB operations in Scotland have failed to compete with the larger, more established banks and are no longer cost-effective. Furthermore, with only 4 per cent of the total population of Scotland recorded as ethnic minorities,[109] the Scottish regions were not deemed a viable source of under-represented HLA-types; and the majority white population were likely to find suitable HLA-matched units within existing reserves. Clearly, smaller, fledgling public banks housing a limited amount of stock with which to generate income face additional financial pressures in trying to absorb costs whilst maintaining efficacy, quantity and genetic diversity of collected UCB.

At the time of writing, the units held by the now defunct SNCBB remain in Glasgow. Those that meet the current clinical standards will be transferred to the NHSCBB and those that do not will in due course be transferred to other SNBTS facilities, such as the Scottish Centre for Regenerative Medicine, for potential future cell therapeutics development. All UCB collections in Scotland have now been discontinued.[110]

Northern Ireland

Public donations of UCB have been made to the Belfast Cord Blood Bank (BCBB) since June 1993 with collections made initially from the Mater Infirmorum Hospital and later from the Royal Jubilee Hospital. For the last ten years, the BCBB has been co-ordinated by the Northern Ireland Blood Transfusion Service (NIBTS) and more recently has accepted donations from the Belfast Health and Care Trust. However, in February 2015, the Northern Ireland Health and Social Care Board embarked upon a consultative exercise to inform the Northern Ireland populace of proposed changes to existing arrangements for the collection and storage of UCB – the main thrust of which was to cease operations at the BCBB with immediate effect.[111] The

109 The Scottish Government, 'Summary: ethnic group demographics, Scotland 2011' www.gov.scot/Topics/People/Equality/Equalities/DataGrid/Ethnicity/EthPopMig, accessed 20 October 2015.

110 I am grateful to Professor Marc Turner, Medical Director of the SNBTS, for his detailed account of the current provisions in Scotland.

111 Health and Social Care (HSC) Board, Directorate of Commissioning (27 February 2015) www.hscboard.hscni.net/consult/Previous%20Consultations/Cord%20Blood%20Bank%20Services/Consultation%20Letter.pdf accessed 20 October 2015.

12-week public consultation was opened in March 2015 and closure of the BCBB was approved at the HSC Board meeting held on 10 September 2015.[112]

The consultation document[113] cites its rationale for closure as being twofold: first – and akin to Scotland – changes to the laboratory accreditation standards underwritten by the UK Stem Cell Forum has impacted upon the BCBB's ability to absorb the additional costs of high resolution testing involved in HLA-typing currently required to produce high-quality units. It is anticipated that an additional £600,000 per year would be required for the BCBB to meet current testing standards. Second, the demand for units stored at the BCBB has been very low – so low that only two UCB units have been selected for use over the last ten years and were utilised by patients outside of Northern Ireland. Like Scotland, they attribute the decline in demand to the genetic makeup of the population in Northern Ireland whose personal demographic resonates with that of donors situated in Europe and the US. As such, the requisite HLA-matched units required by patients from Northern Ireland are likely to be readily available from a larger bank within those countries and the BCBB no longer conferred an advantage either locally or internationally.

The UK strategy to increase productivity by being more selective about the UCB units it preserves perhaps makes greater sense when viewed in terms of Quality Adjusted Life Years (QALYs). The QALY model is used to assess the value for money of a medical intervention, which takes into account the quality and quantity of life to be lived. Rather than blindly conserving large quantities of indiscriminate HLA-type UCB units, a more focused approach is likely to be more cost-effective in the long term. An economic health analysis conducted by the UK Stem Cell Strategic Oversight Committee in 2014 found that an inventory of 50,000 high-quality, ethnically diverse donations would achieve a cost per additional QALY in the region of £9,400 and generate better cost outcomes than previously anticipated. The Committee proclaim that this figure:

> [i]s significantly below the £15,000 threshold used by the Department of Health to evaluate the effectiveness of spending decisions, and a significant improvement on the Strategic Forum's 2010 cost per QALY estimate of £27,000, reflecting ongoing improvements in patient outcomes and the streamlining of the UK's stem cell supply chain.[114]

112 HSC Board, 'Minutes of HSC Board meeting' (10 September 2015) Item 127/15 at p 3, www.hscboard.hscni.net/board/meetings/September%202015/Minutes%20-%2010%20September%202015.pdf, accessed 20 October 2015.

113 HSC Board, 'Consultation on future arrangements to cord blood bank services in Northern Ireland' (March 2015) www.hscboard.hscni.net/consult/Previous%20Consultations/Cord%20Blood%20Bank%20Services/Consultation%20document%20-Cord%20blood%20bank%20services.pdf, accessed 20 October 2015.

114 NHSBT, UK stem cell strategy oversight committee, November 2014.

In addition to geographical restrictions and running costs, funding for the routine collection of UCB may also be influenced by the fact that the saving of cells satisfies a speculative future need rather than an immediate clinical need. At a micro-level, clinicians are required to make an assessment of each patient and determine what treatment is appropriate within the available resources. Based on their particular clinical need, they are either treated immediately or placed on a waiting list according to the level of urgency and the kind of available treatment necessary to meet that need. The evaluation of a clinical need for UCB collection, however, is problematic because there remains no guarantee that collected UCB will actually be needed in the future. In other words, it is too difficult to establish a clinical need for UCB collection since it is based simply on a *possible* future need.

Whilst internal funding difficulties remain, the cost of importing UCB units for transplant purposes from outside the UK has also met with controversy. In 2009, a review by the Technopolis Group for the Department of Health revealed that the cost of imported and tested UCB in preparation for transplant in the UK was in the region of £17,000 per unit.[115] By 2014, this figure had increased to a staggering estimated £30,000 per imported unit.[116] In contrast, the UK fails to generate anywhere near the same amount of income from UCB exports, with only a tiny fraction of exports made per year. The costs of a UK cord blood donation falls in the region of £16,000 per unit to provide; and it is reported that had the requisite units been locally sourced, the NHS would have saved in the region of £270,000 in the year 2014.[117] The disparity in the costs/income analysis provides greater support for a streamlined strategy focused upon high-quality, diverse stocks, and while the adoption of this approach is undoubtedly a step in the right direction, continued efforts need to be deployed to ensure that the target of a 50,000 strong registry of high-quality units is achieved if we are to alleviate financial tensions and personal suffering.

Whilst financial implications have undoubtedly impacted upon the procurement of UCB becoming routine, scepticism also exists with regard to the efficacy of banking UCB for private use – an area that has generated a quagmire of controversies.

Unravelling the (dis)cord: private cord blood use and the sceptics

Perceived failings in the public health sector, lack of public funding and the desire for choice have promulgated the growth of private healthcare.[118] It is

115 Technopolis Group, 2009.

116 NHSBT, UK stem cell strategy oversight committee, November 2014.

117 Ibid.

118 C Propper, 'The demand for private health care in the UK' (2000) 19 *Journal of Health Economics* 6, 855.

against this backdrop that commercial cord blood companies originated, offering expectant parents a 'once in a lifetime opportunity'[119] to preserve their baby's cord blood 'to protect [their] long-term health'.[120] However, UCB use has not been universally welcomed, and in particular, private banking has generated a great deal of discord amongst the sceptics who doubt its utility and question the motives of the private banks. Critics have argued that parents who seek private storage should be made aware that there are financial risks involved because the odds of using one's own UCB are low. Indeed, the American Congress of Obstetricians and Gynecologists (ACOG) advised in the late 1990s that, 'parents should not be sold this service without a realistic assessment of their likelihood of return on their investment'.[121]

Advocates on either side of the debate appear steadfast in their claims. ACOG[122] estimate the chance of a child ever needing his or her own UCB to be 1 in 2,700 and the American Academy of Pediatrics (AAP) place their estimation in the region of one in 200,000.[123] Fisk and others put this figure at one in 20,000,[124] whilst the European Group on Ethics in Science and New Technologies (EGE) claims the private banking of UCB to be 'of no real use', the chance of its subsequent use as 'negligible', and purported future uses for UCB stem cells as 'hypothetical'. Indeed, the position of the EGE is clear:

> The legitimacy of commercial cord blood banks for autologous use should be questioned as they sell a service, which has presently no real use regarding therapeutic options. Thus, they promise more than they can deliver. The activities of such banks raise serious ethical criticisms.[125]

119 Stemcyte online website, 'Why save cord blood?' www.stemcyte.com/why-save-cord-blood-tissue/, accessed 20 October 2015.

120 Ibid.

121 American Congress of Obstetricians and Gynecologists (ACOG), 'Routine storage of umbilical cord blood for potential future transplantation' *ACOG Committee Opinion No. 183* (Washington DC, 1997).

122 ACOG, 'Umbilical cord blood banking' *ACOG Committee Opinion No. 399* (Washington DC, 2008) www.acog.org/-/media/Committee-Opinions/Committee-on-Obstetric-Practice/co399.pdf?dmc=1&ts=20151015T0949081298, accessed 20 October 2015. This view was re-affirmed in 2012.

123 American Academy of Pediatrics (AAP), 'Cord blood banking for potential future transplantations: subject review' (1999) 104 *Pediatrics* 1, 116. This view was later confirmed in 2011, See: Editorial, 'Should you save your child's own cord blood?' *CNN News* (30 May 2011) http://edition.cnn.com/2011/HEALTH/05/30/saving.blood.cord.p/, accessed 20 October 2015.

124 N M Fisk and others, 'Can routine commercial cord blood banking be scientifically and ethically justified?' (2005) 2 *Plos Medicine* 2 www.ncbi.nlm.nih.gov/pmc/articles/PMC549592/, accessed 20 October 2015.

125 European Group on Ethics in Science and New Technologies (EGE) to the European Commission, 'Ethical aspects of umbilical cord blood banking' (Opinion No.19, March 2004).

The RCOG,[126] and the Royal College of Midwives (RCM)[127] echo the same concerns. In their view, there remains no evidence to recommend personal collection in the absence of family history or medical indication as a worthwhile course of action. The French National Consultative Ethics Committee for Health and Life Sciences reiterated this stance in 2002[128] and in France and Italy,[129] the practice of private banking has been banned.

In stark contrast, statistics provided by the private cord blood industry tend to present a more optimistic picture: both CorCell[130] and Insception Lifebank[131] estimate the chance of future use of one's own cells as one in 5,000 while Cells4Life rate the odds that a child will someday need his or her own newborn stem cells to one in 400.[132] Perhaps more controversially, however, Viacord evidence the probability as 1 in 217 by the age of 70 years.[133] With the current disparity in available statistical evidence regarding autologous UCB's utility, it is little wonder that confusion and distrust has permeated the debate on storage for private use.

Notwithstanding the conflicting statistics, the sceptics also argue that with the increasing quantities of publicly available units – currently in the region of over 600,000 units banked worldwide – failure to store UCB at birth is unlikely to be disastrous.[134] Furthermore, advancements in conventional therapy and improvements in allogeneic transplantation are continuing to reduce the need for autologous cells to be available and have therefore made private UCB banking less necessary.

Another concern for the sceptics is that for certain medical conditions, it may not even be advisable to use one's own UCB. For example, if the disease to be treated originates from the immune system, autologous UCB may contain the same genetic defect and if it were re-infused into the body's system, it would predispose the recipient to the same disease.[135] For this reason, autologous UCB cannot be used to treat inherited metabolic diseases

126 RCOG, 2006.

127 RCOG/RCM, 2011. This view reaffirms the RCM's opinion in 2002 and 2008.

128 French National Consultative Ethics Committee for Health and Life Sciences, 'Umbilical cord blood banks for autologous use or for research' (Opinion No. 74, 2002).

129 Article 1 of Law No. 107/1990 (11 January 2002).

130 CorCell online website, 'What are the odds my child will use their cord blood?' www.corcell.com/blog/what-are-the-odds-my-children-will-use-their-cord-blood/ accessed 20 October 2015.

131 Insception Lifebank online website, 'Factsheet' http://parentsguidecordblood.org/docs/FactSheet_Insception.final.pdf accessed 15 October 2015.

132 Cells4Life online website, 'Common misconceptions' www.cells4life.co.uk/common-misconceptions-faq accessed 20 October 2015.

133 ViaCord online website, 'Benefits of banking: current odds of use' www.viacord.com/healthcare-providers/benefits-of-banking/current-odds-of-use/ accessed 25 November 2015.

134 Fisk and others, 2005.

135 Meyer, Hanna and Gebbie, 2005 p 5.

such as Hunter's disease, Hurler's disease, Krabbe disease and Tay–Sachs' disease because the genetic mutation is already present in the cells. Furthermore, research has indicated that some subtypes of leukaemia are linked to certain chromosomal translocations found in foetal blood. The presence of pre-leukaemic mutations reinforces the concerns expressed by those opposed to UCB use and have led some paediatric haematologists to reject the use of autologous stem cells in the treatment of leukaemia.[136] Ballen and others make a convincing case by spelling out the odds in statistical terms: they claim that there is only a 0.04 to 0.0005 per cent chance that by the age of 21 years, an individual will develop a blood-borne disease that would be treatable with their own (autologous) stored UCB.[137]

The techniques used to preserve UCB have also raised concern with regard to the long-term efficacy of the stored units. Whilst collected UCB can withstand room temperature for up to 48 hours with minimal effect on cell viability, it must be properly stored within 72 hours to ensure non-depletion of the cells, although a 24-hour period is preferable.[138] Various techniques are used to freeze either the viable UCB stem cells within the sample or the entire cord blood unit. The methodology for its conservation has developed over time but, typically, cryopreservation is performed by storing the UCB unit at very low controlled temperatures in either liquid or a vapour-phase nitrogen to maintain its viability.[139]

Controversy has also been witnessed in relation to the optimal conditions required in the storage of UCB.[140] Early studies carried out on cryopreserved UCB units indicated that samples could survive for up to ten years from the initial point of freezing,[141] a view that continues to be held today.[142] Even more promisingly, a report published in 2011 revealed that UCB stem cells could survive for up to 23.5 years.[143] However, it should be noted that this

136 M F Grieves and J Wiemels, 'Origins of chromosome translocations in childhood leukaemia' (2003) 3 *Nature Reviews Cancer* 639.

137 K K Ballen and others, 'Collection and preservation of cord blood for personal use' (2008) 14 *Biology of Blood Marrow Transplant* 356–363.

138 A Hubel and others, 'Liquid storage, shipment, and cryopreservation of cord blood' (2004) 44 *Transfusion* 4, 518.

139 N M Reboredo, 'Collection, processing and cryopreservation of umbilical cord blood for unrelated transplantation' (2000) 26 *Bone Marrow Transplant* 1263–1270.

140 N Ketheesan, and others, 'Effect of cryopreservation on the immunogenicity of umbilical cord blood stem cells' (2004) 30 *Transfusion and Apheresis Science* 1, 47.

141 H E Broxmeyer and S Cooper, 'High efficiency recovery of immature haematopoietic progenitor cells with extensive proliferative capacity from human cord blood cryopreserved for 10 years' (1997) 107 *Clinical and Experimental Immunology* 107 (Suppl. 1), 45.

142 S Yamamoto and others, 'Quality of long-term cryopreserved umbilical cord blood units for hematopoietic cell transplantation' (2011) 93 *International Journal of Hematology* 1, 93–105.

143 H Broxmeyer and others, 'Hematopoietic stem/progenitor cells, generation of induced pluripotent stem cells, and isolation of endothelial progenitors from 21- to 23.5-year cryopreserved cord blood' (2011) 117 *Blood* 18.

conclusion was derived from a study involving the generation of iPSCs from cryopreserved UCB and not during clinical application. In the absence of more conclusive evidence of UCB's longevity it is therefore too early to predict with absolute certainty whether the cells will survive indefinitely. It is therefore extremely speculative for private cord blood companies to advertise the storage of UCB as a 'biological life insurance',[144] and a service that preserves 'a perfect lifetime match'[145] for your beloved child. Given the uncertainty of cryopreserved UCB's future viability and medical potential, such controversial statements based on future hypotheses – that personally stored UCB stem cells hold the key to future health for the entire length of one's life – cannot at this time be substantiated and only seeks to give credence to the critics of private UCB banking.

Meanwhile, patients seeking a suitable UCB transplant from public reserves may be only too aware that whilst public stocks of the requisite HLA-type, quality and cell-dose are somewhat limited, suitable but inaccessible privately stored units may never be utilised. The knowledge that a potentially life-saving resource may exist somewhere in a private account but its exclusivity prohibits its use by a patient in need may for some be too much to contemplate. This may of course be no different from knowing that a suitable bone marrow donor may exist but who is either unwilling to donate or is simply unaware that they are a match. Like privately stored UCB, access to bone marrow is in this sense denied; but what sets these two examples apart is the fact that bone marrow will only be procured once a donor has been located and contacted, whereas a UCB unit will have already been collected and stored. Whilst the search for a potentially life-saving treatment is a traumatic prospect for anyone in need, it is arguable that to be denied access to a resource that has been collected, stored and made readily available for use but may never be utilised may have an even greater psychological effect on those who require the UCB unit for treatment.

Conclusion

This chapter has provided the background to UCB collection and highlighted many of the underlying controversies that surround its use. It has presented UCB stem cells as a powerful biological resource that can be used to treat many blood disorders, immunodeficiency and inherited metabolic diseases, and may in the future be useful in regenerative medicine. UCB has become a major player in transplant services with a greater choice of high-quality UCB amongst the 600,000 cord blood units currently stored for transplantation worldwide; combined with a more robust system of

144 Cord Blood Bank of Canada online website, http://cordbloodbankofcanada.com/step-2-collect-your-familys-biological-insurance-2/, accessed 20 October 2015.

145 Cryo-Cell International online website, 'Frequently asked questions' www.cryo-cell.com/cord-blood/frequently-asked-questions, accessed 20 October 2015.

preparing patients for treatment and advancements in high resolution HLA-typing[146] and the use of techniques such as PGD and TT further enhancing its utility for directed transplantation purposes. In terms of twenty-first century medicine, UCB has been firmly put on the map.

In spite of its resourcefulness, however, its collection is not routine and, like many resources within the NHS, access to available stored UCB units is limited, particularly for those within the BAME group. This is further exacerbated by the low number of collecting hospitals. Certainly, the cost/benefit analysis has impacted significantly on the expansion of public UCB banks within the UK – not only in terms of the finances involved in the day-to-day running of the organisation but also the costs of keeping pace with the new regulatory and accreditation standards required of them. Both Scotland and Northern Ireland have found this particularly challenging and have failed to compete with the larger national and international banks in terms of their ability to produce diverse, HLA-typed, high-quality units not already banked elsewhere. It would appear that the UK's perceived reluctance to set up more public banks and to expand the number of collecting hospitals can be attributed to the prioritising of its endeavours. Rather than collecting and storing an unlimited amount of donated units that may never be used, the UK is internalising its efforts by focusing on raising the quality and efficacy of a more streamlined stock that offers a greater chance of being successfully utilised. Essentially this is a matter of 'improving quality rather than quantity'.[147]

Private banking has also met with its fair share of criticism. The sceptics have argued that private storage of autologous cells offers little in return for the account holder's investment because there are very few blood disorders and diseases that can be treated with autologous cells. Furthermore, its long-term efficacy has not been proven, and suitable UCB (or alternative resources) may already be available on existing registries and within public banks. The ethics of their advertising methods have also fallen into question – the methods deployed by some banks have led to confusion amongst prospective parents over whether or not there is any great need to save one's own cells, and whether they would be of greater utility in a public bank.

But what is important for those who choose to bank privately is that for them, it is a potentially worthwhile act. Regardless of the arguments surrounding the need for greater public stocks, if parents have the necessary finances and are suitably informed, then that is their choice. That said, it is just as important that the decision to save UCB is made based on not only its potential benefits, but also its associated risks. The risks involved in the collection process are addressed in the next chapter.

146 Ballen, Gluckman and Broxmeyer, 2013.
147 NHSBT, UK stem cell strategy oversight committee, November 2014.

2 The risks of cord blood collection

> Whatever the scientific merits or demerits, commercial collection and banking of cord blood presents many other risk factors that need to be taken into account … parents need to know how their care, and the care of other women, can be affected by cord blood collection and what could go wrong during collection.[1]

Since the first successful UCB transplant almost 29 years ago, UCB has generated great excitement amongst those in the stem cell field. As demonstrated in Chapter 1, cord blood advocates have been keen to point out the benefits of using UCB for transplant purposes, in addition to espousing the potential for its future use in regenerative medicine. Meanwhile, private banks have been quick to promote UCB as a readily available resource that should be safeguarded for your family's future use instead of discarding it as biological waste. Their advertising mantra is that the cells can be collected at birth in a completely safe, 'non-invasive and risk-free'[2] manner; the process is presented as 'the most risk-free methodology of stem cells collection'[3] and the service offered is one that enables you to 'give your child the gift of a lifetime'.[4] These are certainly powerful claims and if the ability to save a potentially valuable resource poses 'absolutely no pain or risk to mother and child',[5] as claimed by the commercial UCB banks, then those who can afford to may simply say 'Why not?' To do so would be entirely their choice, but as one troubled prospective parent has expressed:

1 L C Edozien, 'NHS maternity units should not encourage commercial banking of umbilical cord blood' (2006) 333 *British Medical Journal* 801.
2 CryoSave online website, 'Our process' http://cryo-save.com/en/about-cryo-save/our-process, accessed 20 October 2015.
3 ProteanCells online website, 'Benefits of banking cord blood' http://proteancells.com/why-bank-stem-cells/benefits-of-banking-cord-blood/, accessed 20 October 2015.
4 CorCell online website, 'The process' www.corcell.com/the-process/ accessed 21 October 2015.
5 Cryo-Cell International online website, 'The banking process' www.smartcells.com/en/list-of-faqs/is-there-any-chance-of-harm-to-me-or-my-baby.htm, accessed 20 October 2015.

> [w]e are just trying to understand and get our head around everything that is available. There is just so much conflicting information out there, we are just trying to gather as much of its [*sic*] we can so we can make an informed decision.[6]

Conducting individual research is of course very wise. As private banking can be expensive, consumers need to satisfy themselves – with the help of their health professional – whether it is a price worth paying. But in order to make such a decision, one must first unravel the mass of variant material available and unpick the information that the commercial cord blood companies *don't* focus on in their advertising literature. Such a process is important because it has a direct impact upon the quality of informed consent, which is a legal requirement of any clinical procedure. Moreover, in its Scientific Opinion Paper of June 2006, the Royal College of Obstetricians and Gynaecologists (RCOG) highlighted several risk factors involved in UCB collection and from its findings recommended that greater research is needed to determine its full effects. It is with this in mind that I examine the potential risks and key areas of conflict in the context of their scientific, practical and legal application.

Scientific risks

One of UCB's major limitations for transplant purposes is the low volume of blood in a single collected unit and the subsequent number of nucleated stem cells that the unit contains. At its best, harvested UCB typically totals in the region of 75 ml, compared to a litre of bone marrow required to perform a bone marrow transplant,[7] which critics argue renders transplants using UCB in its current form suitable only to benefit paediatric patients or small adults weighing approximately 40–45 kg.[8] While techniques to improve total volume have shown great promise (as we shall see later), it is difficult to convincingly claim that cells collected today will be of use to your newborn child into adolescence or adulthood, as the private UCB sector suggests.

The total nuclear cell (TNC) dose[9] of the unit has proven to be a critical

6 BubHub online forum, www.bubhub.com.au/community/forums/showthread.php?453132-Has-anyone-used-their-babies-cord-blood-for-treatment-for-their-baby, accessed 23 October 2015.

7 S Trotter, 'Cord blood banking and its implications for midwifery practice: time to review the evidence?' (2008) 18 *Midirs Midwifery Digest* 2, 159.

8 Alberta Heritage Foundation for Medical Research, *Cord Blood Transplantation* (Canada: University of York, 1996) Technical Note TN3, 6.

9 The term 'TNC dose' refers to the total number of nucleated stem cells within a cord blood unit.

determinant of success in UCB transplants.[10] Studies[11,12,13] have indicated that transplants using high-nucleated cell dose units improve the chances of engraftment and ultimate patient survival.[14] Engraftment is the term given to the post-transplant phase when the donated cells start to grow and make new blood cells, a major sign of which is the absolute neutrophil count (ANC), also known as neutrophil recovery. This means that there are 500 or more neutrophils, which are a type of white blood cell important for fighting infections, present in the bloodstream for more than three days in a row.[15] Until neutrophil recovery occurs, the recipient is open to viruses and disease because there are not enough neutrophils present in the body's immune system to resist infection.

Critics purport that as engraftment typically occurs around 14–20 days after a bone marrow transplant compared to that of UCB, which is between 25–42,[16] patients may find themselves susceptible to disease for a longer period of time. In a study[17] in adults being treated for leukaemia, neutrophil recovery occurred approximately seven days later in patients who had UCB transplants than those who had bone marrow, and 31 days later for platelet recovery.[18] Although the overall success rates of engraftment using UCB are comparable to that of adult stem cells from bone marrow,[19] the body would lack sufficient immune defences for a greater length of time than in bone marrow transplants and thus there is a greater risk of contracting a potentially fatal disease.

10 R C Wadlow and D L Porter, 'Umbilical cord blood transplantation: where do we stand?' (2002) 8 *Biology of Blood and Marrow Transplantation* 12, 637–647.

11 E Gluckman and others, 'Outcome of cord blood transplantation from related and unrelated donor: Eurocord Transplant Group and the European Blood and Marrow Transplantation Group' (1997) 337 *New England Journal of Medicine* 373.

12 J E Wagner and others, 'Transplantation of unrelated donor umbilical cord blood in 102 patients with malignant and non-malignant diseases: influence of CD34 cell dose and HLA disparity on treatment-related mortality and survival' (2002) 100 *Blood* 1611.

13 P Rubinstein and others, 'Outcomes among 562 recipients of placental-blood transplants from unrelated donors' (1998) 339 *New England Journal of Medicine* 22, 1565.

14 Wadlow and Porter, 2002.

15 This refers to 500 or more neutrophils counted in a cubic millimetre of blood.

16 National Marrow Donor Program, 'Engraftment: Days 0–30' *Be the Match* https://bethematch.org/for-patients-and-families/getting-a-transplant/engraftment—days-0-30/, accessed 20 October 2015.

17 M J Laughlin and others, 'Outcomes after transplantation of cord blood or bone marrow from unrelated donors in adults with leukaemia' (2004) 351 *New England Journal of Medicine* 22, 2265.

18 Platelets are blood cells responsible for clotting, which helps control bleeding. A count of 20,000 to 50,000 platelets per microlitre of blood indicates platelet recovery.

19 S Takahashi and others, 'Comparative single-institute analysis of cord blood transplantation from unrelated donors with bone marrow or peripheral blood stem-cell transplants from related donors in adult patients with hematologic malignancies after myeloablative conditioning regimen' (2007) 109 *Blood* 3, 1322.

While collecting the maximum volume of UCB units (and hence the optimal number of nucleated cells) is paramount, what also needs to be considered are the risks associated with current collection methods and what effect they may have on the procurement of nucleated cells. There are two distinct methods of collection – while the placenta remains inside the uterus (in-utero) and once the placenta has been delivered (ex-utero).

In-utero versus ex-utero collection and cell expansion

Typically, in-utero collection involves the cord being clamped after delivery of the child. The cord is then wiped clean and sterilised with a solution of alcohol and iodine, and a needle (with attached syringe) is inserted into the umbilical vein. The needle is connected to a closed collection bag containing an anticoagulant to inhibit blood clotting into which the blood is drained.[20] Using the ex-utero method, the clamped cord and placenta are delivered intact. The placenta is then transferred either to a collection tray to allow gravity to drain the UCB from the cord into the collection bag, or onto sterilised absorbent sheets where the needle is inserted into the vein as per the in-utero method.

It is a contested issue as to which collection method most efficiently produces greater volume. Lasky and others report that UCB can be collected successfully using either method,[21] a view supported by Sparrow and others in a separate study.[22] However, Solves *et al.* refute this view based on the findings of their own research.[23] Solves claims that unlike their study, the research carried out by Lasky and others failed to take into account obstetric data, which had been shown to boost the quality of UCB.[24] These factors include first-born infants, prolonged labour, an increase in gestational age and increased birth weight, which appear to contribute to high cell dose.[25] In contrast, smoking during pregnancy is associated with a decrease in cell quality.[26]

20 K J Moise, 'Umbilical cord blood stem cells' (2005) 106 *Obstetrics and Gynaecology* 6.

21 L Lasky and others, 'In utero or ex utero cord blood collection: which is better?' (2002) 42 *Transfusion* 10, 1261.

22 R L Sparrow and others, 'Influence of mode of birth and collection on WBC yields of umbilical cord blood units' (2002) 42 *Transfusion* 2, 210.

23 P Solves and others, 'In-utero or ex-utero cord blood collection: an unresolved question' (2003) 43 *Transfusion* 8, 1174.

24 C Donaldson and others, 'Impact of obstetric factors on cord blood donation for transplantation' (1999) 106 *British Journal of Haematology* 1, 128.

25 C P McGuckin and others, 'Cord blood revelations – the importance of being a first-born girl, big, on time and to a young mother!' (2007) 83 *Early Human Development* 733.

26 K K Ballen and others, 'Bigger is better: maternal and neonatal predictors of hematopoietic potential of umbilical cord blood units' (2001) 27 *Bone Marrow Transplant* 1, 7.

From the results of his study, Solves concluded that the in-utero method of collection significantly influences the quality of the procured unit, a view confirmed by the findings of two additional studies conducted by Surbeck and others in 1998[27] and Wong and others in 2001.[28] Similarly, higher volumes of UCB and greater cell dose are more likely to be obtained during Caesarean sections when the samples are collected before placental expulsion.[29] However, this is clearly a controversial and hotly contested issue; and one that raises a risk that failing to adopt the optimal collection may mean that the collected UCB unit lacks efficacy for transplant purposes.

To address this problem, pilot trials in 2005 were conducted by combining two[30] and even three UCB units[31] to increase the number of available nucleated cells with some initial success. These outcomes have continued to be improved upon in clinical trials today,[32] as well as those that combine UCB with peripheral blood stem cells.[33] Furthermore, there has been some progress in the field of cell expansion, which may further help the problem of low cell dose. In 1997, a new cell expansion device called the Replicell System secured the successful UCB transplant of a 52-year-old man suffering chronic myelogenous leukaemia.[34] In 2003, the Aastrom Replicell System was successfully used to treat 27 patients with malignant and non-malignant disorders,[35] and more recently, Israel-based Gamida Cell, in a joint venture with Teva Pharmaceutical Industries Ltd, announced that they are witnessing 'a

27 D V Surbeck and others, 'Optimizing cord blood mononuclear cell yield: a randomized comparison of collection before vs after placenta delivery' (1998) 22 *Bone Marrow Transplant* 3, 311.

28 A Wong and others, 'Cord blood collection before and after placental delivery, levels of nucleated cells, haematopoietic progenitor cells, leukocyte subpopulations and macroscopic clots' (2001) 27 *Bone Marrow Transplant* 2, 133.

29 D V Surbeck and others, 'Umbilical cord blood collection before placental delivery during Caesarean delivery increases cord blood volume and nucleated cell number available for transplantation' (2000) 183 *American Journal of Obstetricians & Gynecology* 1, 218.

30 J N Barker and others, 'Transplantation of 2 partially HLA-matched umbilical cord blood units to enhance engraftment in adults with hematologic malignancy' (2005) 105 *Blood* 3, 1343.

31 W Wiktor-Jedrzejczak and others, 'Simultaneous transplantation of three cord blood units in adults with high risk acute leukaemia' (2005) 106 *Blood American Society of Hematology Annual Meeting*, Abstract 5457.

32 V Rocha and others, 'Double cord blood transplantation: extending the use of unrelated umbilical cord blood cells for patients with hematological diseases' (2010) 23 *Best Practice Research Clinical Haematology* 2, 223–229.

33 J N Barker and others, 'Double-unit cord blood (CB) transplantation combined with haplo-identical CD34+ cell-selected PBSC results in 100% CB engraftment with enhanced myeloid recovery' (2013) 122 *Blood* 21.

34 Editorial, 'New device may make cord blood transplants possible for more adults' (2000) 11 *Blood and Marrow Transplantation* 3 (Newsletter 51).

35 J Jaroscaka and others, 'Augmentation of umbilical cord blood (UCB) transplantation with ex-vivo expanded UCB cells: results of a phase 1 trial using the Aastrom Replicell system' (2003) 101 *Blood* 5061.

paradigm shift in transplantation'[36] following Phase I/II Trials of the new Nicord® using a single UCB configuration with Phase III trials planned for 2017.

While transplants using multiple double cord blood units and expansion techniques have undoubtedly shown great promise, the use of such methods is not uncontentious. Notwithstanding the possibilities of combining two UCB units, even greater quantities of cell dose (the preferred threshold being in the region of 37 million cells per kilo) is required for heavier transplant patients of approximately 80–100 kg; for example, most adults. Furthermore, results of a study published by Wagner and others in 2014 reveal that patient outcomes following double UCB transplants demonstrate a higher incidence of GVHD and slower platelet recovery, highlighting areas that need further investigation.[37] Meanwhile, medical scientists conducting clinical trials in the US using ex-vivo expansion have indicated that the ex-vivo expansion of low-quality stem cells occurs at the expense of the higher-quality cells.[38] In other words, whilst expansion of cell dose quantity is possible, cell quality may be compromised and the efficacy of the procured unit is put at risk.

However, in October 2015, scientists at the Antony Nolan Research Institute revealed that they had developed a technique that could revolutionise cell engraftment. They discovered that by adding the protein IL-15 into the natural killer cells within a UCB unit they could greatly enhance its utility, which would speed up the engraftment process, ultimately aiding the patient's recovery process and reducing the risk of infection.[39] Natural killer cells are a type of white blood cell responsible for the body's immune system and help to detect and fight disease. Overall, the ability to enhance the quality of these cells would promote better UCB cell function and optimise transplant outcomes. However, caution is urged. While the technique has shown promise, it is still in the clinical trials phase and is yet to be trialled in human application. As the commonly held view is that the total number of nucleated cells that can be transplanted strongly correlates with clinical outcome, it is imperative that further studies using human subjects are carried out to test the full extent of natural killer cells' ability to affect UCB before stronger conclusions can be drawn.

36 Gamida Cell online website, (Press Release 9 September 2013) www.gamida-cell.com/press_item.asp?ID=57&t=Gamida-Cell-Announces-the-Successful-Transplantation-of-the-First-Patient-in-The-Company%E2%80%99s-Phase-I/II-Study-of-NiCord%C2%AE-in-a-Single-Cord-Configuration accessed 23 October 2015.

37 J E Wagner Junior and others, 'One-unit versus two-unit cord-blood transplantation for hematologic cancers' (2014) 371 *New England Journal of Medicine* 18, 1685–1694.

38 S Robinson and others, 'Ex-vivo expansion of umbilical cord blood' (2005) 7 *Cytotherapy* 3, 243.

39 M Escobedo-Cousin and others, 'Natural killer cells improve hematopoietic stem cell engraftment by increasing stem cell clonogenicity in vitro and in a humanised mouse model' (2015) 10 *PLoS One* 10.

Practical risks

The RCOG cite the timing of cord clamping as one of the major risk factors involved in UCB collection.[40] There are two methods used in cord clamping: early (immediate) or deferred (delayed), both of which carry some kind of health risk to mother and/or baby.[41] For decades, early cord clamping has been commonly practised in the UK despite the lack of consensus amongst professionals as to its advantages.[42,43,44] However, in response to mounting evidence that questioned the safety of the practice, the RCOG acknowledged in its latest Scientific Impact Paper that immediate cord clamping had become 'routine practice without rigorous evaluation'.[45] As a consequence, the RCOG now advocates deferred clamping as part of its routine midwifery care[46] based on a review of the Cochrane Database[47] and the latest advice from the National Institute for Health and Care Excellence (NICE). NICE recommends that under regular conditions, the cord should not be clamped any earlier than 1 minute and no later than 5 minutes in order to minimise health risks to the foetus.[48]

However, whilst deferred clamping is the current recommended standard in maternity care, for the purposes of UCB collection, early clamping is necessary to ensure maximisation of the resource,[49,50,51] which presents those

40 Royal College of Obstetricians and Gynaecologists (RCOG), Scientific Impact Paper No. 2, 'Umbilical cord blood banking' (2006) at 5(1) www.rcog.org.uk/globalassets/documents/guidelines/scientific-impact-papers/sip_2.pdf accessed 6 October 2015.

41 The phrase 'early' (or 'immediate') clamping is commonly associated with clamping the cord within 30 seconds of birth and 'deferred' (or 'delayed') refers to waiting for at least two minutes after birth before clamping.

42 P F Van Rheenan and B J Brabin, 'A practical approach to timing cord clamping in resource poor settings' (2006) 333 *British Medical Journal* 954.

43 F Bertolini and others, 'Placental blood collection: effects on newborns' (1995) 85 *Blood* 11, 3361.

44 N Ende, 'Cord blood collection: effects on newborns (Medical-Legal)' (1995) 86 *Blood* 12, 4699.

45 RCOG, Scientific Impact Paper No. 14, 'Clamping of the umbilical cord and placental transfusion' (February 2015) www.rcog.org.uk/globalassets/documents/guidelines/scientific-impact-papers/sip-14.pdf accessed 24 October 2015.

46 Ibid.

47 S J McDonald and others, 'Effect of timing of umbilical cord clamping of term infants on maternal and neonatal outcomes' (2013) *Cochrane Database of Systematic Reviews* 7 Art No. CD004074

48 National Institute for Health and Care Excellence (NICE) Guideline [CG190] 'Intrapartum care for healthy women and babies' (December 2014) www.nice.org.uk/guidance/cg190/chapter/1-recommendations, accessed 22 October 2015. At the time of writing, the Royal College of Midwives (RCM) have established an 'Optimal Cord Clamping Working Group' to review and report on their current recommended advice.

49 Ende, 1995.

50 T Levy and I Blickstein, 'Timing of cord clamping revisited' (2006) 34 *Journal of Perinatal Medicine* 4.

51 D Farrar and others, 'Measuring placental transfusion for term babies: weighing babies with cord intact' (2011) 118 *British Journal of Obstetrics and Gynaecology* 70–75.

who choose to preserve UCB with a very difficult decision. Should they request early clamping to procure the maximum volume/optimal number of cells (because, as we saw above, to do otherwise may render the collected unit unsuitable for transplant purposes) or follow professional opinion to minimise the health risks? Although UCB can be procured using either method, neither is without risk.

Delayed versus early cord clamping

First, a delay in the clamping process has been associated with the risk of the baby developing hyperbilirubinemia,[52] which causes jaundice, and has been linked to the precipitation of other birth-related conditions such as hypothermia[53] and polycythaemia.[54] Neonatal polycythaemia is of particular concern as it can cause neurological complications.[55] However, as Mercer and Erickson-Owens acknowledge:

> A widely held belief, often unreferenced in obstetrical and neonatal textbooks, is that there is a link between DCC [delayed cord clamping], hyperbilirubinemia, and symptomatic polycythemia. Clinicians are concerned that babies will be "overtransfused." This belief is unsubstantiated by the current research. Recent evidence suggests DCC is a harmless practice.[56]

In contrast, early clamping has been linked to the risk of hypovolemia, a blood disorder caused by an excess of fluid in the blood[57] and the risk of intraventricular haemorrhage (IVH)[58] in pre-term infants.[59] IVH is a serious condition as it can ultimately lead to brain damage.

Perhaps the biggest controversy surrounding early cord clamping is the various risk factors associated with placental transfusion, a term given to the

52 S Saigal and others, 'Placental transfusion and hyperbilirubinemia in the premature' (1972) 49 *Pediatrics* 3, 406.
53 Hypothermia is a dangerously low body temperature of below 95 degrees fahrenheit (35 degrees celsius).
54 Polycythaemia is caused by an overload of red blood cells, which thickens the blood and makes it harder to circulate through the body. This in turn can cause the baby to experience breathing difficulties.
55 T Ze-Zhong and others, 'Relationship between neonatal polycythemia and brain damage' (2006) 44 *Chinese Journal of Pediatrics* 11, 845–849.
56 J S Mercer and D A Erickson-Owens, 'Rethinking placental transfusion and cord clamping issues' (2012) 26 *Journal of Perinatal and Neonatal Nursing* 3, 202–217.
57 J S Mercer, 'Current best evidence: a review of the literature on umbilical cord clamping' (2001) 46 *Journal of Midwifery and Women's Health* 6, 402.
58 Bleeding within the brain, which places pressure on the nerve cells and can cause brain damage.
59 G J Hofmeyr and others, 'Periventricular/intraventricular haemorrhage and umbilical cord clamping. Findings and Hypothesis' (1988) 73 *South African Medical Journal* 2, 104.

transfer of foetal blood from the placenta to the baby at birth. Placental transfusion is an important phase of the birthing process as it provides the baby with up to 30 per cent more blood volume and up to 60 per cent more red blood cells,[60] and if this process is interrupted by early cord clamping – which forces the umbilical arteries to close prematurely – the baby will be denied up to a six-month supply of the red blood cells needed to provide oxygen for normal growth and development.[61]

A lack of red blood cells, or iron deficiency, in neonates has been shown to hinder neurodevelopment, which may be irreversible even after iron supplementation[62] and lead to a greater chance of anaemia in later life.[63] Clinical trials have also shown that children with low iron counts demonstrate decreased cognitive abilities, poor school performance and behavioural problems,[64] and may be shy and withdrawn.[65] In clinical trials conducted in Sweden to compare the effects of early versus deferred clamping in 400 full term infants, those subjected to early cord clamping demonstrated lower iron status at birth and a higher prevalence of iron deficiency at four to six months development;[66] and conversely, those in the delayed clamping group were found in a follow-up study to demonstrate a higher degree of fine motor skills at four years of age.[67] As Rabe *et al.* have recently warned:

> Infants who have received early [cord clamping] have demonstrated lower iron stores at 6 months of age. This time co-incides with the most critical period of brain growth and myelin development, during which most of the brain's eloquent neural pathways are established. We can no longer ignore the effects of low iron stores and neurodevelopment.[68]

Of course, it is not only red blood cells that placental transfusion transfers. Of comparable importance are the stem cells themselves that are housed within the placental blood that the baby may need in later life – the very cells

60 Mercer, 2001.

61 Mercer and Erickson-Owens, 2012.

62 B Lozoff and others, 'Long-lasting neural and behavioural effects of iron deficiency in infancy' (2006) 64 *Nutrition Reviews* S34–S43.

63 S J McDonald and P Middleton, 'Effects of timing of umbilical cord clamping of term infants on maternal and neonatal outcomes (Protocol)' (2003) *Cochrane Database of Systematic Reviews* 1 Art No. CD0040747.

64 J Beard, 'Recent evidence from human and animal studies regarding iron status and infant development' (2006) 137 *Journal of Nutrition* 524S–530S.

65 B Lozoff and others, 'Dose-response relationships between iron deficiency with or without anemia and infant social-emotional behaviour' (2008) 152 *Journal of Pediatrics* 696–702.

66 O Andersson and others, 'Effect of delayed cord clamping on neurodevelopment at 4 months of age: a randomised clinical trial' (2011) 343 *British Medical Journal.*

67 O Andersson and others, 'Effect of delayed cord clamping on neurodevelopment at 4 years of age: a randomized clinical trial' (2015) 169 *JAMA Pediatrics* 7, 631–638.

68 H Rabe and others, 'Long term follow-up of placental transfusion in full term infants' (2015) 169 *JAMA Pediatrics* 7, 623–624.

that are collected for private banking. Tolosa *et al.* rather aptly refer to this transfer of cells from mother to child during the third stage of labour as 'mankind's first natural stem cell transplant'.[69] Controversially, rather than collecting the cells 'as a wise investment towards the family's future health'[70] it may transpire that the baby needs them all, at the moment of birth, rather than in a hypothetical future. Any artificial loss of stem cells at birth, Tolosa *et al.* argue, could lead to a vast number of health conditions in the child ranging from asthma, to diabetes, Parkinson's disease and cerebral palsy.[71]

In addition to these findings, the results of a study carried out in animals, reported in 2001, showed that blood loss at birth could result in harm.[72] In the study, 25 per cent of the total blood volume in newborn rats was removed and compared to those rats whose birth had not been subject to any intervention. At only three hours old, the presence of proinflammatory cytokines, indicating tissue damage, was detected in the lungs and liver of the rats whose blood had been removed, whereas none was detected in those that had not. The researchers concluded that the removal of 25 per cent of the rat pup's blood had damaged their vital organs, causing the production of cytokines. Interestingly, the presence of cytokines was also noted in early blood samples of human newborns who later developed the motor neurone condition, cerebral palsy.[73] If the results of the rat model are an indication of what *could* occur in human infants whose cords are clamped too early, then this should be fully investigated, substantiated and communicated to those contemplating UCB banking. This is especially poignant given the warnings of Mercer who suggests that early clamping denies the newborn 30 per cent of its total blood volume, a figure that Hutchon places as 40 per cent[74] and Morley claims to be 'between 30 to 50 per cent of its natural blood volume'.[75]

The precise aetiology of cerebral palsy (an umbrella term for the effects of damage to the developing brain), however, is very difficult to determine,[76]

69 J N Tolosa and others, 'Mankind's first natural stem cell transplant' (2010) 14 *Journal of Cell Molecular Medicine* 488–495.

70 Cryo-Cell International online website, 'Cord blood banking' www.cryo-cell.com/cord-blood-banking accessed 25 November 2015.

71 Tolosa and others, 2010.

72 M Rajnik and others, 'Early cytokine expression induced by hemorrhagic shock in a non-resuscitated rat model' (2001) 49 *Pediatric Research*, 4S and 44A.

73 K B Nelson and others, 'Neonatal cytokines and coagulation factors in children with cerebral palsy' (1998) 44 *Annals of Neurology* 4, 665.

74 D J R Hutchon in: C Fox, 'The great clamping debate' (4 April 2013) *Bioscience Technology* www.biosciencetechnology.com/articles/2013/04/great-clamping-debate accessed 24 October 2015.

75 G M Morley, 'Premature clamping of the umbilical cord may result in brain damage to newborns' *Mercola.com online website* (8 March 2013) http://articles.mercola.com/sites/articles/archive/2003/03/08/umbilical-cord-part-two.aspx, accessed 24 October 2015.

76 In addition to development and birth-related causes, researchers have very recently claimed that up to 45 per cent of cases could be attributed to genetic causes. See: Editorial, 'Genetic causes of cerebral palsy trump birth causes' (2 June 2015) *Science Daily* www.sciencedaily.com/releases/2015/06/150602074725.htm accessed 26 October 2015.

but can occur during pregnancy or during the intrapartum period, from the onset of labour to soon after birth.[77] Hypoxic-ischemic encephalopathy (HIE), which is also known as intrapartum asphyxia, can arise from oxygen deprivation during birth caused by an interruption of the placental blood flow, and is the most common birth injury claim.[78] Thankfully, cerebral palsy caused by intrapartum asphyxia has been shown to be extremely rare[79] and the contribution of intrapartum events and obstetric mismanagement to overall cerebral rates is low.[80] Moreover, for the unlucky few who do develop the condition, the good news is that clinical trials have shown some exciting results using UCB *to treat* cerebral palsy patients,[81] with a world first medical trial using UCB being conducted in a two-year study at the Royal Children's Hospital in Melbourne, Australia.[82] In 2008, *The Los Angeles Times* reported on the extraordinary improvement in health of a little boy in the US who suffered from the condition. The article recalled how doctors had reinfused the child's own UCB cells and he transformed from being unable to walk, sit or crawl to walking and reaching within five days of the treatment, prompting his parents to declare the cells as 'liquid gold'.[83]

Meanwhile, in the UK, a three-year-old female sufferer was busy having her own privately stored stem cells reintroduced into her body.[84] She too demonstrated vastly improved motor skills – and it would appear that these children are not alone. A quick search of *Google* reveals an abundance of children with similar stories, many gracing the websites of private cord blood companies eager to share their experience with other families.[85] But what

77 J M Perlow, 'Intrapartum hypoxic-ischemic cerebral palsy injury and subsequent cerebral palsy: medico-legal issues' (1997) 6 *Pediatrics* 851–859.

78 S Donn, 'Medico-legal implications of hypoxic-ischemic birth injury' (2014) 19 *Seminars in foetal and neonatal medicine* 5, 317–321.

79 E Blair and F S Stanley, 'Intrapartum asphyxia: a rare cause of cerebral palsy' (1988) 112 *Journal of Pediatrics* 4, 515–519.

80 Donn, 2014.

81 C M Cotton, 'Feasibility of autologous cord blood cells for infants with Hypoxic-ischemic encephalopathy' (2014) 164 *Journal of Pediatrics* 5, 973–979.

82 M Dobbin, 'Children to receive umbilical cord blood in world first cerebral palsy trial' *The Sydney Morning Herald* (9 March 2016) www.smh.com.au/national/health/children-to-receive-umbilical-cord-blood-in-world-first-cerebral-palsy-trial-20160309-gney2t.html accessed 10 March 2016.

83 E Davis, 'Cord blood: a weapon against cerebral palsy?' *Los Angeles Times* (Los Angeles, 7 April 2008) http://articles.latimes.com/2008/apr/07/health/he-cpalsy7 accessed 26 October 2015.

84 S Templeman, 'Stem cell first for cerebral palsy girl' *The Sunday Times Online* (London 7 November 2010) www.thesundaytimes.co.uk/sto/news/article439988.ece accessed 26 October 2015.

85 Examples such as: Lifeline, www.lifelinecordblood.com/cgibin/hweb?-A=1866&-V=media, Smartcells, www.smartcells.com/blog/2010/11/08/sasha-3-is-infused-with-stem-cells-from-her-own-umbilical-cord-to-treat-cerebral-palsy/ CordLife, www.cordlife.com/news/pdf_articles/Singapore_First_Cerebral_Palsy_treatment.pdf CryoSave, www.cryo-save.co.ke/six-year-old-girl-with-cerebral-palsy-treated-with-own-stem-cells-from-cord-blood/ Smartcells, www.smartcells.com/our-clients-their-stories-

these children have in common – besides having their cord blood collected and saved at birth – is that they all have cerebral palsy or anoxic brain injury. This begs the question: is there a connection between saving a child's cord blood and developing neurological problems?[86] There is of course no conclusive evidence to connect the two, and we know little of the collection methods used in any of these cases referred to, or of the children's familial backgrounds or birth experiences – yet it does make you think. If early clamping is deployed to collect UCB (which is needed to maximise blood and cell volume), preventing full transfer of blood, which in turn can cause tissue damage indicative of cerebral palsy (or any type of red blood loss induced harm), this is particularly worrying. Notwithstanding the follow-up studies conducted in relation to the timing of cord clamping, there do not appear to be any research studies that have specifically examined the health outcomes of children subjected to UCB collection. That said, we would be wise to adopt the RCOG's call to better understand the effects of all third stage practices, which includes UCB collection, and the potential consequences these practices have on newborns to determine its potential long-term consequences.[87]

In spite of challenged cord clamping opinions, recent reviews of available literature[88] and news reports[89] support delayed cord clamping for both full- and pre-term infants. Although early cord clamping has been shown to maximise cord blood volume[90] and is thus beneficial for UCB collection, it also presents a greater risk for the child.[91] As David Hutchon, consultant obstetrician and gynaecologist, advises:

> Cord blood collection must not be allowed to restrict the [delayed cord clamping] practice. The value of delayed cord clamping has been shown whereas the value of commercial cord blood banking is still hypothetical at present.[92]

kyle-carla-poppleton/ ViaCord, http://blog.viacord.com/lillians-story-cerebral-palsy-treated-with-cord-blood/ accessed 26 October 2015; and for a selection of cerebral palsy patients who had their cord blood collected at one UCB bank, see: The Cord Blood Registry, www.cordblood.com/shared-stories accessed 26 October 2015.

86 K Devine, 'Cord blood collection and cerebral palsy – is there a connection?' *Bionews* (22 November 2010a, Progress Educational Trust) www.bionews.org.uk/page_82436.asp accessed 26 October 2015.

87 RCOG, 2006.

88 Mercer and Erickson-Owens, 2012.

89 D Campbell, 'Hospitals warned to delay cutting umbilical cords after birth' *The Guardian Online* (London 11 July 2013) www.theguardian.com/society/2013/jul/11/hospitals-nhs-umbilical-cords-babies-delay-cutting accessed 23 October 2015.

90 Levy and Blickstein, 2006.

91 Rajnik and others, 2001.

92 D J R Hutchon (Letter), 'Commercial cord blood banking – immediate cord clamping is not safe' (2006) 333 *British Medical Journal* 919.

What present as additional problems, however, are the practical risks associated with collecting the UCB either in-utero or ex-utero.

In-utero versus ex-utero collection methods

In-utero collection is performed with the placenta still in situ, whilst ex-utero collection is performed after the placenta and clamped cord have been delivered. As with the early cord clamping method, studies have indicated that greater volume and a higher incidence of nucleated cell dose occurs when UCB is collected via the in-utero method and demonstrates a lower incidence of bacterial contamination than the ex-utero method.[93] The in-utero method is therefore preferable for UCB banking.

However, there might be practical reasons[94] why the ex-utero method is preferable. First, in-utero collections can be both invasive and distressing for the pregnant woman,[95] while the logistics of the ex-utero method ensures that the number of people within the delivery room is kept to a minimum, thus creating a calm atmosphere for everyone involved in the birth process. Second, ex-utero collection is less likely to interfere with the third stage of labour, the phase between the baby being delivered and up to and including the delivery of the placenta. This is a particularly vulnerable phase of the labour process when the risk of maternal haemorrhage[96] is at its greatest and severe pre-eclampsia[97] is of concern.

In 2011, a retrospective analysis of data gathered from 529 consecutive vaginal full term births across 14 European countries revealed that maternal bleeding after birth was significantly greater in women who had donated cord blood compared to those who had not.[98] Analysis of the data collected as part of the European project on obstetric, reduction, attitudes, trial and early warning system, commonly known as the EUPHRATES Project, concluded that, 'Cord blood collection can increase intrapartum blood loss, especially at instrumental deliveries.'[99] Similarly, a study conducted by Cohen and others between 2007 and 2009 on a cohort of 92 women who chose to

93 Solves and others, 2003.

94 Lasky and others, 2002.

95 D Dickenson and P Vineis, 'Evidence-based medicine and quality of care' (2002) 10 *Health Care Analysis* (2002) 10, 243.

96 Maternal (or post-partum) haemorrhage is a potentially life threatening complication of vaginal and Caesarean section births resulting in blood loss in excess of 1,000 ml. Between 1–10 per cent of all pregnancies experience complications associated with PPH and approximately 17 per cent of maternal mortality is caused by PPH.

97 Severe pre-eclampsia is the most serious of common pregnancy related conditions. It is caused by a defect in the placenta, which results in the mother experiencing symptoms such as high blood pressure, protein in the urine and severe swelling in parts of the body.

98 L Amat and others, 'Cord blood collection for banking and the risk of maternal haemorrhage' (2011) 90 *Acta Obstetricia et Gynecologica Scandinavica* 1043–1045.

99 Ibid., 1043.

have UCB collected while undergoing a Caesarean section, produced equivalent results. They concluded:

> The collection of UCB was found to be associated with a drop in maternal haemoglobin levels. Although it has been suggested that in utero collection makes it possible to increase the total volume of collected cord blood, the current results indicate that this might also increase the risk of maternal haemorrhage during caesarean section, probably due to delayed uterine incision closure.[100]

Clearly, in-utero collection for the purposes of preserving UCB is a controversial issue in both vaginal and Caesarean deliveries with regards to the health and wellbeing of the birthing woman.

One final area of controversy is raised by the RCOG who fear that collecting UCB during the third stage of labour may distract the midwife from essential routine checks and maternal or neonatal observations may be delayed or overlooked.[101] For the baby, such procedures would include immediate checks to ensure a clear airway, normal body temperature and check for any physical abnormalities. For the birthing mother, the routine monitoring of blood pressure, pulse, temperature, uterine fundal height[102] and her general wellbeing would normally be a priority. In addition, the placenta and umbilical cord are checked as soon as practicable to ensure that they are complete[103] and do not demonstrate abnormalities.[104] Any or all of these routines may be disrupted in the process of saving UCB. UCB collection increases the workload of hospital staff during this critical time and without adequate resources, this additional procedure could jeopardise the patient's primary care, putting both mother and baby at risk. This is particularly poignant given the current shortage of midwives within the NHS.[105]

100 Y Cohen and others, 'Umbilical cord blood collection carry increased maternal bleeding risk during cesarean section' (2012) 25 *The Journal of Maternal-Fetal and Neonatal Medicine* 9, 1549–1551.

101 RCOG, 2006.

102 The 'Uterine Fundal Height' is the distance between the top of the pubic bone and the uterus, calculated in centimetres. This is measured during pregnancy to estimate the number of gestational weeks of the foetus. After birth, it can be used to monitor the contraction of the uterus. Observations with regard to fundal height and blood loss are particularly important to the wellbeing of the mother because if the uterus contracts insufficiently, blood may accumulate within the uterus.

103 Checking that the placenta has expelled completely is crucial because retained placental tissue can be associated with maternal haemorrhage and infection.

104 Abnormalities detected in the placenta and umbilical cord may indicate abnormal foetal development and perinatal morbidity.

105 Commons Select Committee, 'NHS midwives shortage remains despite increasing numbers' (31 January 2014) www.parliament.uk/business/committees/committees-a-z/commons-select/public-accounts-committee/news/maternity-services-report/, accessed 28 October 2015.

Although the practical risks of UCB raise possible health implications for the patient, those who collect the cells (and their employers) are also themselves potentially at risk of legal liability for any negligent execution of the collection process.

Legal risks – an overview[106]

While it is the parent, child and/or beneficiary that bears the risks associated with the scientific and practical implications of UCB collection, it is the facilitators of the collection process – typically midwives – who face the potential legal consequences of performing the procedure. They are at risk of being held personally liable if they perform any part of the collection process negligently, and cause physical harm to mother, baby or others in their care, or fail to obtain valid consent. Furthermore, their employers will be held vicariously liable for any torts they commit provided that collection took place during the course of their employment,[107] or even directly liable for failing to provide competent staff. For a claim in clinical negligence to succeed, the patient must show that the UCB collector owed them a duty of care, which was breached and resulted in harm.

Legal harms

Legal harms capable of compensation in the tort of negligence include personal injury, damage to property and, in limited circumstances, psychological harm and economic loss. As previously discussed, personal harm to the pregnant woman and/or baby can manifest during the third stage of labour if essential checks and observations and/or other necessary treatment is delayed or overlooked, in addition to potential harm from the collection process. Furthermore, needlestick injury pursuant of the use of multiple needles used for collection may arise, or the essential care of other patients within the labour suite may be compromised if medical attention is diverted in favour of UCB collection.

Other than personal injury, a claim in negligence may be formulated in a number of other forms; from damage to the procured unit (such as blood spillage during collection or from damage to the blood bag) or from inadequate labelling of the UCB or maternal samples that prevent its storage because it fails to meet the recommended cryopreservation standards. Labelling mix-ups are not uncommon. In 2002, it was revealed that mixed-

106 The legal risks that can arise through the tort of negligence and the doctrine of informed consent are examined in detail in later chapters. However, an overview is given here to provide context and to indicate the enormity of the possible consequences of collection to health professionals early in the book.

107 See: *Lister v Helsey Hall* [2001] UKHL 22, later confirmed by Lord Phillips in *Various Claimants v Catholic Child Welfare Society and Others* [2012] UKSC 56.

race twins had been born to a white couple after sperm at an IVF clinic had been mislabelled. This led to the introduction of a 'bar-coding' system of labelling to prevent further mishaps. Despite the new system, the same mistake occurred in 2007 and again in May 2009 at the Guy's and St Thomas' Hospital, London.[108] In a case that centred on a different type of insufficient labelling, a white couple sued a defendant trust in 2011 following the birth of their twins who were born with skin colour that did not match the requested donor sperm. The trust had assured the couple that they would only use sperm from a white or Caucasian donor; however, imported sperm labelled 'Caucasian (Cape-coloured)' was used in error.[109]

Since 2008, the collection and storage of UCB has been regulated by the Human Tissue (Quality and Safety for Human Application) Regulations 2007, which transpose the European Union Tissues and Cells Directive (EUTCD)[110] into UK law. These regulations place stringent guidelines on hospitals that procure UCB and require all collected cells to be fully traceable for identification and monitoring purposes. Any labelling error that would impact upon the unit's utility would prevent it from being stored and raise the risk of a subsequent claim against the collector. Furthermore, a breach of the requirement for a UCB collector to act under a licence or observe its provisions may attract specific liability under the Regulations. Section 10(3) provides that non-compliance may attract a sanction that constitutes a fine, up to two years' imprisonment, or both.

Non-injury claims of this type may be difficult to pursue, particularly because the mother must demonstrate that she and/or her child has legal ownership over the 'damaged' UCB unit and that the cells are property capable of giving rise to compensation.[111] Whilst the existing case law shows that property rights over extracted biological material are recognised in limited circumstances,[112] their exact legal status remains somewhat unprincipled and unclear.[113] As we shall see later, UCB may be *viewed* by some parents as 'property' for which they may wish to seek compensation if it should become damaged and rendered unusable. Furthermore, ownership rights over the cells would directly impact upon who the claimant should be in a negligence action.

108 N Shaikh, 'Fertility watchdog investigates serious IVF mix-ups at London hospital' (Progress Educational Trust, 3 May 2009) *Bionews* www.bionews.org.uk/page_13787.asp, accessed 28 October 2015.

109 *A (a minor) and B (a minor) by C (their mother and next friend) v A Health and Social Services Trust* [2010] NIQB 108.

110 Council Directive (EC) 2004/23 on setting standards of quality for the donation, procurement, testing, processing, preservation, storage and distribution of human tissues and cells [2004] OJ L102/53 art 8.

111 The issue of UCB ownership is discussed in Chapter 6.

112 See: *R v Rothery* [1976] RTR 550 (CA) and *Roche v Douglas* (2000) 22 WAR 331 (WA SC).

113 See generally: *Moore v Regents of the University of California* 793 P 2d 479 (Cal, 1990).

One final point is that the Limitation Act 1980 places certain restrictions on the ability to commence a claim. While Section 2 of the Act provides that actions in torts (including trespass to the person torts) must be brought within six years of the tort being committed, personal injury cases arising from negligence, nuisance or a breach of duty must be brought within three years.[114] The time period in these cases runs from either the occurrence of the damage[115] or if later, the date of knowledge that the tort was causative of the harm.[116] Section 14 defines the 'date of knowledge' as the date the claimant became aware that they were suffering from a significant harm resultant of the negligence, nuisance or breach of duty from an identifiable defendant(s).[117] This is taken as when the claimant became aware, or ought reasonably to have been aware (constructive knowledge),[118] of the harm suffered from a negligent act that causes damage that is only later recognised or is 'discoverable'. The test of constructive knowledge is a mainly objective one, which takes into account all the circumstances of the case, and considers that in cases of significant injury the claimant would enquire as to the aetiology of the injury and seek specific knowledge about the circumstances of the harm and any other relevant information from experts.[119]

The time frame involved in connecting the discovered harm with the negligent act is therefore crucial to a pregnant woman seeking redress in a UCB-related personal injury claim because if she falls outside of these time limits, the claim will be statute barred. For minors, however, there is a further exception – for them, the time period runs from when they reach their eighteenth birthday.[120] These provisions are important for children whose personal injury was not prevalent at birth, such as occurs with some brain injuries, yet become discoverable later in life. For example, in *Whiston v London Strategic Health Authority* [2010],[121] an adult claimant commenced civil proceedings in 2006 against the Queen Charlotte's Hospital, London for cerebral palsy allegedly caused by a lack of oxygen at his birth in 1974, a condition that worsened considerably later in life. At trial, the judge ruled that he was not statute barred because the time limit ran from when his mother had told him of the suspected negligence in 2005.

However, on appeal the Health Authority successfully argued that Whiston would have appreciated that his injury was 'significant' (despite

114 Limitation Act 1980 ss 11–13.

115 Ibid., s 11(4)(a).

116 Ibid., s 11(4)(b).

117 Ibid., s 14(1)(a)–(d).

118 Ibid., s 14(3). For example, see: *Ministry of Defence v AB and others* [2012] UKSC 89.

119 See Lord Hoffmann's judgment in *Adams v Bracknell Forest BC* [2004] UKHL 29, confirmed in *Whiston v London Strategic Health Authority* [2010] EWCA Civ at 54 (Dyson, LJ).

120 Also note that under Section 33, the court has the discretion to increase the time limits in certain circumstances. See: *A v Hoare* [2008] UKHL 6.

121 *Whiston v London Strategic Health Authority* [2010] EWCA Civ.

his stoic attitude to his disability) from his early twenties when his condition began to significantly deteriorate and that a reasonable person in the claimant's position would have sought details from his mother, who was a nurse and trained midwife, about his birth and that information would have been communicated. That said, the court held that the claimant had constructive knowledge[122] by approximately 1998 and should have at that point commenced a claim, whereas he was now outside the time limitations. But in a final twist, the court allowed the claim to proceed by exercising its discretion under Section 33 of the Act, which permits the extension of time limits where, on consideration of all the circumstances, it is deemed equitable to do so. Clearly, the 1980 Act can have far-reaching consequences for pregnant women and their offspring in a UCB-related personal injury claim.

Legal duty and standards

For a successful clinical negligence claim, the patient must show that the UCB collector owed them a duty of care, which was breached and resulted in harm. Establishing a legal duty between the professional UCB collector and the mother is generally unproblematic due to the nature of the relationship. Once a duty is established, the court would then examine how the UCB had been collected to determine whether or not there was a breach of that duty, and the pregnant woman would have to show that the requisite standard had not been met. Since *Bolam v Friern Hospital Management Committee* [1957],[123] the standard owed by any medical professional to their patient was set as follows: the professional

> is not guilty of negligence if he has acted in accordance with a practice accepted as proper by a responsible body of medical men skilled in that particular art.[124]

Thus, under the *Bolam* standard, the standard of care required by the midwifery profession is that of a reasonable midwife who acts in accordance with the particular practice accepted as proper by a professional body of midwives. The midwife must show that (s)he had acted within the remit of protocols, policies and guidelines laid down by the profession both locally and nationally.[125] In contrast, lower standards might be expected of those who do not purport to possess the same professional skills as a collector who

122 Ibid., at 61–63 (Dyson, LJ).
123 *Bolam v Friern Hospital Management Committee* [1957] 2 All ER 118.
124 Ibid., at 587 (McNair, J).
125 Nursing and Midwifery Council (NMC), 'The Code: professional standards of practice and behaviour for nurses and midwives' (January 2015). The Code should be read in conjunction with the Midwives Rules and Standards (2012).

is also a midwife. Such an 'informal collector'[126] may include an independent nurse or phlebotomist, who would instead be judged to the standard by reference to the degree of care and skill that a reasonably competent UCB collector might be expected to apply to the collection process.[127]

In terms of professional guidance, health professionals who collect UCB are guided by the RCOG Scientific Advisory Committee Opinion Paper on UCB banking[128] and more recently, the joint statement from the RCOG and the Royal College of Midwives (RCM) position statement on UCB collection and banking.[129] The advice given is that the ex-utero method should be adopted and for the collection process to take place away from the delivery room. Regarding cord clamping, they state:

> There is also the issue of the timing of the clamping of the cord as this will have an effect on the collection of cord blood. Evidence suggests that immediate cord clamping in preterm babies may be harmful to them. In healthy newborns, deferred clamping may enhance placental transfusion and reduces jaundice and low iron stores at birth. Both the RCOG and RCM strongly believe that interference with the third stage of labour needs to be kept at a minimum to ensure good outcome for both mother and baby.[130]

Clearly, the Colleges espouse the dangers of early clamping (although this is confined to pre-term infants) and the advantages of delayed clamping for babies born at full term, but in contrast to the in-utero versus ex-utero methods, they do not *expressly* state which clamping technique should be adopted when collecting UCB. The best that is offered is the recommendation that, 'interference with the third stage of labour needs to be kept to a minimum' – and whilst this phrase presumably presents a preference for delayed clamping to ensure a better health outcome than early clamping (as is now more commonly accepted in general midwifery care), it is by no means a clear expression of best practice in the context of UCB collection.

The application of *Bolam* to cases of clinical negligence, however, does not appear to be an exact science in any context because decided cases will operate on questions of fact, which take into account 'all the circumstances'[131] of

126 While an independent nurse and phlebotomist are professionals within their own field of expertise, the term 'informal' is used in this context to denote a UCB collector who is not a midwife and one that would not have the skills associated with the birthing process.

127 *Wells v Cooper* [1958] 2 QB 265 at 271(Jenkins, LJ).

128 RCOG, 2006.

129 RCOG and Royal College of Midwives (RCM), 'RCOG/RCM statement on umbilical cord blood collection and banking' (2011). www.rcm.org.uk/sites/default/files/Joint%20Statement%20-%20UCB%20-%20aug%2011%20%286%29%20v2.pdf accessed 29 October 2015.

130 Ibid., 1.

131 *Bolam v Friern Hospital Management Committee* [1957] 2 All ER 118 at 587 (McNair, J).

each case. Moreover, the impact of the significant qualification to *Bolam* developed in *Bolitho v City and Hackney Health Authority*[132] must also be considered. Here, the House of Lords held that in spite of professional endorsement, there might be circumstances in which a doctor could still be liable. While this would only occur in 'a rare case',[133] nonetheless, liability in negligence could arise when the accepted practice was deemed unable to withstand logical analysis and would entitle the judge to declare the body of opinion as neither 'reasonable nor responsible'.[134] To satisfy the threshold of logic, medical (and midwifery) experts must now demonstrate that the defendant's actions had been carried out after careful consideration of all the 'comparative risks and benefits'[135] involved and that they had reached a 'defensible conclusion'.[136]

This 'test of logic' places UCB collectors in a precarious position, particularly as there are perceived risks associated with competing collection methods. Whichever method they deploy – in-utero or ex-utero and early or delayed clamping – would need to be defended as the logical choice should harm result. The point here is that to be *Bolitho*-compliant, it is imperative for UCB collectors to demonstrate that equal weight had been given to the risks and benefits involved in each method and this is arguably an arduous task.

Legal consent

As with all other forms of healthcare, consent to UCB collection provides the legal justification for intrusive interventions and, as collection involves the physical touching of the umbilical cord and insertion of a needle into the umbilical vein, consent is vital.[137] Lack of consent would undermine a patient's autonomy[138] and may invoke a number of legal consequences, namely in the trespass to the person torts and possibly even criminal liability in assault and battery. However, most medical malpractice litigation is brought under the tort of negligence.[139]

The duty of a medical professional applies not only to treatment and diagnosis but also extends to the provision of information, including disclosure of risks.[140] The law has developed over the years and what is regarded as relevant information to be disclosed has changed, culminating in the recent Supreme Court risk disclosure case of *Montgomery v Lanarkshire Health*

132 *Bolitho v City and Hackney Health Authority* [1998] AC 232.
133 Ibid., at 233 and 243 (Lord Browne-Wilkinson).
134 Ibid., at 243 (Lord Browne-Wilkinson).
135 Ibid., at 242.
136 Ibid.
137 Moise, 2005.
138 M A Jones, 'Informed consent and other fairy stories' (1999a) 7 *Modern Law Review* 103.
139 J Herring, *Medical Law and Ethics* (5th edn, Oxford: Oxford University Press, 2014) 104.
140 *Sidaway v Board of Governors of the Bethlem Royal Hospital* [1985] 1 All ER 643.

Board [2015].[141] As part of this process, the courts have long held that a patient should be informed of substantial risks inherent in a procedure that can produce 'a substantial risk of grave adverse consequences', as seen in *Sidaway v Board of Governors of the Bethlem Royal Hospital* [1985],[142] which can be taken to constitute a '10 per cent risk' of serious harm[143] and where the nature of the risk in question so obviously justifies disclosure in order for the patient to make a considered decision. In the same way, risks should be communicated to the patient who 'would be likely to attach significance to' them during their decision-making process or has enquired about them.[144] The Court of Appeal in *Pearce* stated that:

> [i]f there is a significant risk which would affect the judgment of a reasonable patient, then in the normal course it is the responsibility of a doctor to inform the patient of that significant risk, if the information is needed so that the patient can determine for him or herself as to what course he or she should adopt.[145]

To assert simply that a pregnant woman should be informed of a risk that she has asked about, however, is to assume that she had sufficient knowledge and understanding to know what questions to ask. This is particularly worrying given that pregnant women are taken to have a poor knowledge and understanding of UCB and its use.[146] But, perhaps more worryingly, the principle set out in *Pearce* seems to suggest that although the standard of risk disclosure is based upon what a reasonable patient would want to know, 'the reasonable patient' is still determined by the doctor – and what information is ultimately disclosed may be different from what the patient wants to know. That said, the UCB collector may still retain control over what information is communicated to the pregnant woman. On the *Pearce* model of risk disclosure, a midwife collecting UCB must inform the pregnant woman of any 'realistically'[147] significant risks involved in the process, which may affect her health or that of her newborn child. What is not immediately apparent, however, is whether the actual risks inherent in the procedure would constitute the classification of 'a significant risk' for liability purposes and how the

141 *Montgomery v Lanarkshire Health Board* [2015] UKSC 11.
142 *Sidaway v Board of Governors of the Bethlem Royal Hospital* [1985] 1 All ER 643 at 900 (Lord Bridge).
143 Ibid., Lord Bridge provided the example of a 10 per cent risk of a stroke from an operation to demonstrate what he considered a serious harm that required risk disclosure.
144 *Sidaway v Board of Governors of the Bethlem Royal Hospital* [1985] at 902 (Lord Templeman).
145 *Pearce v United Bristol Healthcare NHS Trust* [1999] PIQR 53 at 59 (Lord Woolf).
146 N Fox, C Stevens and R Ciubotariu, 'Umbilical cord blood collection: do patients really understand?' (2007) 4 *Journal of Perinatal Medicine* 35.
147 *Pearce v United Bristol Healthcare NHS Trust* [1999] PIQR 53 at 59 (Lord Woolf).

risk is actually quantified. While risks as low as 1 per cent[148] have been declared as sufficient enough to warrant disclosure, the risk of stillbirth, given as between 0.1 and 0.2 per cent, was not.[149]

Perhaps of equal significance to UCB collectors is that Lord Bridge's adaptation to the '*Bolam* Test' in *Sidaway* – that a blanket application of the test would not apply to all cases of risk disclosure, particularly where disclosure of a risk was so obviously necessary to a patient's informed choice – suggests a move towards acknowledging the rights of the patient to information. Essentially, if a patient is to gamble with a high risk of serious harm, then they have the right to be informed of it and to make up their own minds whether to run that particular risk, a judicial endorsing of the patient-centred approach first seen in American[150] and Australian[151] rulings. The Australian court in *Rogers* held that it was the doctor's duty to disclose all material risks inherent in the proposed treatment and that a material risk was one that:

> [i]n the circumstances of the particular case, a reasonable person in the patient's position, if warned of the risk, would be likely to attach significance to it or if the medical practitioner is or should reasonably be aware that the particular patient, if warned of the risk, would be likely to attach significance to it.[152]

What is suggested in *Rogers* is that the risk should be communicated if it would be likely to have a bearing on the patient's decision whether or not to consent to the treatment. Such scenarios call for autonomous decision-making by the patient based upon full and frank disclosure of information.

In England, this approach was adopted by the House of Lords ruling in *Chester v Afshar*.[153] Carole Chester brought a negligence action against her surgeon for failing to inform her of a small risk of paralysis inherent in a spinal operation, a risk that subsequently materialised. Although she had not specifically enquired about that particular risk, she had made numerous requests for information and had communicated her fear of surgery. Furthermore, she gave evidence that she would not have given consent to the operation on that day had she known of the risk, but conceded that she might still have had the operation at another time, which would likely see her fall outside of traditional 'but for' causation rules.

However, the court not only found the surgeon in breach of his duty for denying her the ability to decide for herself whether or not she would run the risk but also that the failure to warn was the *cause* of her harm. The

148 *Chester v Afshar* [2004] UKHL 41.
149 *Pearce v United Bristol Healthcare NHS Trust* [1999] PIQR 53 at 59 (Lord Woolf).
150 *Canterbury v Spence* (1972) 464 F 2d 772.
151 *Rogers v Whitaker* (1992) HCA 58 (1992)175 CLR 470.
152 Ibid., at 16 (Mason, CJ).
153 *Chester v Afshar* [2004] UKHL 41.

majority held that in the interests of her right to autonomy and dignity, her ability to make an informed choice was so important that traditional causation principles could be departed from in order to effect a remedy. Clearly, a shift towards patient autonomy and patients' rights with regards to information provision was beginning to be championed – and a shift that was robustly settled in the more recent case of *Montgomery*.

Mrs Montgomery's claim against Lanarkshire Health Authority hinged on whether she had been given proper advice regarding the birth of her son, Sam. Mrs Montgomery, who is of small build and a Type 1 diabetic, carried a 9–10 per cent risk of shoulder dystocia (where the baby can become lodged within the birth canal) – a fact that her doctor failed to inform her of because even if this did happen, the chance that it would result in 'grave adverse consequences' (as per *Sidaway*) was extremely small. The doctor also claimed that had she informed her of the risk, she would likely have opted for a Caesarean section, which did not carry the risk of dystocia, but that in her opinion 'it was not in the maternal interests of women to have Caesarean sections'.[154] Sadly, for Mrs Montgomery, dystocia did occur and as a result the baby was starved of oxygen and suffered brain damage, later developing cerebral palsy.

In the lower courts, the claim failed. The doctor's failure to inform had met the requirements of the *Bolam* test and a strict application of *Sidaway* meant that the doctor had not breached her duty because there was not a substantial risk of significant harm present. The Supreme Court, however, disagreed. They held that in modern-day healthcare, *Sidaway* had ceased to reflect the current nuances of the doctor–patient relationship and that, 'patients are now widely regarded as persons holding rights, rather than as the passive recipients of the care of the medical profession'.[155] That said, the courts held that the doctor is under a duty to inform a patient of any 'material risks' involved in the treatment and that:

> The test of materiality is whether, in the circumstances of the particular case, a reasonable person in the patient's position would be likely to attach significance to the risk, or the doctor is or should reasonably be aware that the particular patient would be likely to attach significance to it.[156]

Such a finding certainly reflects the rulings of *Rogers* and marks as a milestone in the law on risk disclosure and informed consent. No longer is there a requirement for the harm endured to have been highly probable – or even probable. It is merely a question of whether when faced with the chance of

154 *Montgomery v Lanarkshire Health Board* [2015] UKSC 11 at 13 (Lords Kerr and Reed).
155 Ibid., at 75 (Lords Kerr and Reed).
156 Ibid., at 87 (Lords Kerr and Reed).

a particular harm occurring, the patient is still likely to go ahead with the procedure if they had been informed of that chance beforehand. Undoubtedly, *Montgomery* is a landmark decision and *Sidaway* is now dead.[157] In their judgment the courts have expressly acknowledged that patients have a right to information in order to make autonomous choices – a right that is ever more important in childbirth when the decisions that a woman makes can affect not only her own health but that of her child.

Given the gravity of the possible harm that could arise from UCB collection, as both *Chester* and *Montgomery* demonstrate, communication should be in place to ensure that an informed decision is made prior to collection. The majority in *Montgomery* were clear that it was ineffective to consider risks in terms of percentages and that the only way to sufficiently determine whether a patient would attach significance to a risk is to engage in dialogue. In the context of UCB collection, that engagement should specifically relate to the personal risks that both mother and baby undertake during the procedure as even though the risks may be small, the potential health consequences, if known, would significantly influence their decision whether or not to collect the cells, especially where no family history of disease exists. Above all else, I argue that the *possible* consequence of removing up to 50 per cent of the baby's natural blood if the cord is clamped too early and/or the risk of maternal haemorrhage if the mother adopts the in-utero method in favour of collecting the optimal volume of UCB, are potential consequences that fulfil the *Montgomery* test of materiality.

What is significant for those who collect UCB is that as Lord Steyn in *Chester* pointed out, 'the result [of the case] ought to come as no surprise to the medical profession',[158] because the profession had already subscribed to the duty to warn a patient in general terms of significant risks in its guidelines on consent.[159] For example, the General Medical Council (GMC) declares that information given to patients about their proposed treatment should include the risks and serious side-effects of treatment.[160] In an additional guidance policy, it advises that the doctor should 'explain the options to the patient, setting out the potential benefits, risk, burdens and side-effects of each option, including the option to have no treatment'.[161] While clinical

157 D Hart, 'Supreme Court reverses informed consent ruling: *Sidaway* is dead' *UK Human Rights Blog* (London 13 March 2015) http://ukhumanrightsblog.com/2015/03/13/supreme-court-reverses-informed-consent-ruling-sidaway-is-dead/ accessed 31 October 2015.

158 *Chester v Afshar* [2004] UKHL 41 at 26 (Lord Steyn).

159 The Royal College of Surgeons, *Good Surgical Practice Guidelines* (2002) to which Lord Steyn refers has now been replaced by *Good Surgical Practice* (2014) www.rcseng.ac.uk/standards-and-research/gsp accessed 29 October 2015.

160 General Medical Council (GMC), 'Consent: patients and doctors making decisions together' (June 2008) at paras 28–32 www.gmc-uk.org/guidance/ethical_guidance/consent_guidance_index.asp accessed 29 October 2015.

161 Ibid., at para 5(b).

guidelines do not set legal standards of care, but simply provide supportive evidence of customary practice,[162] the findings of a survey published in 2006 by Samanta and others[163] suggest that the use of clinical guidelines in legal practice is more than minimal and predict their increased use in future litigation.[164]

In addition to their personal involvement in the collection process, there may be an additional risk of liability faced by the midwife and NHS. Even though the procurement of UCB is now regulated by the Human Tissue (Quality and Safety for Human Application) Regulations 2007 and the EUTCD, the new regulations permit the collection of UCB on unlicensed premises where the UCB collector acts under what is called 'a third party agreement'.[165] This means that licensed third party collectors – such as independent nurses and phlebotomists – can collect the cells on NHS premises during the third stage of labour, a stage in which the midwife remains actively involved. This, however, places the midwife in a vulnerable position because if problems arise during the collection of UCB by a third party, as (s)he owes a duty of care to the birthing mother, there may be circumstances in which (s)he would be expected to assist.

Yet once assistance is given, negligent procurement may result in an action against the midwife directly or jointly with the informal collector and the NHS (and even the private bank) vicariously.[166] However, the patient may still encounter difficulties in recovering damages because it is for the claimant to show that, on the balance of probabilities, UCB collection had been a cause of their harm. Proving causation – particularly in cases such as birth-related brain injuries, where there is more than one possible cause[167] – can be extremely difficult to establish.

Conclusion

Given the diversity of evidence regarding the risks and benefits of UCB collection and its use, it is little wonder that the cord blood debate has raged

162 B Hurwitz, 'How does evidence-based guidance influence determinations of medical negligence?' (2004) 329 *British Medical Journal* 1024. Also, the principle in *Thompson v Smiths Shiprepairers (North Shields) Ltd* [1984] 1 All ER 1 is that common practice does not equal the standard of care in negligence.

163 A Samanta and others, 'The role of clinical guidelines in medical negligence litigation: a shift from the Bolam Standard?' (2006) 14 *Medical Law Review* 3, 321.

164 Ibid., the authors propose a 'half-way house' between the '*Bolam* Test' and one in which guidelines rigidly define the standard of care. This, they suggest, would allow 'evidence-based science into judicial decision-making whilst at the same time permitting expert testimony to assess the exercise of clinical judgment'.

165 Human Tissue (Quality and Safety for Human Application) Regulations 2007 r 6.

166 K Devine, 'Tying the cord around the midwife's neck: the problem with umbilical cord blood collection' (2010b) 26 *Professional Negligence* 2, 83–95.

167 For example, see *Wilsher v Area Essex Health Authority* [1988] AC 1074.

on. While it is acknowledged that some of the scientific and practical risks highlighted here have been challenged, it is argued that where the science remains equivocal, UCB collection cannot be regarded as a procedure that is 'risk-free'[168] and 'is completely harmless to both mother and child'[169] as some private UCB banks suggest. The difficulty for any parent using this service is whether, for them, the benefits of saving the cells outweigh the risks and whether they receive and understand adequate information to make that decision. As there are potential risks involved in the procedure and the low odds that the cells will ever be used, it is questionable whether the benefits do in fact outweigh the risks.

For the UCB collector, the dilemma is just as great – by facilitating the patient's request, the collector carries the legal risks associated with the collection process, while the cord blood industry reaps the financial rewards of their efforts. This chapter has shown that by collecting UCB – or even by assisting in a procedure carried out by an informal collector acting under a third party agreement – midwives are placing themselves and their employer at risk of incurring liability. In the current judicial trend towards patients' rights, a dialogue between midwife and patient discussing the best course of action for them should be undertaken. Despite the equivocacy of evidence regarding the risks of UCB collection, if there is a chance that there may be a risk, albeit a small one, then current case law dictates that where the harm is of a serious nature, the pregnant woman should decide for herself whether or not to accept that risk. This legal requirement, however, places the UCB collector in the vulnerable position of having a lack of scientifically validated data with which to impart and ensure informed consent.

In 2006, the RCOG recommended that 'research be performed to understand better the short- and long-term neonatal effects of third stage practices'.[170] Since then we have benefitted from the follow-up studies into the timing of cord clamping, which has directly influenced current best practice, as well as a regulatory overhaul into who can procure UCB and where. However, there has been no such follow-up of children who have had their cord blood collected – a process that is conducted during the third stage of labour. That said, while it cannot be concluded that UCB collection is positively harmful to the child, it is safe to say that there is enough evidence to place serious doubts over whether denying a child up to 50 per cent of its total blood volume and 60 per cent of its red blood cells in pursuit of the best chance to preserve a 'future gift' for the child is really a gift worth pursuing.

168 CryoSave online website, 'Our process' http://cryo-save.com/en/about-cryo-save/our-process accessed 29 October 2015.

169 Ibid.

170 RCOG, 2006.

3 The rise of the cord blood industry

> The Council of Europe and most professional associations and physicians do not recommend private cord blood banking and have declared the use of cord blood as 'biological insurance' to be 'ill-advised'. In contrast, donating your baby's cord blood for public use is the best and most efficient alternative, having the potential to provide life-saving treatment for the many patients in need.[1]

Since the mid-1990s, public and private UCB banking services have been introduced worldwide.[2] While bodies such as the RCOG support the promotion of public UCB banks, a view concurred by the RCM, the Council of Europe, the American Medical Association, and the International Federation of Gynaecology and Obstetrics, the over-riding opinion of its scientific advisory committee is that there is currently insufficient evidence to recommend collection and storage for private use. In spite of these claims, the private cord blood industry has continued to grow. The emergence of private banks began predominantly in the US, but soon saw a rapid expansion of for-profit enterprises open to a global market.

There are two main types of UCB bank – public and private. Public banks are non-profit making and collect from altruistic donors for use by unrelated patients worldwide. In the UK, the NHS Blood and Transplant (NHSBT) services has carried out the public banking of UCB since 1996 in a similar way to donations of bone marrow. In contrast, private banks offer a for-profit service whereby the UCB unit is sequestered into a private account that is held exclusively for the account holder, commonly marketed as a form of personal 'biological life insurance'[3] for the future. The NHSBT facilitates an

1 The Council of Europe, 'Umbilical cord blood banking: a guide for parents' (2015) *European Directorate for the Quality of Medicines and Healthcare* www.edqm.eu/sites/default/files/parents_guide_to_umbilical_cord_blood_banking_organ_transplantation_2015.pdf accessed 26 November 2015.

2 D Nelkin, 'Banking on blood: the strange made familiar and the familiar made strange' (1998) 5 *Civilisation* 3, 24.

3 M Sullivan, P Browett and N Patton, 'Private umbilical cord blood banking: a biological insurance of future benefit' (2005) 118 *New Zealand Medical Journal* 1208.

additional form of collection and banking known as 'directed donations'. As the name suggests, these donations are made on behalf of an identified recipient, usually a family member. The Newcastle upon Tyne NHS Trust, which has a stem cell research facility at Newcastle University, also conducts directed donations, mainly on behalf of paediatric patients. In addition, a third type of banking known as either 'mixed' or 'hybrid' banking was introduced in 2007, which combines a system of both private and public banking.

Public banks

The first public UCB bank was established in 1993 in New York and there are now an estimated 54 public banks worldwide.[4] In the UK, the NHS Cord Blood Bank (formerly known as the London Cord Blood Bank),[5] was set up by NHS and Blood Transport (NHSBT) in 1996 with the aim of supplying donated cord blood units for use anywhere in the world. The ability to donate to the NHS Cord Blood Bank, however, is not open to all. The Bank collects only from maternity departments at the Barnet General, the Northwick Park, the Watford General, the Luton and Dunstable, and University College Hospital, London. These hospitals were specifically selected on the basis of their high rates of normal deliveries and the ethnic diversity of potential donors.

The Antony Nolan Bone Marrow Trust launched its public bank, the Antony Nolan Cell Therapy Centre (which houses the Antony Nolan Cord Blood Bank) in September 2008. It has a combined stem cell research centre at Nottingham Trent University, a world leader in the biosciences. UCB donations at the centre are used both for transplant purposes and as a source for approved research centres. Mothers giving birth at the King's College Hospital, London were the first to be recruited as donors after the hospital was chosen for the wide demographic of its population and as a means of enhancing HLA-matches for ethic minority groups.[6] Public awareness of the scheme has been heightened by the publicity surrounding the altruistic donation of UCB from TV actress and *EastEnders* soap star Kellie Shirley, who specifically chose to give birth at King's College Hospital in order to donate.[7]

4 NHS Cord Blood Bank, 'What the professionals say' www.nhsbt.nhs.uk/cordblood/cordblood/professionals/cristinanavarette/ accessed 2 November 2015.

5 Not to be confused with the New England Cord Blood Bank UK, which is a commercial cord blood company based in Harley Street, London offering storage overseas at the New England Cord Blood Bank.

6 King's College Hospital NHS Foundation Trust, 'Women who give birth at King's College Hospital can save lives by donating cord blood' (14 February 2008) www.kch.nhs.uk/ news/archive/2008/women-who-give-birth-at-kings-college-hospital-can-help-save-lives-by-donating-cord-blood/ accessed 10 February 2009.

7 W Manger, 'Eastenders star's twins will become life-savers as soon as they're born' *Daily Record* (London 4 August 2015) www.dailyrecord.co.uk/entertainment/celebrity/eastenders-stars-twins-become-life-6189916 accessed 3 November 2015.

As the Anthony Nolan is a charity, its operations can be affected by financial difficulties,[8] but in spite of this, the scheme continues to flourish and now accepts additional UCB donations from the Leicester General Hospital, the Leicester Royal Infirmary and Saint Mary's Hospital, Manchester and Birmingham Women's Hospital. Volunteers and staff at the Birmingham hospital celebrated the thousandth donation to the Antony Nolan Cell Therapy Centre in June 2013.[9] The Centre is currently financed by charitable donations from individuals and organisations, with its start-up costs supported by charitable grant company, the James Tudor Foundation and the East Midlands Development Agency.[10]

In addition to the traditional public banks, hybrid banking (discussed later in this chapter) blends a mix of public with private banking. These can take many forms – public banking facilitated by the private sector; dividing the UCB unit, partly for private use and the larger proportion for public use; and finally, the sequential model. The sequential model sequesters the whole UCB unit for private (autologous) use but the unit is also recorded on the international stem cell registries and released if matched to a patient for an allogeneic (unrelated) UCB transplantation. Consent using this model, however, must be re-sought from the donor should a non-related match be found, and this may prove difficult if the donor relocates and becomes untraceable.[11]

As we saw in Chapter 1, Northern Ireland's public cord blood bank was set up in 1993, collecting from the Mater Infirmorum and the Royal Jubilee Maternity Hospitals. It ceased operations in September 2015 due to the cost-effectiveness of its facility exacerbated by low usage. Donations made by the Northern Irish population tended to mirror the HLA-types of UCB reserves already held in larger banking facilities and therefore continuing collections became unnecessary. For similar reasons, the Scottish National Cord Blood Bank, collecting from the Princess Royal Maternity Hospital in Glasgow, closed in January 2015. There are no public banks available in Wales.

The ability to donate UCB, however, presents an extra concern for the donor in that they must agree to the testing of the unit and maternal samples – which usually consists of testing for infectious diseases such as HIV, syphilis

8 P Blackburn, 'Antony Nolan Trust to cut cord on pioneering blood bank' *Nottingham Post* (Nottingham 1 January 2015) www.nottinghampost.com/Charity-cut-cord-pioneering-blood-banks/story-25791882-detail/story.html accessed 3 November 2015.

9 M McLeod, '1000th cord blood donation collected' *Birmingham Women's NHS Foundation Trust* (25 June 2013) www.bwnft.nhs.uk/news/born-lifesavers accessed 3 November 2015.

10 Antony Nolan, 'How we are funded' www.anthonynolan.org/clinicians-and-researchers/cord-blood-services accessed 3 November 2015.

11 G Manegold and others, 'Controversies in hybrid banking: attitudes of Swiss public umbilical cord blood donors toward private and public banking' (2011) 284 *Archives of Gynaecology and Obstetrics* 99–104.

and human T-lymphotropic virus – and for any positive results to be communicated back to them. This in itself presents two additional areas of controversy. First, the donor can only participate in the programme if (s)he agrees to be availed of the personal health information derived from the UCB screening, thus putting a type of 'condition' on the ability to donate. Second, and perhaps most importantly, there would undoubtedly be psychological implications for the donor informed for the first time that they were the carrier of an infectious disease. As with all blood donations, there is an obligation to communicate the identification of infectious diseases back to the donor and offer counselling and advice.[12]

That said, the act of making an altruistic donation of UCB may be a high price to pay for the donor, especially as the information that they are a carrier of a sexually transmitted serious communicable disease would also affect the donor's sexual partner(s). In such circumstances, the General Medical Council (GMC) has provided guidance to health professionals that they may disclose information to a known sexual contact if they 'have reason to think that they are at risk of infection and that the patient has not informed them and cannot be persuaded to do so'.[13] Clearly, blood testing can have ramifications for the person being screened for either personal health reasons or to test its suitability for transplant purposes; and in particular, a blood donor donating for altruistic reasons may find that they 'gain' more than they bargained for.

Private banks

With increased public awareness of the benefits of UCB, and the option to donate open only to those residing within the vicinity of a small number of collecting hospitals, an opportunity was created for the commercial UCB sector to capitalise on this potentially valuable resource. By 2008, approximately 881,000 UCB units were being privately stored for exclusive use across 112 private banks worldwide,[14] each bank 'fighting harder for a market share'.[15] In the UK there are currently six commercial cord blood companies in operation. These are: Cells4Life, Precious Cells, Future Health, Smart Cells International, Biovault Family and the Virgin Health Bank. The cost of

12 NHSBT, 'Information for donors: tests on your blood' (December 2014) www.blood.co.uk/pdf/tests_on.pdf accessed 4 January 2015.

13 General Medical Council (GMC), 'Supplementary guidance – confidentiality: disclosing information about serious communicable diseases' (September 2009) www.gmc-uk.org/Confidentiality_disclosing_info_serious_commun_diseases_2009.pdf_27493404.pdf accessed 2 November 2015.

14 P Martin, N Brown and A Turner, 'Capitalizing hope: the commercial development of umbilical cord blood stem cell banking' (2008) 27 *New Genetics and Society* 2, 127–143.

15 JSB Market Research, 'Complete 2015–16 global cord blood banking industry report' (4 August 2015) www.jsbmarketresearch.com/healthcare-medical/r-complete-global-cord-blood-banking-industry-report-65397 accessed 2 November 2015.

private storage varies from £1,500 to £3,000 for a 25-year storage term, depending on the type of package and payment plan selected.

With a target audience responsive to baby-related services and products, direct marketing approaches have in the past been used to obtain mailing lists of prospective parents from baby product manufacturers, magazine-subscription departments and hospitals.[16] Although the introduction of the Data Protection Act 1998[17] now prohibits such practices, pregnant women are still marketed to directly via advertisements on pregnancy-related websites, within magazines, the use of pregnancy apps, and via leaflets included in 'Bounty Packs'. These packs are distributed free by the Bounty Organisation to parents attending antenatal classes and postnatal check-ups and contain free baby product samples, vouchers and service information that includes the ability to bank UCB.[18]

However, it is not the distribution of information that has provoked the most controversy. Rather, as we saw earlier, it is from the unsubstantiated promise of future medical possibilities that the brochures and leaflets contain. The general sales pitch is that the stored cells are of an exact HLA-type match for the child, which circumvents the need to locate a suitable donor unit within the public banks and registries should the need arise, acting as a form of personal risk-management.[19] Of course, this claim is true. Such a precise need just *might* materialise – albeit by only a slim chance. But this remote possibility does little to quell the concerns of RCOG who chastise the industry for its use of emotive language and imagery to sell a service that may not fulfil their clients' expectations.[20] As Querol and Torrabadella elucidate on a cost/benefit analysis of autologous banking:

> [i]n our opinion, justifying private [banking] only for that possibility is not sufficient to support their development. If we translate this into a cost/benefit equation, the handful of procedures reported until now may have cost more than 100,000 euros each if divided by total fees paid by parents that used such organisations.[21]

Clearly then, the promise of storing 'a biological life insurance'[22] when the only certainty is the return of a vial full of stem cells, which may or may not

16 Nelkin, 1998.

17 Data Protection Act 1998 s 11.

18 N Brown and A Kraft, 'Blood ties: banking the stem cell promise' (2006) 18 *Technology Analysis & Strategic Management* 3, 313–327.

19 J L Erickson, D Barry and A Doyle, 'The moral hazards of neoliberalism: lessons from the private insurance industry' (2000) 29 *Economy and Society* 4, 532–558.

20 Royal College of Obstetricians and Gynaecologists (RCOG), (2006) 'Umbilical cord blood banking' (Scientific Impact Paper No. 2) www.rcog.org.uk/globalassets/documents/guidelines/scientific-impact-papers/sip_2.pdf

21 S Querol and M Torrabadella, 'Session 13: Debate: is umbilical cord blood banking for autologous treatment useful? 0-050 Con' (2012) 27 *Human Reproduction* Supplement 2.

22 Sullivan, Browett and Patton, 2005.

be of any practical use, is viewed by the critics as misleading and unethical.

Amidst the criticism, commercial cord blood companies argue that they are simply 'plugging a gap by providing a service which is popular with some parents',[23] and like any other private enterprise, they are merely seizing a profit-making opportunity within the open market. As the ability to donate UCB to public banks is only available to those who reside within specific locations, the private sector cannot be criticised for simply providing an alternative option. Moreover, in an era of 'personalised medicine', where direct-to-customer services are sold under the marketing guise of offering future treatment that is customised for each individual, private UCB banking is no different from other forms of 'Me Medicine'[24] such as the banking of baby teeth for stem cells within dental pulp,[25] the banking of menstrual blood for its reported stem cell content,[26] and the personal genetic testing and genome analysis services such as 23andMe, My Genome and deCODEme.

However, it should also be noted that the private industry marketing messages have softened in the last 15 years. Promises that were once prominent amongst the glossy brochures such as, 'save the key components to future medical treatment', 'like freezing a spare immune system', 'storing a kind of spare-parts kit' and 'saving a lifeline for a lifetime'[27] are now rarely used and have, *on the whole*, been replaced with much less speculative language.

In the UK, it is likely that the threat of scrutiny from the Advertising Standards Authority (ASA) has something to do with this more moderate approach. The ASA is the independent regulator for all forms of media within the UK. Its role is to monitor, investigate complaints, and take action against misleading, harmful or offensive adverts, including direct marketing. Notwithstanding the possibility of a claim for breach of contract by a consumer against a private UCB banking service provider (or vice versa) for non-fulfilment of a term of the contract, or for misrepresentation by a consumer who was misled into purchasing a collection kit and service, it is the private banks who have publicly fought amongst themselves over the contents of their advertising as they jostle for prime position within the market.

23 J Dreaper, 'Concern over cord blood banking' *BBC News Online* (London 13 May 2005) http://news.bbc.co.uk/1/hi/health/4541515.stm accessed 3 November 2015.

24 D Dickenson, *Me Medicine vs We Medicine: Reclaiming Biotechnology for the Common Good* (New York: Columbia University Press, 2013).

25 H Nicholl, 'Baby tooth bank opens its doors' *Bionews* (Progress Educational Trust, 23 July 2006) www.bionews.org.uk/page_12799.asp, accessed 3 November 2015.

26 Cryo-Cell International online website, 'Banking menstrual stem cells' www.cryo-cell.com/menstrual/stem-cells accessed 3 November 2015.

27 These are all examples taken from advertising brochures (primarily from the UK and the US) during the course of my undergraduate research in 2002 through to my postgraduate research in 2008.

Advertising standards and misrepresentation

In June 2014, Smart Cells International and Cells4Life asked the Advertising Standards Authority (ASA) to investigate several alleged breaches of the ASA's Code of Practice[28] by Precious Cells International in its online advertising brochure citing four separate issues. The first issue related to Precious Cells' claim that they were the world's first accredited biobank; the second that they had released more UCB units for transplant than all other UK biobanks combined; the third that their insolvency policy *guaranteed* the safe storage of the unit; and finally, that they were the only bank to hold 35 unique licences from the licensing authority.[29]

With the exception of issue three regarding insolvency, which Precious Cells was able to substantiate via a pre-existing contract with a major international storage company guaranteeing a transfer of stocks should the bank become insolvent, all other complaints were upheld. Precious Cells were unable to substantiate the claims made and had therefore breached the Code under rules 3.1 (Misleading advertising), 3.7 (Substantiation) and 3.33 (Comparisons with identifiable competitors) on these three issues. The ASA declared that the brochure must no longer appear in its current form and warned that all future material should be properly evidenced. In response, Precious Cells complained about three issues relating to Smart Cells' advertising, a claim that was heard on the same day. However, the ASA found them not to be in breach of any of the three issues cited.[30]

February 2015 saw Precious Cells return to the ASA asking it to adjudicate on three issues contained in Cells4Life's advertising brochure and a page on its website. The ASA held that Cells4Life's claim to store more units than any other bank, and that they operated a 24-hour 365 days a year collection service, had been substantiated and therefore did not breach the Codes, as Precious Cells had argued. However, it was found to be in breach of rules 3.1 (Misleading advertising), 3.7 (Substantiation) and 3.33 (Comparisons with identifiable competitors) for the statement regarding their storage method. It said that their 'superior method can greatly increase the success of treatment should your child need it'.[31] The ASA found that Cells4Life had

28 Advertising Standards Authority (ASA) 'The CAP Code: The UK Code of Non-broadcast Advertising, Sales Promotion and Direct Marketing' (Edition 12, 2014a) www.cap.org.uk/Advertising-Codes/~/media/Files/CAP/Codes%20CAP%20pdf/The%20CAP%20Code.ashx, accessed 6 November 2015.

29 ASA, 'ASA ruling on Precious Cells International Ltd' (18 June 2014b) www.asa.org.uk/Rulings/Adjudications/2014/6/Precious-Cells-International-Ltd/SHP_ADJ_252000.aspx#.VjxilK9OeUk accessed 6 November 2015.

30 ASA, 'ASA ruling on Smart Cells International' (18 June 2014c) www.asa.org.uk/Rulings/Adjudications/2014/6/Smart-Cells-International-Ltd/SHP_ADJ_258261.aspx#.Vjxkl69OeUk accessed 6 November 2015.

31 ASA, 'ASA ruling on Precious Cells International Ltd' (18 February 2015) www.asa.org.uk/Rulings/Adjudications/2015/2/Cells4Life-Group-LLP/SHP_ADJ_259676.aspx#.VjxvPK9OeUk accessed 6 November 2015.

not provided sufficient evidence to support its claim and subsequently it faced the same sanctions meted out to Precious Cells International Ltd the year before.

In addition to the ASA, private banks should also be mindful of their customer base, who may have a claim for breach of contract or for misrepresentation if a statement either within the advertisement itself or made during discussions leading up to the contractual agreement to UCB banking proves to be untrue. For example, the consumer may feel aggrieved if (s)he only entered into an agreement with a particular private bank because it had represented itself to have released the largest number of units for transplant; had boasted to be the world's first accredited bank or that its storage method was deemed to be superior to its competitors', and any of these claims proved untrue. In such a situation, the court would look to whether the untrue statement was a term of the contract or a representation[32] and whether words used had caused (or 'induced') the consumer to enter the contract. In doing so, the court would assess how the UCB bank had expressed its words,[33] with the presumption that anything in writing is a term,[34] or if it had a degree of importance to the consumer,[35] whether the bank accepted responsibility for the truth of its statement[36] or whether either party had any special skill or knowledge in UCB banking.[37] These factors are likely to be relevant in the case of UCB banking, especially as the private bank is likely to be in a stronger position than the average consumer seeking its services.

One issue that may present a bar to a remedy[38] is that in the context of misrepresentation, statements may be regarded as either a 'sales puff' or a statement of opinion. The assumption in contract law is that reasonable people do not take most statements made in advertisements seriously, which allows sellers

32 The difference between the two is often expressed as 'a misrepresentor's statement is either a term if it is *inside* the contract or a representation if it is *outside* the contract'. Thus, anything within the written contract is likely to be a term of the contract and statements during verbal discussions are more likely to be representations, which affect the type of remedies available.

33 For example, private banks purporting the use of their products and services as a *potential* biological life insurance or cure for the future are more likely to escape a claim for misrepresentation.

34 *Helibut, Symons and Co v Buckleton* [1913] AC 30, HL.

35 *Bannerman v White* (1861) 10 CB NS 844.

36 In *Ecay v Godfrey* (1947) 80 Lloyd's Rep 286, a boat seller advised the buyer to have the boat surveyed before purchase, and in doing so the court held that his statement was a representation rather than a term. However, see: *Schawel v Reade* [1913] 2 IR 64, HL in which the court reached the reverse outcome.

37 *Bentley (Dick) Productions Ltd v Harold Smith (Motors)* [1965] 1 WLR 932, HL.

38 Misrepresentation falls into four types: fraudulent, negligent under Section 2(1) of the Misrepresentation Act 1967, negligent in common law and innocent. For a claim under the Act, the burden of proof is reversed and is on the representor to prove the statement was made honestly. Remedies for fraudulent, Section 2(1) of the Act and negligent in common law are rescission of the contract and/or damages (for the latter, where they are reasonably foreseeable); and for innocent misrepresentation, rescission or damages.

to make exaggerated claims. For example, a washing powder claim to make clothes 'whiter than white' is likely to be nothing more than a 'puff', which no reasonable consumer would take to be true. It could therefore be argued that private banks who present the banking of UCB as 'a cure for all' are not expected to be taken seriously. However, the more specific the statement, the more likely it will be regarded by the courts as a statement of fact.[39]

Second, an actionable misrepresentation cannot arise from a mere statement of opinion, unless it is dishonest, unreasonable or the opinion becomes a term of the contract. For example, in *Bisset v Wilkinson* (1927)[40] the buyer negotiated the purchase of land that he required to farm sheep. Although neither party knew the likelihood of successful farming on the land (as neither had special knowledge), the seller stated that he *thought* the land would hold approximately 2,000 sheep, which turned out to be a rather optimistic estimate. However, the court held that the seller had merely passed an opinion rather than stating a fact. In contrast, an estimation of a petrol station selling 200,000 gallons per year led directly to its lease. When it transpired that this figure was wildly over-estimated, the court treated this as a term of the contract as the opinion was made by a company with vast amounts of skill and experience in the petrol industry.[41] That said, while it is possible that UCB banks who comment on the likelihood of needing UCB in the future may be regarded as merely expressing opinion, they may still fall foul of the law if the strength of their knowledge of the UCB industry exploits the consumer's ignorance; and the court may find that the consumer was not at fault for trusting the UCB bank despite the ability to seek further information elsewhere.[42]

Clearly, the private UCB industry would do well to avoid any form of negative publicity from the use of its advertising material. While the ASA watchdog has only a limited number of sanctions available to it,[43] any exposed attempts to mislead the public can court controversy. This may lead to damaged reputations and a lowering of status within the industry, in the same way that claims for breach of contract or misrepresentation can damage the industry by way of becoming a matter of public record or media reporting. Negative publicity can be further disseminated via the weekly publishing of adjudications on the ASA website. Given that the term 'Cord Blood' falls within the top 20 most expensive keywords in *Google* AdWords Advertising,[44]

39 *Carlill v Carbolic Smoke Ball Company* [1893] 1 QB 256, 57 JP 325, CA.

40 *Bisset v Wilkinson* (1927) AC 177.

41 *Esso Petroleum v Mardon* [1976] 2 All ER 5.

42 *Redgrave v Hurd* (1881) 20 Ch D 1, CA. For a contrasting outcome, see: *Peekay Intermark v Australia and ANZ Banking Group* (2006) 2 Lloyds Rep 511.

43 The ASA can order problematic adverts to be removed, offer advice on future compliance with the CAP Code and refer complaints to the Office of Fair Trading (OFT) and the independent regulator for the UK communications industries, Ofcom, both of which can issue fines. In addition, Ofcom can revoke advertising licences.

44 Wordstream, 'Top 20 most expensive keywords in Google AdWords Advertising' www.wordstream.com/articles/most-expensive-keywords accessed 6 November 2015.

commanding up to $27.80 per click, private companies have every reason to remain in a strong market position.

Public versus private banks

The debate between whether society should opt for public or private banking has in itself raised controversies. Those that bank privately do so in the hope that the UCB will act as 'a good investment in case the child needs it'[45] but this type of personal investment is made in the knowledge that only those who contract with the storage facility have access to, and might benefit from, the stored cells. Such displays of individual self-interest, however, provoke a dichotomy between public and private access to healthcare in the respect that it conflicts with the altruistic nature of public donation, which resonates as an act of selfless goodwill for the benefit of others.[46]

Contrary to NHS principles of community welfare, the private UCB storage model solely promotes personal interests, and this has led the French National Consultative Ethics Committee to declare that, '[t]he gravest danger for society in so far as setting up such [private] banks is [that it is] likely to contradict the principle of solidarity, without which no society can survive'.[47] These conflicting principles portray the ideologies of self-interest and altruism as diametrically opposed and in stark contrast to the ideals of the French creators of UCB cryopreservation, who developed the technique in 1987.[48] Their aim was to preserve UCB as a communal resource, in pursuit of which they secured financial assistance from the American National Institutes of Health (NIH) and formed a European consortium of cord blood banks, known as Eurocord.

Set against a model of social utility and akin to the 'gift relationship' of blood donations first espoused by Richard Titmuss,[49] the cryopreservation technique that they developed was soon to take a change of direction as the vision of preserving cells for public use driven by French idealism became usurped by the commercialisation of a capitalist society. While the reasons why parents choose to bank privately may be self-evident, why the public choose to donate UCB is less clear.

45 C V Fernandez and others, 'Knowledge and attitudes of pregnant women with regard to testing, collection and banking of cord blood stem cells' (2003) 168 *Canadian Medical Association Journal* 6, Table 2: 'Choice and reasons for storing cord blood in private versus public bank'.

46 C Fung, 'Is altruism a vice?' (1988) 17 *Journal of American Medical Association* 2509.

47 French National Consultative Ethics Committee for Health and Life Sciences, 'Umbilical cord blood banks for autologous use or for research' (Opinion No. 74, 2002).

48 Nelkin, 1998.

49 R Titmuss, *The Gift Relationship* (London: Allen & Unwin, 1971).

Altruism, self-interest and UCB donor motivations

Altruism has been described by Fung as caring for someone else when there is no obvious reward for doing so, other than that it will benefit that person or will avoid harm to him or her.[50] Whilst this may be the traditional view, other academics[51] have suggested that incurring an advantage or avoiding a detriment may also be motivational factors for acting altruistically. For example, reciprocation may be enjoyed by the donor whose status is raised within the community as a direct response to his or her actions.[52] Conversely, the individual may only choose to act in a positive manner out of guilt or in order to avoid being shamed or frowned upon by society.[53]

Altruistic behaviour can be witnessed in all forms of donation for public health benefits. Bodily matter such as blood, organs, tissue and gametes are all given voluntarily in the UK in the pursuit of helping someone in need.[54] For donors of reproductive material, however, there may be consequences for making the decision to help another. Donors of eggs and sperm that are donated for use in assisted reproduction are no longer afforded anonymity status – any children borne of gametes donated after 1 April 2005 are entitled by law to have access to the donor's identity once they reach the age of 18 years.[55] Acting altruistically in this context can therefore have far reaching consequences for the donor and may adversely affect a willingness to donate. However, while this concern has been realised in egg donation, which has witnessed a steady decline since 1997,[56] the Human Fertilisation and Embryology Authority (HFEA) reports that there has been a steady increase in sperm donors since 2004, but that demand still outstrips supply.[57]

In the context of UCB, those who wish to donate to a public bank are not subject to the same issues associated with gamete donors. UCB can be donated anonymously,[58] and as it lacks the reproductive qualities of gametes, it can be given without fear of future contact from (or on behalf of) a biologically related child or any financial obligations that such an encounter may entail. As discussed in Chapter 1, as UCB is non-reproductive in quality, its

50 Fung, 1988.
51 G E Switzer and others, 'Understanding donors' motivations: a study of unrelated bone marrow donors' (1997) 45 *Social Science and Medicine* 137.
52 M Mauss, *The Gift* (London: Cohen & West, 1966) pp 66–67.
53 B Schwartz, 'The social psychology of the gift' (1967) 73 *American Journal of Sociology* 1.
54 In November 2008, the government shelved plans to introduce an 'opt-out' system for organ donation after experts cast doubt on whether the system would work. An 'opt-out' system would give doctors the right to presume consent had been given to organ removal after death unless objections had been made in advance.
55 The HFEA (Disclosure of Donor Information) Regulations 2004 SI 2004/1511.
56 In response to the decline in egg donors, egg-sharing schemes have been set up.
57 J Gallagher, 'UK national sperm bank opens for business' *BBC News Online* (London 30 October 2014) www.bbc.co.uk/news/health-29815524 accessed 7 November 2015.
58 Human Tissue (Quality and Safety for Human Application) Regulations 2007 r 13(2).

donation also fails to evoke the same level of controversy that surrounds the use of gametes and embryos for use in either clinical applications or research.

So why do women choose to donate UCB? A study carried out in Canada in 2003 into the knowledge and attitudes of pregnant women with regard to collection, testing and banking of UCB cells[59] does provide limited insight. The results showed that 70 per cent of the women involved reported very poor knowledge of the existence of UCB banking and a staggering 86 per cent said that they would have chosen to donate to a public bank had they been aware of the facility, many citing altruism and the expense of private banking as the reasons for this choice.[60] Similarly, studies carried out in Switzerland[61] and Turkey[62] examining parental attitudes to UCB banking also found strong support for public donation.

More recent studies show that these attitudes remain largely unchanged. In a comparative study,[63] collected data revealed that 59 per cent of participants across five European countries cited a desire to make a personal contribution to public health resources as a key motivational factor for donating, with 26 per cent stating that their decision-making had been influenced by the fact that public donation was free of charge. In addition, a willingness to donate UCB to research initiatives was homogeneous with 91.8 per cent predominantly motivated by the desire for advancements in medical therapies.

In the UK, an analysis of semi-structured interviews with a sample of pregnant women in England conducted by researchers at the universities of York and Lancaster has provided an intriguing insight into modern day perceptions of donating UCB to a public bank.[64] Common themes of aiding society and the ability to donate freely as opposed to the expense of private banking were once again prevalent, but what is interesting is that there appears to be a heavy emphasis placed on the donated unit remaining available to the donor should it be needed. Participants demonstrated a strong perception that they *will* be able to reclaim the unit, which they based on the belief that as the unit is 'matched' specifically to the donor, it is unlikely that it will be of any practical use to anyone else and would therefore remain available to them if required.

59 Fernandez and others, 2003.

60 Ibid., at Table 2: 'Choice and reasons for storing cord blood in private versus public bank'.

61 E Danzer and others, 'Attitudes of Swiss mothers toward unrelated umbilical cord blood banking 6 months after donation' (2003) 43 *Transfusion* 604.

62 H Dinç and N H Şahin, 'Pregnant women's knowledge and attitudes about stem cells and cord blood banking' (2009) 56 *International Nursing Review* 250–256.

63 G Katz and others, 'Banking cord blood stem cells: attitude and knowledge of pregnant women in five European countries' (2010) 51 *Transfusion* 3.

64 L Machin, N Brown and D McLeod, 'Giving to receive? The right to donate in umbilical cord blood banking stem cell therapies' (2011) 104 *Health Policy* 296–303.

There are two issues here: first, the decision to donate the UCB would have been based on a misconception because although there is a strong chance that the unit will remain available, there is no guarantee that it will not have been utilised and thus unable to be returned to the donor. Moreover, the interviewees might have been either misinformed, or had misunderstood the information provided by the UCB collector, prior to donation. Either way, this can have an effect on the quality of consent given and places its validity in law in doubt. Second, UCB given to a public bank under this reasoning says very little for the altruistic nature of donation, which is commonly viewed as non-reciprocal 'gift-giving'. As noted by the researchers, there appears to be a notion of the donors 'giving to receive'[65] in this context. An element of reciprocity can be seen within the act of donating because although publicly banked UCB is made accessible to anyone who needs it, this also includes the donor.[66] We shall return to this issue in a later section when we explore whether such motivations also characterise 'good' and 'bad' behaviour.[67]

In other areas of human tissue donation, financial inducement may affect the potential donor's decision-making. Whilst this has been a cause for uneasiness in the context of eggs[68] and sperm,[69] the donation of UCB does not raise the same concerns. Although the European Tissue Directive[70] prohibits direct payment for eggs and sperm, Article 12 of the Directive permits the reimbursement of reasonable expenses including lost earnings, and sperm donors may receive a nominal fee for their contribution. Furthermore, those who participate in egg-sharing schemes or agree to donate surplus embryos created via IVF may receive their treatment at a reduced rate – a further incentive to donate. Such rewards have raised fears that financial hardships will be an influential factor for donation.[71] For UCB, however, as the donation is made free of charge at the moment of birth, inducements and loss of wages are unlikely to be an issue for the pregnant woman. Yet while financial inducements are therefore unlikely to affect UCB

65 Ibid.

66 NHS Cord Blood Bank online website, 'Public versus private cord blood banks' www.nhsbt.nhs.uk/cordblood/about/publicvprivate/ accessed 8 November 2015.

67 See generally, K Devine, 'Ethics and choice in healthcare: the case of public v private cord blood banking' in: N Priaulx and A Wrigley (eds), *Ethics, Law and Society* Volume V (Surrey: Ashgate, 2013) pp 55–68.

68 I Sample, 'Row over cash for women donating eggs' *The Guardian Online* (London, 21 February 2007) www.guardian.co.uk/society/2007/feb/21/health.genetics accessed 20 February 2009.

69 M Johnson, 'Payments to gamete donors: position of the Human Fertilisation and Embryology Authority' (1997) 12 *Human Reproduction* 1839.

70 Council Directive (EC) 2004/23 on setting standards of quality for the donation, procurement, testing, processing, preservation, storage and distribution of human tissues and cells [2004] OJ L102.

71 Johnson, 1997.

donors, there may be an emotive impetus that underpins the decision to donate – one that is based on family ties.

Family matters, private banks and the vulnerable consumer in a risk-based society

In today's world of stem cell innovation, making medical remedies and regenerative medicine a possibility, there are arguably good reasons to donate. Emotional commitments to a relative and a sense of duty have been cited as key influences in the decision to donate to a family member or for research purposes.[72] Such emotions can be simultaneously powerful, all-encompassing, and provoke feelings that families *matter*, and it is upon such emotive issues that the courts have been finding themselves adjudicating – from parents and family members that go to great lengths to ensure funding for the continued health and wellbeing of loved ones[73] to the extraordinary efforts made by those who create so-called saviour siblings, such as the Nash and Hashmi families discussed in Chapter 1. Such displays of human devotion, however, are not only expended towards those who are in poor health now, but also those we wish to protect from future ill health.

It is with such familial sensitivities in mind that private UCB banks urge expectant families to have the foresight to personally save their 'elixir of life',[74] packaged as a 'once in a lifetime opportunity to protect [their] child's long-term health'.[75] The marketing departments eager to promote a clear family connection between the collected unit and the cord blood company capture images of newborn babies cradled in the protective arms of their parents. Pictures of babies wrapped in blankets or clutching flowers – images typically associated with security and the life cycle – remind the potential consumer that stem cells can offer both protection and possibly the future health of their child. As one mother who banked her baby's cord blood with UK based Smart Cells exclaimed, 'The medical world is evolving so quickly. It's possibly the best investment you could make for your child's future.'[76]

72 Switzer and others, 1997.

73 Such as in *R v Cambridge HA ex parte B* (1995) 25 BMLR 5. For a modern-day example, however, see the actions of the parents of Ashya King who sought proton beam therapy abroad to treat a malignant brain tumour against their treating hospital's advice. See, A Craft, 'What exactly happened in the hospital treating Aysha King?' *The Telegraph Online* (London 5 September 2014) www.telegraph.co.uk/news/health/11078199/What-exactly-happened-in-the-hospital-treating-Aysha-King.html accessed 8 November 2015.

74 S Hall, 'Elixir of life claims of cord cell storage firms speculative, mothers-to-be warned' *The Guardian Online* (London 14 June 2006) www.guardian.co.uk/uk/2006/jun/14/health.healthandwellbeing accessed 8 November 2015.

75 StemCyte online website, 'Why save cord blood?' www.stemcyte.com/why-save-cord-blood-tissue/ accessed 8 November 2015.

76 Smart Cells International online website, 'Our customers' stories' www.smartcells.com/our-customers-and-their-stories/ accessed 8 November 2015.

Photographs of happy familial settings are prominent – depictions that could portray any family unit with sufficient funds to purchase it. Even the extended family is not left untouched from the snare of the industry.[77] In an attempt to further endorse the perception that stem cells are a perfect gift for the newest, most precious member of the family, close friends and family are advised that they too can create contractual relations for the storage of UCB. As Smart Cells International are keen to point out to anyone looking for a gift idea, 'Stem cells are not just for life – they're for Christmas.'[78] The message here is explicit – stem cells can act as a lifesaver, and you couldn't purchase a more worthwhile gift for that special child.

But what advertising campaigns have failed to mention in their advertising material, particularly in the early campaigns, is the purportedly low odds of the doting family member ever getting a return on their investment or that few paediatric transplant physicians recommend private UCB banking.[79] This has led to fears[80] that the commercial sector is exploiting expectant families at a particularly vulnerable time, with companies having been described as 'hard-nosed'[81] and 'like snake-oil salesmen'[82] who prey on vulnerable targets. Smart Cell's 2005 Christmas advertising campaign, neatly timed to coincide with a typically 'family' time of year, can certainly add weight to this criticism. It is not unreasonable for new parents to want to safeguard their family's future regardless of whether their actions are deemed by the medical profession as necessary and it is the family connection that the industry attempts to exploit.[83] Californian Cryobank Company, FamilyCord, and the UK's Biovault Family's branding certainly capitalises on the 'family' connection.

With an emphasis on the private UCB account acting as a form of personal investment, the potential client is thrust into a whirlwind of commercial extravagance full of mercantile language where they are invited to secure, for a price, a 'gift of life'.[84] With individualistic goals in mind, such marketing

77 J Carvel, 'With love at Christmas – a set of stem cells' *The Guardian Online* (London 6 December 2005) www.guardian.co.uk/news/2005/dec/06/topstories3.genetics accessed 8 November 2015.

78 The slogan used by Smarts Cells International in their Christmas 2005 marketing campaign.

79 I Thornley and others, 'Private cord blood banking: experiences and views of pediatric hematopoietic cell transplantation physicians' (2009) 123 *Pediatrics* 1011–1017.

80 B H Lubin and others, 'Cord blood banking for potential future transplantation' (2007) 119 *Pediatrics* 1.

81 A Hardie, 'Baby blood bank firms prey on the vulnerable' *The Scotsman* (Scotland 23 February 2005).

82 J DeFao, 'Is it worth banking your baby's cord blood? Doctors say hard sell of hope is deceptive' *San Francisco Chronicle* (San Francisco 20 June 2005) www.sfgate.com/cgi-bin/article.cgi?file=/c/a/2005/06/20/MNG9GDBBLS1.DTL accessed 8 November 2015.

83 R Highfield, 'Umbilical cord blood banks are exploiting parents' *The Telegraph* (London 22 February 2008).

84 LifeCell International promotional video, 'Gift of life (umbilical cord blood banking)' on CNN-IBN (published 11 September 2014) *YouTube* www.youtube.com/watch?v=PFkkRs5PlSE accessed 8 November 2015.

techniques would be hard to resist for those who can afford it. What underpins the methods deployed by these banks, however, is their key selling point – one that centres upon a future peppered with health risks, uncertainty, and the future medical possibilities that stored stem cells may avail. The language used is one of probabilities, risks and benefits, statistical odds, contractual obligations and chance, all of which resonate with the nuances typically associated with insurance brokers.

Insurance typifies a risk/benefit analysis, which the cord blood industry capitalises on. The companies suggest that prudent parents can counter possible future health risks in the same way that they take out insurance for other types of unforeseen events, for example, holiday insurance or health cover. However, in insuring against the risk of future ill health, the UCB industry appears to go one step beyond conventional insurance. Not only is a return on your investment offered (albeit in the form of the stored biological 'asset' rather than a financial payout), but also the ability to tap into future technological advancements in medicine. But the difficulty with advertising UCB as a type of insurance is that it is not a conventional model. Unlike typical insurance policies that guarantee an agreed return on the initial investment, the 'return' here is a set of stem cells whose longevity is unknown, they may be damaged or diseased, or may simply fail to produce the required results. Put another way, while conventional insurance provides a certain benefit in an uncertain future, UCB storage provides an uncertain benefit in an uncertain future.[85]

However, it may be argued that the 'return' for consumers of UCB banking is the *potential benefit* that the stored UCB may provide. With conventional health insurance, the cost of treatment is reimbursed to the patient and/or any ongoing costs, minus any excess on the policy, are met by the insurer. In contrast, UCB banking incurs no excess, and whilst conventional treatment can be paid for by conventional insurance or by the NHS, a stored UCB unit offers hope of a cure rather than just palliative treatment. In monetary terms, UCB banking is more akin to premium bonds in the sense that the bond holder is offered a chance of gaining a financial benefit in addition to being able to cash the bond in at any time. Similarly, a private UCB account can be returned to the contract holder whenever the storage company is instructed to do so, and the unit's availability offers the chance of a health benefit to its recipient.

With stem cell research and innovation moving forward at an incredible pace, any premiums paid today in order to cover the risks of tomorrow may benefit from future medical technology. Speaking of a new type of familial insurance relationship, Brown and Kraft write:

85 B Nelson, 'Stem cell banking: lifeline or sub-prime?' *Nature Reports Stem Cells* (13 March 2008) www.nature.com/stemcells/2008/0803/080313/full/stemcells.2008.48.html accessed 8 November 2015.

> In the construction of the stem cell dream and the production of new 'blood ties', new parental duties [are formed] towards the future. Here, parents are encouraged to think themselves into a future in which their newborns are at risk, but also a future populated by an innovative range of regenerative medical treatments.[86]

Although talk of future disease is one of speculation and uncertainty, it is a dialect that can convince expectant families that banking UCB can be:

> [o]ne of the smartest, farthest-reaching decisions you can make when it comes to the health and wellness of your new-born, and to your own peace of mind. Knowing you've taken steps to safely store these incredible, life-affirming cells – and that they're just a phone call away – can put any parent's mind at ease.[87]

Once again, a combination of altruism and self-interest is evident. As potential investors in their child's future, parents act altruistically towards their offspring by expending finances on a form of biological insurance, but in a self-interested manner to ensure that their 'new parental duties'[88] have been fulfilled.

In their attempt to subscribe to the role of dutiful parent, it is feared that pregnant women and their vulnerabilities are being exploited.[89] According to Curtis and Leitner, being pregnant makes women vulnerable. They claim that 'even the most independent, self-reliant woman, irrespective of her home environment or financial status, becomes vulnerable during pregnancy'[90] due to her increased awareness of everyday risks. It is arguable that in her pregnant form, the woman carries dual personal risks – risks to both herself and her unborn child – and is 'vulnerable' in the sense that she is personally and physically responsible for herself and her unborn child's life.[91] This increased awareness of risks, however, may also make pregnant women more open to the idea of future risk, including those of a hypothetical nature. At a time when everyday risks to both themselves and their unborn child are

86 Brown and Kraft, 2006.

87 PacifiCord online website, http://pacificord.com/1_0_Stem-Cells-Family-Cord-Blood-Bank.php accessed 8 November 2015.

88 Brown and Kraft, 2006.

89 J Aleccia, 'Cord blood choice: private fears v public good – parents-to-be must weigh merits amidst barrage of advertising' *MSNBC News* (New York 21 July 2008) www.msnbc.msn.com/id/25723984/ accessed 8 November 2015.

90 A Curtis and M Leitner, 'Are pregnant women really vulnerable?' *Geographic Information Systems and Public Health – Eliminating of Perinatal Disparity* (Hershey, PA: IRM Press, 2005) 275.

91 These 'dual' risks can include those associated with the environment such as environmental toxins and passive smoking, lifestyle choices including the consumption of certain foods, alcohol, drugs and the taking of excessive exercise, and medical decision-making such as elective Caesareans, amniocentesis or blood transfusions.

more prevalent, the fear is that pregnant women are easy prey for the commercial UCB industry and their heightened awareness making them more susceptible to emotion-laden advertising.

Of course, if parents choose to respond positively to the advertising, then that is their choice and they are perfectly entitled to do so, but this simply exacerbates the controversial 'public versus private' debate in that their actions deny the public availability of the cells for the greater good of society. It would appear that contrary to the public health care benefits they first envisaged, the French creators of the UCB cryopreservation technique have unwittingly spawned several sub-species of beneficiaries in the process – those that donate to a public bank and fulfil the original ideal of saving the cells as a communal resource (the good), those who act for their own self-interest and bank the cells for their own private use (the bad), and those that are 'lucky' enough to combine the two.

The good, the bad and the lucky – the multi-facets of cord blood banking

The tensions raised by the public versus private UCB banking debate have been provoked by the accessibility of the stored cells. Such criticisms can spark a dichotomy in UCB collection between individualism and a collective response to healthcare provision, with the decision to bank invoking elements of 'good' or 'bad' behaviour. While such notions are value judgements, these concepts have been adopted here to demonstrate how the ideologies of altruism and self-interest can be characterised within public and private banking.

As discussed above, the exclusivity of private storage is at odds with ideals of community welfare and solidarity.[92] Given that the chance of an individual ever utilising their privately banked cells is purportedly low, and that public reserves of UCB are limited, it may arguably be more beneficial to society if UCB units were placed in a public bank and those that deny public utility have faced criticism for their perceived 'bad' actions in failing to contribute to public stocks.[93,94] As Ecker and Greene point out, '[a]t a societal level

92 An analogy can also be drawn here with the provision of health care in the United States, which is based upon an insurance-type system. The Affordable Care Act (ACA) 2010, officially known as The Patient Protection and Affordable Care Act (PPACA) and more commonly referred to as 'ObamaCare', came into force in 2013 and reforms both healthcare and health insurance industries in the US. Under this system, citizens take personal responsibility for their own health provision via employers' insurance or personal insurance purchased within government regulated health insurance marketplaces, with the government continuing to provide cover via Medicare and Medicaid for senior citizens and the poor.

93 N M Fisk and others, 'Can routine commercial cord blood banking be scientifically and ethically justified? (2005) 2 *PLoS Medicine* 2 www.ncbi.nlm.nih.gov/pmc/articles/PMC549592/, accessed 20 October 2015.

94 J L Ecker and M F Greene, 'The case against private umbilical cord blood banking' (2005) 105 *Obstetrics and Gynaecology* 6, 1282–1284.

privately donated samples is a lost opportunity for the banked blood to serve some individual (as opposed to remaining frozen and unused)'.[95] In fact, the only interested parties *guaranteed* to benefit are the commercial UCB companies who sell their service.

What Ecker and Greene's viewpoint fails to address, however, is that in spite of support for public banks[96] and calls for greater encouragement of UCB donations[97] very few women are actually afforded the opportunity to do so. As previously discussed, there are only a handful of hospitals who participate in collection for public use which dictates that the majority of pregnant women do not have the chance to act altruistically. Even if a mother acknowledged that the UCB unit stood a greater chance of being utilised in a public bank,[98] her ability to do so will be thwarted if she resides outside of the prescribed collection areas. Far from acting in a self-interested manner by banking privately, in such circumstances, this may be the mother's only preservation option in the same way that a lack of finances may influence a choice to donate rather than letting the UCB be destroyed. As Porter and Kerridge argue, to choose between the two banking options is to effectively 'force' women to elect between being 'a good citizen' and a 'good mother', with the latter 'increasingly seen as something enacted through purchasing decisions'.[99]

But as the government's recent efforts to maximise UCB availability gains pace, so too does the probability that the donated unit will remain available to the original donor. In addition, the number of those deemed 'lucky' to still have their cells in storage would undoubtedly be increased and in this sense, self-interest and altruism is cleverly combined. These two contrasting ideals formed the basis of a third type of UCB bank – the first 'mixed' or 'hybrid' banking system emerged in early 2007.

'Mixed banking' – the Virgin Health Bank

Recognising both the need for greater public stocks and to facilitate choice, the world's first 'mixed banking' initiative, the Virgin Health Bank (VHB), was launched on 1 February 2007 amidst a blaze of publicity.[100] Backed by

95 Ibid. An additional analogy may be drawn with those who carry a donor card, are on a donor register, or give permission for a deceased's organs to be used if in a qualifying relationship. Those who do so may be regarded as altruistic ('good') and those that do not may be deemed selfish ('bad').

96 RCOG, 2006.

97 Mr D Burrowes (Enfield, Southgate) (Cons) Hansard HC Vol 470 Cols 157–158 (8 January 2008) 'Umbilical cord blood donation'. Also see: The Umbilical Cord Blood (Donation) Bill 2008.

98 Including personal use subject to the unit remaining available in the public bank.

99 M Porter and I H Kerridge, '"Good mothering" or "good citizenship"? Conflicting values in choosing whether to donate or store umbilical cord blood' (2012) 9 *Bioethical Enquiry* 41–47.

100 Editorial, 'Branson to launch new stem-cell bank' *BBC News Online* (London 1 February 2007) http://news.bbc.co.uk/1/hi/health/6317855.stm, accessed 10 November 2015.

entrepreneur and businessman, Sir Richard Branson, and his multi-billion pound international business empire, The Virgin Group, the launch could not fail to attract widespread media coverage. With Branson himself posing angelically alongside a poster of a giant sized sleeping baby,[101] the use of a high-profile figurehead, emotive imagery complete with the Virgin brand logo and the presence of two leading stem cell experts, Professors Proctor and McGuckin from the North East England Stem Cell Institute,[102] ensured maximum press exposure.

The innovative 'mixed' system stands out from its commercial banking competitors in that it promotes an 'altruistic twist'.[103] Unlike other commercial companies, who store the entire UCB unit solely for the client's use, VHB splits the unit and stores approximately 20 per cent (the first 5 ml of the collected unit) on behalf of the private account holder and the remaining 80 per cent is gifted for public use. The initial venture was jointly funded by Virgin and Merlin Biosciences, a specialised venture investor in life sciences and is currently marketed by VHB as 'Community Banking'. This banking model was the first of its kind, and with its blend of public-private mix went some way towards addressing the concern that private storage denies public banks valuable reserves, a view echoed in the House of Commons, which 'applauded [VHB's] initiative'.[104] In addition to the public-spirited community banking, VHB also offers 'Family Banking' – a totally private banking service offering exclusivity of use to the private account holder for a fee of up to £1,995 for a 25-year storage term. In contrast, community banking can be secured for the discounted price of up to £1,095 for a storage term of the same length.

During the initial launch, Branson provided the media with an insight into his interest in stem cells and the factors that led him to branch into the biotech industry.[105] He communicated how numerous letters from distraught parents unable to find suitable bone marrow donors for their sick children had emotionally affected him and, after conversations with medical experts in the stem cell field, became convinced that UCB had a future in the fight against disease and in regenerative medicine. While the commercial

101 Editorial, 'Branson launches Virgin stem cell bank' (London 1 February 2007) *The Guardian Online* www.theguardian.com/uk/2007/feb/01/science.health accessed 11 November 2015.

102 N M Fisk and R Atun, 'Public-private partnership in cord blood banking' (2008) 336 *British Medical Journal* 642.

103 J Laurance, 'Branson moves into biotechnology with launch of Virgin stem cell storage bank' *The Independent Online* (London 2 February 2007) www.independent.co.uk/life-style/health-and-wellbeing/health-news/branson-moves-into-biotechnology-with-launch-of-virgin-stem-cell-storage-bank-434714.html accessed 10 November 2015.

104 HC Session 2006–7 Early Day Motions 'Stem cells and Virgin Health Bank' 797 (6 February 2007).

105 Editorial, 'Umbilical cord blood stem cell banking service – Richard Branson launches Virgin Health Bank' *Medical News Today* (International, 1 February 2007) www.medical-newstoday.com/articles/62106.php accessed 11 November 2015.

divergence into bio-banking is a world away from some of his other business ventures, which include holidays, trains, mobile phones and record labels, his interest may also have been influenced by his daughter's medical connections. Holly Branson qualified as a junior doctor in 2007 but deferred her hospital training to join Virgin a year later.[106] As a form of social enterprise, all profits from the VHB venture are donated to fund stem cell initiatives.

At first glance, it would appear that a banking model that simultaneously fosters altruism and self-interest while offering choice as well as addressing the critics of private banking, would be free from controversy. However, that is not the case. First, it is unclear why a parent would choose to pay the cost of £995 (or £1,095 if paying via VHB's payment plan) to store only 20 per cent of the unit, especially as sufficient blood volume is vital to transplant success, and has led some critics to question the viability of storing such a small amount for personal use.[107] In a personal interview in 2008 with the then commercial director of VHB, the company's position was explained.[108] VHB, he claimed, relies heavily on the message that banking your own UCB would in all probability be of little use today, but that the stored cells' utility lies in its potential future use in regenerative medicine. Although alternative resources, such as the use of adult stem and induced pluripotent stem cells have shown great promise[109] (and arguably limit the need to preserve autologous UCB cells), current research has shown that UCB demonstrates future potential within the field of regenerative medicine.[110]

For such use, however, the unit is reliant upon cell expansion techniques, regardless of its original size. After taking advice from a number of medical experts, VHB determined that an uneven split was deemed more beneficial than a 50/50 spilt for two reasons; first, a larger public sample would be more beneficial for use in unrelated (allogeneic) transplants due to its higher concentration of nucleated cells, and second, because it is more likely to be used than units stored for personal (autologous) use.[111] Furthermore, in VHB's opinion, parents have become more knowledgeable of UCB's potential and understand the necessity for expansion techniques in future autologous use and thus are now less concerned that the stored UCB unit has been divided. It is purported that a large majority of VHB clients have chosen

106 Editorial, 'Holly Branson quits medicine to work for her billionaire father' *The Mail Online* (London 28 July 2008) www.dailymail.co.uk/news/article-1039174/Holly-Branson-quits-medicine-work-billionaire-father.html accessed 11 November 2015.

107 G M T Guilcher, C V Fernandez and S Joffe, 'Are hybrid umbilical cord blood banks really the best of both worlds?' (2015) 41 *Journal of Medical Ethics* 272–275.

108 A semi-structured interview was conducted on 14 April 2008 in preparation for this author's doctoral thesis and published in: Devine, 2013.

109 S Holm, 'Time to reconsider stem cell ethics – the importance of induced pluripotent stem cells' (2008) 34 *Journal of Medical Ethics* 63.

110 N Foraz and C P McGuckin, 'The umbilical cord: a rich and ethical stem cell source to advance regenerative medicine' (2011) 44 *Cell Proliferation* (Suppl 1) 60–69.

111 Thornley and others, 2009.

this storage option because they appreciate the benefits of public donation as well as being able to keep some of the cells for exclusive use, citing receptiveness towards the altruistic concept involved in mixed banking.

Such generosity demonstrated by those willing to fund a public-private donation may be premised on the hope that the public section remains available, and akin to the women who took part in the study conducted by the universities of York and Lancaster examined earlier in this chapter, anticipate that the unit can be retrieved for private use if they later need it. As VHB estimates the chance of it being unavailable to be in the region of less than 1 per cent,[112] rather than the act of donation being totally altruistic, those who choose this 'mixed banking' option may simply be taking advantage of the discounted price tag and banking on the probability that both components of their unit will be available to them at a later date.

VHB appears to have further disengaged itself from other private banks by breaking with traditional modes of advertising. Whilst rival companies centre their promotional pitch upon the all-important 'lifesaving choice'[113] of preserving personal UCB in a medically uncertain future, VHB adopts a more conservative approach and acknowledges that for certain blood diseases, private (autologous) banking is unhelpful:

> It is likely that your baby's own cord blood stem cells may not be suitable to treat blood disorders such as childhood leukaemia. In fact, the nature of childhood leukaemia means that stem cells from a matched donor (an allogeneic transplant) are more likely to be of use than your child's own stem cells (an autologous transplant).[114]

Instead, the VHB marketing team focus upon the possible future of personally stored units in regenerative medicine and its public potential. As observed by Fisk and Atun, VHB appears to have 'aligned itself with conventional medical wisdom on the benefits of banking'[115] in an attempt to gain the public's trust – a stance that prompted the RCOG to publicly declare that they were 'pleased with the honesty of the Health Bank'.[116] Certainly, Virgin is a reliable brand label, the marketing of which swayed at least one VHB consumer who proudly states that, 'Virgin is a brand I trust'.[117] In

112 Fisk and Atun, 2008.

113 New England Cord Blood Bank online website, 'What is cord blood?' www.cordbloodbank.com/future_potential_of_stem_cells.html accessed 11 November 2015.

114 Virgin Health Bank (VHB) online website, 'FAQs' www.virginhealthbank.com/find-out-more/faqs accessed 11 November 2015.

115 Fisk and Atun, 2008.

116 RCOG, 'RCOG statement on the setting up of the Virgin Health Bank' (1 February 2007) www.rcog.org.uk/en/news/rcog-statement-on-the-setting-up-of-the-virgin-health-bank/ accessed 18 November 2015.

117 VHB online website, 'Why Virgin Health Bank?' www.virginhealthbank.com/why-virgin-health-bank accessed 12 November 2015.

March 2009, VHB extended its operations into the Middle East after announcing a partnership with the Qatar Foundation in Doha and relocating its international headquarters at the Qatar Science and Technology Park, with future plans to develop networks across Asia and Europe.[118]

In January 2012, VHB continued its short-term expansion plans closer to home. In a partnership with the Cambridge University Hospitals (CUH) NHS Foundation Trust, VHB directly marketed to pregnant women delivering at Cambridge's Rosie Hospital offering them the opportunity to buy into the 'mixed' banking option. Their marketing here centred upon the need to address the shortfall in public stocks, exacerbated by the high costs of the infrastructure and imported UCB units. However, while there remained a fee to be paid, women giving birth at this hospital were likely to have encountered an ethical dilemma – that is, the only way that they could act altruistically under the scheme was to pay for the privilege of doing so. The contract with VHB ended in August 2015.[119]

What presents as our second major controversy within this form of hybrid banking centres on the growth of collaborations between businesses and the public sector, particularly the NHS. Since the introduction of the Health and Social Care Act 2012, the NHS is obliged under Section 75 of the Act to competitively tender for the provision of its services in order to increase patient choice and foster competition.[120] This outsourcing of products and services has led to fears that the NHS is being privatised by stealth as NHS providers struggle to compete against tenders from the private sector who secured 33 per cent of all contracts awarded in 2013/14.[121] Companies such as Serco, Circle and Virgin Care (another branch of Virgin's medical care provision) are prominent within the NHS, providing a wide range of services from diagnostic tests to children's services and GP surgeries. The message from VHB, however, is that its collaborative service was provided completely 'free' to the NHS, as emphasised at the London Regenerative Medicine Network event in January 2012.[122] But with the Virgin brand gracing the corridors of NHS maternity units, those concerned that any form of public-private blend pragmatically renders the 'NHS for sale'[123] are unlikely to be reassured.

118 Excalibur Group, 'Virgin Health Bank' http://excalibur-group.co.uk/portfolio-companies/virgin-health-bank/ accessed 12 November 2015.

119 Personal email communication with the Information Governance Co-ordinator, CUH (14 December 2015).

120 Health and Social Care Act 2012 s 75(3)(a).

121 M Roberts, 'A third of NHS contracts awarded to private firms – report' *BBC News Online* (London 10 December 2014) www.bbc.co.uk/news/health-30397329 accessed 12 November 2015.

122 G Deal, 'Cord blood banking: charitable, clinical and commercial' (Cambridge 26 January 2012) *Global Regulatory Services* www.globalregulatoryservices.com/blog/cord-blood-banking-charitable-clinical-and-commercial accessed 13 November 2015.

123 NHS Support Federation, 'NHS for sale? Proving NHS privatisation' (undated) http://nhsforsale.info/private-providers/private-provider-profiles-2/virgin.html accessed 13 November 2015.

The venture into NHS territory has also been made by Precious Cells UK Limited. Its charitable arm, Precious Cells Miracle, announced its partnership with Croydon Health Services NHS Trust in October 2014.[124] Like VHB, it provides a free service to the NHS, but it differs in that its services to pregnant women who wish to donate are also given free of charge. In addition, those delivering in Croydon are also offered the option of a fee-paying private service for exclusive use. Precious Cells have pledged to share *some* of the profits from its private sales with the NHS, which they estimate to be in the region of £2 million over the next five years. But with plans to extend its venture into multiple additional NHS Trusts, one cannot help but wonder if this is more about profit than a social benefit. Furthermore, pregnant women being offered this particular scheme may be faced with a heightened ethical dilemma in that they may find themselves feeling pressurised to take part in the scheme (either to donate or to contract privately), especially as it is offered in the context of standard NHS services, which may add weight to the perceived need to preserve the cells.[125]

Outside of the UK, the mixed model of banking has also been adopted by certain countries, such as Bionet (BabyBanks) in Taiwan and the Shanghai Cord Blood in China.[126] In Taiwan, private banks offer free storage for UCB that is traceable on public registries or for-profit storage with the option of a full refund should they relinquish their private account for public use at a later date.[127] However, Rei has questioned the reliability of the stored cells retrieved from private banks under this type of model because they often fail to meet the stringent quality standards adopted by public banks.[128] It is also reported that some countries, among them Spain, operate under a variation of this model whereby there is a legal obligation to release a unit sequestered within a private account if a match is found on the public registries.[129] Clearly, this version of the mixed banking model plays to public need but in doing so fails to fulfil the exclusivity of its original intended purpose and leaves the element of 'choice' severely hampered.

To secure their child's future health and safety there is huge pressure on parents to make the right decisions, often before the child is born: What foods and supplements should be consumed during pregnancy? Should they bottle or breastfeed? Which sleeping position for the child is deemed best?

124 Ibid.

125 P Brice, 'Public-private partnerships for UK cord blood banking' (6 October 2014) *Phg Foundation* www.phgfoundation.org/blog/16332/ accessed 26 November 2015.

126 H C Chang, 'The third way of umbilical cord blood banking' (2014) 12 *Nature Biotechnology* 4.

127 W Rei, 'Toward a governance structure beyond informed consent: a critical analysis of the popularity of private cord blood banking in Taiwan' (2009) 4 *East Asian Science, Technology and Society: An International Journal* 53–75.

128 Ibid.

129 J Aznar Lucea, 'Umbilical cord blood banks. Ethical aspects. Public versus private banks' (2012) 23 *Cuadernos de Bioetica* 269–285.

To immunise or not? Now, whether or not to bank UCB is just one more thing to add to the expectant family's list of parental decision-making and the emotional burden to make the right choice can be immense. But it is not only expectant parents who have felt the demands from UCB banking. Those who facilitate the process of collection also find themselves under pressure to make the right decisions. As we saw in the previous chapter, UCB must be collected by a qualified health professional – usually a midwife or obstetrician – but with the number of births in the UK increasing, midwives are reportedly dealing with several patients in the labour suite at once.[130] Given that midwives deal not only with the labour process itself, but also the essential checks and observations of both mother and baby post-partum, there is arguably little time to dedicate to UCB collection. The difficulties that midwives face is neatly captured by Louise Silverton of the Royal College of Midwives, who explains that:

> Maternity services are buckling under the pressure. They are understaffed and overstretched. All politicians speak about maternity as a priority, yet the lack of money put into them exposes this as rhetoric, not a reality. We are simply falling into the age-old pattern of boom and bust recruitment, which too often leaves women and their babies suffering the consequences.[131]

In a depleted profession that operates within maternity departments that are seriously understaffed, it is questionable whether scarce midwifery resources should be utilised to collect UCB for private use, especially as its utility is in doubt. If the lack of sufficient funding and resources are to blame for the current crisis affecting the efficient delivery of midwifery services within the UK, then the collection of UCB can only add to its problems. While a regulatory framework for the procurement of UCB now exists, and goes some way towards protecting the safe and efficient collection of the cells, it fails to acknowledge all potential problems for health professionals.

UCB collection, the EUTCD and the Human Tissue Regulations 2007

Prior to the implementation of the European Union Tissues and Cells Directive (EUTCD) (2004/23/EC),[132] which was transposed into UK law via the Human

130 C Irvine, 'Midwives deal with three births at once, says expert' *The Telegraph Online* (London 22 September 2008) www.telegraph.co.uk/news/health/3044749/Midwives-deal-with-three-births-at-once-says-expert.html accessed 15 November 2015.

131 A Epstein and R Ellis, 'Hard labour: the maternity service in crisis' *The Mail Online* (London 11 September 2007) www.dailymail.co.uk/health/article-481102/Hard-labour-The-maternity-service-crisis.html accessed 15 November 2015.

132 The EUTCD is made up of three main Directives: The Parent Directive (2004/23/EC) and two technical directives (2006/17/EC, as amended by 2012/39/EU and 2006/86/EC).

Tissue (Quality and Safety for Human Application) Regulations 2007, the collection of UCB was unregulated in the UK. In response to requests from pregnant women who wished to save the cells, certain NHS Trusts allowed their midwifery staff to perform the procedure on their behalf, and in some cases, permitted collections by unqualified third parties, such as fathers and birth partners.[133] In addition to doubting the merit of storing cells for private (autologous) use, authoritative bodies such as RCOG and the Human Tissue Authority (HTA) were concerned about third parties who lacked suitable medical training being allowed to perform a task that required sufficient competency and expertise.[134] Research carried out by the Institute of Medicine (IOM) in 2004 into the success rates of UCB collectors concluded that those who receive specialist training produced acceptable results.[135] This view was later endorsed by the RCOG who recorded that bacterial contamination rates fall when experienced, trained staff perform collection,[136] and as Sullivan worryingly observed:

> Commercial banks rely on the local healthcare provider, the doctor or midwife, to collect the cord blood at birth and forward it to the bank for long-term storage. Although this may be convenient for the purposes of collection, it introduces the potential for poor quality or low yield cord collections.[137]

However, the implementation of the Human Tissue Regulations by the HTA and its associated General Directions[138] and Guidelines[139] on the requirements and expected standards of tissue establishments changed the way in which UCB can legally be collected. No longer can non-professional collectors, such as birth partners, procure UCB because the strict regulations permit only

133 K Devine, 'Cord blood in the car park: cord blood stem cells, contamination and DIY collection exposed' *BioNews* (Progress Educational Trust, 16 March 2010c) www.bionews.org.uk/page_55941.asp accessed 15 November 2015.

134 RCOG, 'RCOG statement on cord blood collection' (9 March 2010) www.rcog.org.uk/en/news/rcog-statement-on-cord-blood-collection/ accessed 18 November 2015.

135 Institute of Medicine of the National Academies, *Establishing a National Hematopoietic Stem Cell Program* (Washington, DC: The National Academies Press, 2005) 143.

136 RCOG, 2006.

137 M Sullivan, 'Banking on cord blood stem cells' (2008) 8 *Nature Reviews Cancer* 823.

138 Human Tissue Authority (HTA), 'Directions given under the Human Tissue Act 2004 implementing the Human Tissue (Quality and Safety for Human Application) Regulations 2007' 003/2010 www.hta.gov.uk/sites/default/files/2010-11-12_General_Directions_November_2010.pdf accessed 15 November 2015. General Directions 003/2010 consolidate and clarify the standards required under the Human Tissue (Quality and Safety for Human Application) Regulations 2007 and revoke General Directions 001/2006, 002/2007 and 004/2007.

139 HTA, 'Guide to quality and safety assurance for human tissue and cells for patient treatment' (12 November 2010) www.hta.gov.uk/sites/default/files/Annex_-_Guide_to_Quality_and_Safety_Assurance_for_Tissues_and_Cells_for_Patient_Treatment.pdf accessed 15 November 2015.

'sufficient, suitably qualified personnel'[140] to collect the cells and it must only be performed on premises that have received a licence from the HTA. Yet there is little incentive for Trusts who do not collect on behalf of public banks to apply for a licence, which led to a row between the VHB and the HTA in 2008, with the VHB declaring that the new regulations deny many women the opportunity to collect their cells.[141]

The HTA was set up under the provisions of the Human Tissue Act 2004[142] to regulate the removal, storage, use and disposal of human bodies, organs and tissue for certain scheduled purposes. On 5 July 2007, the EUTCD was formally adopted into UK law by the Regulations, with its provisions being implemented in April 2008 and overseen by the HTA. The newly imposed legal requirement for health professionals[143] to procure UCB acknowledges the fact that collection is a complex process and one that necessitates certain knowledge, training and experience[144] in order to complete the task efficiently and safely. The RCOG not only supported this view, but called for additional safety measures in acknowledgement of the logistical difficulties faced by midwives who are asked to collect UCB at a phase of the birthing process that requires their full attention. Instead it recommended that:

> Collection should be by a trained third party (that is, not by the attending obstetrician or midwife) using methods and facilities appropriate to meet the European Tissues and Cells Directive.[145]

Furthermore, as collections can now only be made on HTA licence-holding premises, non-licensed NHS hospitals can no longer permit their own health professionals to facilitate collection – even at their own discretion. This raises a number of issues.

Although the Regulations specifically sets out the necessary qualifications and experience required of a Designated Individual (DI)[146] (the person under whose supervision the licensed activity is authorised to be carried out on), those of the UCB collector are not as comprehensively defined. Instead, more generic terms such as 'suitable persons'[147] and 'should have relevant knowledge of microbiology and hygiene'[148] are used to describe the qualities

140 Ibid., at s 36.

141 K Devine, 'The UK's HTA to regulate the collection of cord blood stem cells' *BioNews* (Progress Educational Trust, 6 May 2008) www.bionews.org.uk/page_13374.asp accessed 15 November 2015.

142 Human Tissue Act 2004 s 13(1).

143 *HTA Guidelines November 2010* s 95.

144 *HTA Guidelines November 2010* ss 36–38.

145 RCOG, 2006.

146 Human Tissue (Quality and Safety for Human Application) Regulations 2007 r 11(3).

147 *HTA Regs 2007* at r 11(a) and *HTA Guidelines November 2010* at s 2(a).

148 *HTA Guidelines November 2010* at s 38.

of a proficient collector possessing 'the necessary experience'[149] to undertake procurement. That level of competency, however, is either evidenced by 'their general job responsibilities',[150] or perhaps more controversially, as determined by the Licence Holder (LH).[151] Where the LH is the NHS Trust, this is unlikely to be problematic. Yet if the LH is a private UCB bank, then it is they who can determine whether a particular UCB collector is deemed a 'suitable person[s] to participate in the carry-on of the licensed activities'[152] and in practical terms, the private UCB bank can set its own standards and levels of competency.

What this form of self-regulation may not take into account, however, is that the collection of blood during the third stage of labour arguably presents a different set of circumstances to the informal collector,[153] such as a phlebotomist – a commonly used UCB collector by private banks. Although a phlebotomist need not possess any formal qualifications to become a trainee, they are required to undertake a six-month training course, after which they are awarded a Certificate of Competence, which allows them to work unsupervised.[154] In this sense, they are a professional within their field of expertise, but one whose competence, knowledge and experience differs to that of a professional midwife or obstetrician. In other words, while they may be suitably qualified and proficient to obtain blood generally, collecting cells during the third stage of labour may present a completely different environment and be unfamiliar territory for the informal collector.

Furthermore, should the mother request that the collection procedure takes place via the in-utero method, which is the favoured method of the private banks due to its purported ability to produce the highest yield of stem cells,[155] then the consent process is likely to fall to the informal collector. As we shall see in the next chapter, the law of informed consent engenders a robust exchange of communication between the patient and health professional covering all known material risks and benefits involved, however small,[156] before they acquiesce to the procedure – a communication process that may not be familiar to an informal collector whose primary task is to procure blood.

149 *HTA Guidelines November 2010* at s 95.
150 *HTA Guidelines November 2010* at s 95.
151 *HTA Guidelines November 2010* at s 95.
152 *HTA Guidelines November 2010* at s 2.
153 For the purposes of this chapter, the term 'Informal Collector' refers to personnel such as a phlebotomist or independent nurse who is employed by the parent or private UCB bank to collect the cells. Although it is acknowledged that informal collectors are professionals in their own field of medical expertise, they are differentiated by this paper from the 'Professional Collector', which refers to those with midwifery or obstetric training.
154 Careers Advisory Service, 'Phlebotomist' http://careersadvice.direct.gov.uk/helpwithyourcareer/jobprofiles/profiles/profile1472 accessed 16 November 2015.
155 B A Armson, D S Allan and R F Casper, 'Umbilical cord blood: counselling, collection and banking' (2015) 27 *Journal of Obstetrics and Gynaecology Canada* 9, 832–844.
156 As determined by the doctrine of informed consent, see: *Chester v Afshar* [2004] UKHL 41; *Montgomery v Lanarkshire Health Board* [2015] UKSC 11.

The second issue raised is that although UCB can only be legally stored on licensed premises, the Regulations permit the *collection* of UCB on *unlicensed* premises under certain circumstances – that is, when the UCB collector (either the midwife or informal collector) performs collection under a 'a third party agreement',[157] which is an agreement between the Licence Holder (LH) and the collector. What this means in practice is that a licensed private bank can enter into an agreement with a third party who can collect on their behalf under the terms of that licence. Personal communications with Smart Cells International[158] revealed that local phlebotomy companies are currently being used to collect on this basis.

Suitably qualified collectors then, even at hospitals that do not possess a licence, can make collections under a third party agreement. This would appear to address the Virgin Health Bank's concerns that prospective clients due to deliver their babies at unlicensed NHS hospitals would be unable to save their UCB. However, although third party agreements allow collections to take place at unlicensed hospitals by non-NHS personnel, it still remains for the NHS Trusts to permit them to do so. The problem is that if permission under these agreements is granted, the midwife and NHS still arguably remain open to potential liability for the torts of that third party collector.

'Two's company – three's a crowd'[159]

The relationship between NHS midwifery staff and informal collectors (such as phlebotomists), privately employed by commercial banks, has been crystallised by Machin, Brown and McLeod in their research specifically focused towards establishing the boundaries between the public and private sphere of UCB collection, published in 2012.[160] Participants in the study included midwives, heads of maternity services, privately employed phlebotomists, donor co-ordinators as well as donors and depositors of UCB. Through their observations and interviews, the researchers made a number of key findings. First, it was made clear that a hierarchical system categorically exists within the labour ward. They expressly describe midwives exerting power over the informal collector with the latter restricted to performing his or her function only when given permission from the midwife to so do.

Second, they noted a clear distinction between the attitudes of midwives 'sharing' the physical NHS space with the informal collectors who the midwives described as 'intruders', 'outside people', 'an inconvenience' and 'a burden to be managed by hospital personnel'. This perception of informal

157 Human Tissue (Quality and Safety for Human Application) Regulations 2007 r 6.

158 Personal communication with Smart Cells online advisor (16 November 2015).

159 L Machin, N Brown and D McLeod, '"Two's company – three's a crowd": the collection of umbilical cord blood for commercial stem cell banks in England and the midwifery profession' (2012) 28 *Midwifery* 358–365.

160 Ibid.

collectors, they deduced, stemmed from the lack of a designated area within which the informal collector could occupy whilst waiting to be summoned by the midwife to perform collection. This is further exacerbated by the discomfort experienced by midwives who witnessed informal collectors transitioning from a member of the public waiting to enter the labour suite into invited personnel working within the maternity area whose official non-NHS status remained unclear.

Third, midwives were expressly positioned within their findings as 'the gatekeepers' of the maternity ward and upon whose trust the birthing mother could rely upon to determine when it was appropriate to summon and grant access to the informal collector. Such determinations by midwives provide further evidence of their control over the collection of UCB, the third stage of labour, and the birthing process as a whole. Of particular relevance is the researchers' reference to the control exerted by the midwife over the UCB collection process itself. The findings of the study revealed that with 'midwifery control' came 'power', referenced by the ability of the midwife to dictate the precise moment that UCB collection could take place, and that control extended to the midwife's ability to prioritise other functions over UCB collection for stem cells, such as collection for cord blood gas analysis purposes.[161] Essentially, the midwife retains authority over the entire birthing process and exerts the necessary control over the timing of UCB procurement. As one senior member of the Royal College of Midwives (RCM) expressed to the researchers, 'the timing of UCB collection and midwives' role in the labour process placed UCB collection squarely within midwives' authority'.[162]

The above finding is particularly important in legal terms. The midwife undoubtedly exerts control over the informal collector in practical terms, but in doing so they also open themselves and their NHS employers to potential litigation should harm result. That said, the introduction of the Regulations only goes so far in offering protection because by allowing third parties access to the maternity department of NHS hospitals to carry out a task at the pregnant woman's request, the NHS is putting its maternity staff, and itself, in a peculiarly vulnerable position. In order to collect UCB, the cord must first be clamped and only the midwife can perform the clamping task.[163] As previously stated, for the optimum number of cells to be collected, the cord must be clamped as soon after delivery of the child as possible and whilst the placenta remains in situ. The problem is that if any of the potential risks associated with early cord clamping and in-utero collection arise, it

161 Cord blood gas analysis is an objective way of assessing a newborn's metabolic condition at birth and provides an insight into the causes of intrapartum foetal distress.

162 Machin, Brown and McLeod, 2012.

163 Personal communication with Parsmedix Ltd, the largest network of cord blood phlebotomists in the UK, confirms that their collectors play no role in the clamping process (15 November 2015).

will be difficult for the midwife to escape potential litigation because his or her involvement and actions are integral to the collection process.[164] Put another way, if the mother or child suffer any form of personal injury and/or damage to the cells, it may be difficult to establish who or what was the legal cause of the harm, and the midwife may therefore find him or herself being held directly liable or jointly liable with the informal third party collector; and the NHS and/or private bank vicariously liable for their actions.

The final point to be made is that in spite of the midwife's authority over the informal collector, the researchers found that within the hierarchical scale, pregnant women themselves exuded ultimate control over the expectations of both midwife and informed collector, with midwives relinquishing their role as 'maternal gatekeepers' in favour of the pregnant woman's demands. Senior midwives that were interviewed described UCB collection as either a woman's 'choice' or a 'wish' that midwives 'bend over backwards' to facilitate. As one consultant midwife explained, '[I]t's the parents' wishes and obviously we're there to support the parents. And they do have a right to choose their type of care.'[165]

While the element of patient choice therefore appears to be upheld by midwifery staff, what does this mean for UCB collection? Although midwifery staff involved in the study expressed a reluctance to accept the existence of informal collectors within the labour suite, in the interests of facilitating the mother's request, they acquiesced with their patient's wishes. This need to comply with requests, however, is made all the more difficult by the fact that as the midwife is responsible for clamping the cord, (s)he may feel pressurised to clamp earlier than would normally be performed in favour of UCB collection, especially if requested by the mother. For the same reasons, midwives may feel morally obliged to allow in-utero collection despite the increased risk of maternal haemorrhage in leaving the placenta attached to the uterine wall.[166] Clearly, the process of collection promulgates differing interests and a conflict of priorities for those tending to the patient. The informal collector's main concern is to obtain an optimal UCB unit in order to maximise utility, whereas the midwife's primary responsibility is to

164 In this situation, the courts have adopted a pragmatic approach. For example, in *Cassidy v Ministry of Health* [1951] 2 KB 343, it was unclear whether it was the negligence of the medical officer, surgeon or nurse that had caused the claimant's injury and the Court of Appeal unanimously held the hospital liable regardless of where the fault lay. However, the traditional approach to causation is by the application of the 'but for' test. In *Wilsher v Essex Area Heath Authority* [1988] AC 1074, a claim was made that the negligent administration of excess oxygen to a newborn infant had been causative of his blindness. While negligence was proved, the claim nonetheless failed because there were several other potential causative agents and the claimants were therefore not able to show that 'but for' the defendant's negligence the harm would not have occurred.

165 Machin, Brown and McLeod, 2012.

166 D Dickenson, *Body Shopping: The Economy Fuelled by Flesh and Blood* (Oxford: Oneworld Publications, 2008) 46–49.

ensure the health and wellbeing of the mother and child; and the pregnant woman's interests fall squarely between the two. Such conflicting priorities may compromise not only the parties involved in collection, both legally and ethically, but NHS Trusts themselves may also remain open to liability for any tortious acts carried out by third party UCB collectors, either from third party liability in negligence, or vicarious liability from the torts of their employees. In the same way, private banks would also be held vicariously responsible for the torts of informal collectors under their charge. Indeed, there could be multiple defendants open to a claimant should a negligence action be pursued.

Third party liability

What is problematic in the area of third party liability are the inconsistent approaches and criteria applied by the courts, which have led McIvor to declare that the current law on third party liability generally is 'unstructured, unprincipled and incoherent'.[167]

It would appear that for liability in the tort of negligence, any type of collector who is not an NHS employee would be classed as either an independent contractor or a third party. Whilst NHS health professionals would be held personally liable for the negligent procurement of UCB, and the NHS vicariously liable for the torts of their employees,[168] the position with regard to the liability of the NHS for the torts of informal collectors is less clear.

While contractual obligations generally exist between the informal collector and the private bank or the commissioning patient, no formal contract exists between the informal collector and the NHS. In the absence of contractual relations, an informal collector may for liability purposes be regarded as a third party in a negligence action. A third party can be described as a person or body that is independent of the legal relationship between the NHS and the patient, but may become involved in that relationship if they cause them harm. Liability in negligence for the acts of third parties has evolved from case law in a manner that has set out exceptions to the general rule that a defendant is not liable for omissions or the actions of others, and differs from vicarious liability in that legal responsibility flows from the fault of the defendant.[169] The traditional approach arises from the judgment in *Home Office v Dorset Yacht Co. Ltd*,[170] where it was held that the Home Office guards were legally responsible for the acts of prisoners in their charge.[171]

167 C McIvor, *Third Party Liability in Tort* (Oxford: Hart Publishing, 2006) p 1.
168 *Lister v Helsey Hall Ltd* [2001] UKHL 22.
169 McIvor, 2006 at 1.
170 *Home Office v Dorset Yacht Co. Ltd* [1970] AC 1004.
171 Later clarified by Lord Goff in *Smith v Littlewoods Organisation Ltd* [1987] 1 AC 241 who laid out four grounds when an exception to the general principle regarding third parties can be found.

The court determined that the Home Office guards owed a duty of care to the neighbouring yacht owners and were responsible for the damage caused by the prisoners as third parties in negligence for the following reasons. First, the guards had a special relationship with the prisoners in that they exercised a degree of authority and control over their actions, and it was due to the guards' negligence that the prisoners had been able to cause the damage. Second, the prisoners' escape was a foreseeable act towards a foreseeable class of victim (the yacht owners) and the type of damage that had occurred was 'the very kind of thing'[172] that the prisoners were likely to do if negligently allowed to escape. Essentially, the prison guards' failure to prevent the damage being caused to the yachts by prisoners in their charge warranted a duty to be owed to the victims for that damage.

For the same reasons, the NHS may be legally responsible for the negligent acts of the informal UCB collector as a third party because all the elements of third party liability can be met. First, a special relationship between the NHS and the collector can be said to arise by authorising collection to take place on NHS premises. Second, the type of harm (physical harm resultant of negligent collection) and the class of victim (the pregnant woman who commissions UCB collection) are foreseeable. But does the NHS exert *sufficient* control and authority over the way that UCB is procured by an informal collector to give rise to liability? As I have argued earlier in this chapter, the findings of the research conducted by Machin, Brown and McLeod point clearly towards the midwife (and therefore the NHS) retaining ultimate control over the collection process. That said, any liability that may arise from the informal collector's negligence may therefore fall jointly to the NHS.

However, it still remains an issue as to whether the NHS would actually be at fault and whether a court would take the view that the NHS *should* be held to account for not preventing the negligence of the informal collector. There are two issues here: first, direct liability may arise if the NHS fails to provide competent staff and/or a safe system of working,[173] and second from their non-delegable duty to ensure that reasonable care is taken in the provision of medical care to patients.[174] If fault is apportioned to the NHS in either of these two contexts, then liability may not be out of the question.

172 *Home Office v Dorset Yacht Co. Ltd* [1970] AC 1004 at 1030 (Lord Reid).

173 For example, see: *Bull v Devon Area Health Authority* [1993] 4 Med LR 117.

174 For example, see: *M v Calderdale Kirkless Health Authority* [1998] Lloyd's Rep Med 157, where the health authority was held liable for the negligent performance of an abortion that it had commissioned at a private hospital. While this view was later doubted by the Court of Appeal in *A (a child) v Ministry of Defence* [2004] EWCA Civ 641, the point does not appear to have been finally settled, especially as the case concerned negligent treatment performed at an overseas hospital. In a different context, the issue has more recently been examined in *NA v Nottingham County Council* [2015] EWCA Civ 1139 where the court held that a non-delegable duty was not imposed upon the defendant local authority for failing to remove a child from the home of an abusive foster parent in the absence of any negligence on the defendant's part.

In addition to acts of third parties, the NHS may also be held legally responsible for the torts of an independent contractor who carries out work on its premises. An independent contractor is generally regarded as a person who provides goods or services to the NHS on a one-off or ad-hoc basis, as opposed to having a permanent contract of employment. An example can be seen in the case of *Gwilliam v West Hertfordshire Hospitals NHS Trust* [2002][175] where the hospital Trust contracted the services of an independent contractor to provide an entertainments structure known as a 'splat-wall' for a fundraising event. The court held that the Trust had discharged its duty to the claimant who had been injured when using the structure because it had confirmed the operator's competency[176] by clarifying that he held insurance. The Trust was therefore not held liable for the injury.

It would be difficult to class an informal UCB collector as an independent contractor of the NHS because they are unlikely to hold a formal contract of employment. Rather, the contract would be between the collector and the private bank or patient. However, there are two points to be made here. First, although *Gwilliam* was essentially an Occupiers' Liability case and a contract existed between the NHS and the contractor, it is arguable that as informal collectors provide a service on NHS premises on behalf of the pregnant woman, by analogy, if the NHS was held to owe a duty to check the competency of a splatt-wall operator when providing a service on their grounds, then the duty should also extend to checking the suitability of those who procure UCB from its patients, whether a contract exists or not. This point is particularly relevant given Howarth's view: he argues that whilst most cases involving independent contractors have some kind of contract between the parties, it is not a formal requirement.[177] This suggests that the absence of a contractual relationship between an informal collector and the NHS would not present a bar to a potential claim in negligence against the relevant Trust.

Indeed, Gilmour has noted that as a matter of policy, the NHS has tended to ignore the distinction between employees and independent contractors in cases where the patient has been injured in the course of receiving NHS treatment.[178] Furthermore, Markesinis and Deakin argue that victims of torts should not be adversely affected by contract terms that deny employee status to a worker.[179] Notwithstanding that for policy reasons the courts may be reluctant to impose liability in these circumstances, in the interest of patient protection, direct and joint liability remains a possibility.

175 *Gwilliam v West Hertfordshire Hospitals NHS Trust* [2002] EWCA Civ 1041.
176 Occupiers' Liability Act 1957 s 2(4).
177 D Howarth, *Textbook on Torts* (London: Butterworths, 2005) p 649.
178 J M Gilmour, 'Patient safety, medical error and tort law: an international comparison' (May 2006) *Health Policy Research Programme, Health Canada* No. 6795-15-203/5760003 www.hc-sc.gc.ca/hcs-sss/alt_formats/hpb-dgps/pdf/pubs/2001-patient-securit-rev-exam/2001-patient-securit-rev-exam-eng.pdf accessed 16 November 2015.
179 S Deakin, A Johnston and B Markesinis, *Markesinis and Deakin's Tort Law* (7th edn, Oxford: Oxford University Press, 2013) p 559.

The relationship between informal collectors and the private bank (as opposed to the NHS) would be one of either an employee or independent contractor, depending upon their employment status and other relevant factors, of which there is no exhaustive list.[180] An element of control over the work activities has been taken to be one of the determining factors. For example, if an informal collector provides the service as part of their own business for which they retain control over the performance of tasks,[181] the hours that they work, provide their own equipment, and invoice for payment of the work they carry out, they are more likely to be classed as an independent contractor. Conversely, they are likely to be employees of the private bank if they hold a formal contract of employment,[182] carry out the collection procedure in accordance with their specific instructions, are paid by the company, and are offered company benefits such as holiday and sick pay and pensions schemes. However, informal collectors working on behalf of an agency who allocates work to them may fall under the auspices of the agency rather than the private bank.

Vicarious liability

Vicarious liability is the principle by which one person can be held legally responsible for the torts of another and typically arises in employment situations when an employee commits a tort whilst carrying out a work-related task during the course of their employment.[183] For the midwife, his or her role is confined to active involvement in the birthing process but as collection is made during the third stage of labour, (s)he will be working alongside the informal collector and, as argued earlier, retains control over UCB collection. As the midwife owes a duty of care to the patient, if problems occur during collection which impacts upon the mother's health, there is a duty to respond regardless of how the problems are caused. Yet once assistance is given, the midwife becomes directly involved in the process, and if harms result, litigation may follow, with the NHS vicariously liable. What is particularly worrying for a midwife at an unlicensed hospital acting under a third party agreement is that the National Health Service Litigation Authority

180 *Market Investigations Ltd v Minister of Social Security* [1969] 2 QB 173 at 184–185 (Cooke, J).

181 Although unlikely to be relevant here, Horsey and Rackley have noted that in other contexts, employees are often encouraged (and even rewarded) for exercising discretion and showing initiative on behalf of their employers and therefore this element of 'control' may be viewed as out of touch with a modern day workforce. See K Horsey and E Rackley, *Tort Law* (4th edn, Oxford: Oxford University Press, 2015) pp 591–592.

182 Such as can be seen in the job advert for a phlebotomist posted by Precious Cells International on 1 March 2016, see: www.reed.co.uk/jobs/phlebotomist/29090705?utm_source=adzuna&utm_medium=aggregator&utm_campaign=health_medicine&cmpid=124 accessed 19 March 2016.

183 *Lister v Helsey Hall Ltd* [2001] UKHL 22 at 70 (Lord Millett).

(NHSLA) is unable to confirm whether s(he) will be indemnified under the Clinical Negligence Scheme for Trusts (CNST) should anything go wrong and (s)he is later sued.[184]

In August 2011, the RCOG issued a joint statement with the RCM which went some way to addressing this type of concern. It recommended that collection should be made 'in a designated area away from the delivery room'[185] to encourage a clear division of tasks during the third stage of labour (which would also necessitate the ex-utero method). However, even this is not problem free because it does not address the timing of cord clamping, a task that falls to the midwife alone. As it is a commonly held view that early cord clamping procures the optimal blood volume,[186] it is certainly conceivable that in the haste to transfer the placenta to the 'designated area', the midwife may feel pressured to adopt early cord clamping, which in itself carries risks to the child; and akin to the midwife who feels morally obliged to allow in-utero collection on the pregnant woman's request despite the risks, (s)he becomes entangled in a 'joint' collection process. Whichever way you look at it, the midwife and NHS Trust are placed in a potentially precarious position as they take on all the legal responsibilities UCB collection can entail for the financial benefit of the private banks.

Conclusion

This chapter has shown that increased knowledge of UCB's potential and its acceptance by the medical community as a viable clinical resource for transplantation purposes have led to a growth in the cord blood industry. The 'public versus private' debate highlights the burgeoning dichotomy between altruism and self-interest; whether we should provide greater opportunities for public donation and increase public stocks in the interests of solidarity and to uphold the 'community welfare' ideals of the NHS, pitted against the fear that banking privately denies much-needed public reserves in favour of furthering our own self-interested goals. The emotive marketing techniques of the private sector have certainly added another dimension to the debate in that expectant parents may face the dilemma of

184 Personal communications with the Access Manager, NHSLA, and the Claims Department throughout November 2015 has revealed that the NHSLA are unable to confirm whether the Clinical Negligence Scheme for Trusts would be available to health professionals facing litigation in this type of scenario. The assumption is therefore made that indemnity would be decided on a case-by-case analysis.

185 RCOG and RCM, 'RCOG/RCM joint statement on umbilical cord blood collection and banking' (August 2011) www.rcm.org.uk/sites/default/files/Joint%20Statement%20-%20UCB%20-%20aug%2011%20(6)%20v2.pdf accessed 12 March 2016.

186 For example, see HTA online website 'F&Qs' where the HTA endorses the RCOG's view that '...delaying cord clamping can prevent a successful cord blood collection' www.hta.gov.uk/faqs/cord-blood-procurement-faqs#sthash.87t2klqf.dpuf accessed 17 November 2015.

being regarded as a 'bad' citizen if they contract with a private bank, and a 'bad' parent if they do not. This can be particularly problematic for those unable to do either, especially as the market advocates that, 'Stem cells are too valuable to be discarded.'[187]

In contrast, mixed banking models have shown that there is room for the private sector to work in parallel with public banks in a bid to utilise welfare principles, to build up a more comprehensive and ethnically diverse range of available units; and to facilitate choice. While these models are not free from criticism, they do provide a more ethical alternative to banking solely with a for-profit bank.

As we have seen, the collection of UCB perpetuates a number of legal issues for the NHS, its midwifery staff and informal collectors. While the HTA's licensing system for hospitals offers midwives some protection by prohibiting unqualified staff, I have argued that it does not go far enough. As UCB must be collected during the third stage of labour – an integral part of the birthing process and one in which the midwife is directly involved – the task is ultimately performed under the midwife's guidance, co-operation and supervision. We have also seen how midwives are keen to facilitate pregnant women's requests where it is practicable to do so. Yet, if anything should go wrong, the midwife, as arbiter of the collection process, may be found liable not only for his or her actions, but also for the actions of an informal collector, with the NHS potentially liable for both. Ultimately, while UCB facilitators and their patients run the risks associated with the collection process, it is the private industry that reaps the financial rewards for their efforts.

187 CryoSave online website, 'Why save stem cells?' http://cryo-save.com/en/what-are-stem-cells/why-save-stem-cells accessed 16 November 2015.

4 Cord blood and the role of informed consent in law in the UK

> Whether deciding to donate UCB to a public bank or to pay to store UCB in a private bank, informed choice and consent for the collection, banking and future use of the UCB should be central to the process. To ensure transparency, openness, and accountability, information about UCB should be discussed broadly between women and their healthcare providers.[1]

One of the fundamental principles that underpins medical law and ethics is the doctrine that a competent[2] patient must voluntarily provide valid consent to any medical procedure performed upon them. Not only is this a requirement in common law, but more recently the ideal has been given legislative effect in the form of the Human Tissue Act 2004,[3] the Human Tissue (Scotland) Act 2006[4] and the Medicines for Human Use (Clinical Regulations) 2004,[5] which transpose the provisions of the European Clinical Trials Directive[6] into UK law. This chapter examines the tragic events that primarily took place at the Bristol and Alder Hey hospitals, their effect on the law of consent in the UK and the importance of informed consent for those involved in the procurement of UCB.

Prior to the enactment of these pieces of legislation, the role of consent in English law was unhappily emphasised by the Bristol Royal Infirmary Inquiry,[7] a report into the events that occurred between 1984 and 1995 in

1 L Kharaboyan and others, 'Understanding umbilical cord blood banking – what women need to know before deciding' (2007) 17 *Women's Health Issues* 277.

2 A competent patient is taken to be one that has the mental capacity to process and retain the information given and to comprehend the decision to be made.

3 Human Tissue Act 2004 ss 2, 3 and 4.

4 Human Tissue (Scotland) Act 2006 ss 5–10.

5 SI 2004/1031.

6 Council Directive (EC) 2001/20 on the approximation of the laws, regulations and administrative provisions of the Member States relating to the implementation of good clinical practice in the conduct of clinical trials on medicinal products for human use [2001] OJ L121/ 37–39 arts 3, 4 and 5.

7 The Bristol Royal Infirmary Inquiry, 'Learning from Bristol: the report of the public inquiry into children's heart surgery at the Bristol Royal Infirmary 1984–1995' (Cm 5207, 2001).

paediatric cardiac surgical services at the Bristol Royal Infirmary. The Report, chaired by Professor Ian Kennedy, highlighted the huge discrepancies in mortality rates and incidents of brain damage following heart surgery performed at the Bristol Royal Infirmary compared to other centres. It transpired that parents had not been informed of the risks involved in heart surgery, had been misled with regard to the chances of success and that the hospital had fostered, and operated within, a culture where questions were not invited. Furthermore, it reported on the systematic removal of organs without parental consent from the children who had died.

Details were soon to emerge of the extent of organ retention not only in Bristol, but also at hospitals around the country. Professor Anderson, Professor of Morphology at the Great Ormond Street Hospital for sick children, gave evidence to the Inquiry panel on 7 September 1999 and revealed that the practice of removing organs for medical education and research purposes without consent was widespread and routine. He identified the Alder Hey Hospital in Liverpool as having the largest number of organs stored, which subsequently sparked an additional public inquiry, led by Mr Michael Redfern QC. The Redfern Report[8] concluded that there had been a wholesale removal and retention of organs from children who had died in the period 1988–1995 at the Alder Hey Hospital. While some parents had given consent for a post mortem examination on their deceased child, they had not understood that any removed organs would not be returned to the body. At the centre of the scandal was Dutch senior pathologist, Dr Dick Van Velzen, who systematically ordered the 'unethical and illegal stripping of every organ from every child who had had a post-mortem'[9] during his time at the hospital. The report recommended the introduction of proper informed consent procedures for the removal and retention of all organs and tissues for post mortem examinations.

The issue of consent also featured highly[10] in the Bristol Inquiry. Its extensive list of recommendations focused heavily on the partnership between the healthcare professional and the patient, where 'the patient and the professional meet as equals with different expertise'.[11] During the process of the Inquiry, the General Medical Council (GMC)[12] revised its document *Good Medical Practice*[13] that set the standards that doctors are expected to meet;

8 M Redfern, 'The Royal Liverpool Children's Inquiry Report' (2001) www.gov.uk/government/uploads/system/uploads/attachment_data/file/250934/0012_ii.pdf accessed 30 November 2015.

9 Redfern, 2001.

10 Of the 198 recommendations, 19 were devoted to consent. Compare the situation in Scotland discussed later in this chapter.

11 Redfern, 2001 at recommendation 3.

12 The General Medical Council (GMC) is the independent regulator for medical practice in the UK. Its purpose is to protect, promote and maintain the health and safety of the public by ensuring proper standards in the practice of medicine.

13 General Medical Council (GMC), *Good Medical Practice* (London: GMC, 1998).

non-compliance of which may result in a revocation of their licence to practise. In doing so, the profession received specific guidelines on what constitutes good medical practice, guidance that Smith purports should be viewed by medical professionals as their 'social contract with patients and the public'.[14]

A number of hospitals across NHS Scotland were also found to have retained organs following post mortem examinations without the permission of the deceased relatives, the practices of which were independently reviewed with the final report in November 2001.[15] The review committee's remit, chaired by Professor Sheila Maclean, was to examine current practices relating to post-mortems, consent and guidelines, and to develop a Code of Practice for Scotland taking into account developments across the UK with regard to informed consent.

The aftermath of the Bristol and Alder Hey scandals led to the promulgation of numerous documents and guidelines to ensure best practice within healthcare and in which consent is specifically addressed. These include the revised version of *Good Medical Practice* in 2006, *Good Medical Practice for General Practitioners*,[16] *Consent: Patients and Doctors Making Decisions Together*[17] and the *Guidelines on Consent: Reference Guide to Consent for Examination or Treatment*.[18] These documents emphasise the need for good communication, ethical behaviour and the need to treat patients with dignity and respect. They also led to legislative change in the form of the Human Tissue Act 2004 in what was previously deemed an uncertain and unprincipled area of law. As Brazier had observed:

14 R Smith, 'Re-negotiating medicine's contract with patients' (1998) 316 *British Medical Journal* 7145, 1622.

15 Scottish Government Health and Social Care Directorates, 'Independent Review Group on Retention of Organs at Post-Mortem: Final Report' (2001) www.sehd.scot.nhs.uk/scotorgrev/Final%20Report/ropm-01.htm accessed 30 November 2015. An additional audit review was produced by Audit Scotland in March 2002, see: 'Organ Retention Validation Review' (March 2002) www.audit-scotland.gov.uk/docs/health/2001/nr_020314_organ_retention.pdf accessed 30 November 2015.

16 Royal College of General Practitioners, 'Good medical practice for general practitioners' (July 2008) www.rcgp.org.uk/~/media/Files/Revalidation-and-CPD/CPD%20Credits%20and%20Appraisal/GoodMedicalPracticeforGPsJuly2008ashx.ashx accessed 30 November 2015.

17 GMC, 'Consent: patients and doctors making decisions together' (June 2008) www.gmc-uk.org/guidance/ethical_guidance/consent_guidance_index.asp accessed 30 November 2015. This replaces the previous guidance 'Seeking patients' consent: the ethical considerations' (1998).

18 Department of Health (DH), 'Guidelines on consent: reference guide to consent for examination or treatment' (2009) 2nd edn www.gov.uk/government/uploads/system/uploads/attachment_data/file/138296/dh_103653__1_.pdf accessed 30 November 2015.

> [t]here is little dissent from the view that law reform is urgent. The confused and tangled web of different statutes and outdated common law principles must be clarified, preferably in a single Act of Parliament.[19]

While the events surrounding organ retention were undoubtedly awful and at times verging on 'the grotesque',[20] their repercussions have led to the prioritisation of the need for more informed decision-making in health care and the fostering of trust and confidence between patients, relatives and health care staff thought the UK.

Cord blood collection and the role of informed consent

Before UCB can be collected, valid consent of the pregnant woman for clinical or research use must be obtained. The doctrine of consent is inextricably linked to the ethical principle of respect for a patient's autonomy – the ability of people to exercise free will, to decide and act on their own thoughts and judgements, and to make independent decisions about their own lives.[21] In the context of healthcare, this principle translates as the capacity to decide for oneself whether to accept a particular treatment or service provision. The decision to collect UCB, whether for public or private use, rests solely with the pregnant woman as the consent of both parents is not legally necessary.[22] As the Royal College of Obstetricians and Gynaecologists (RCOG) observed in its Opinion Paper of June 2006, '[e]ither parent is competent to consent to anything done to or for the baby, but only the mother can consent to anything done to her own body, including cord blood collection.'[23]

Informed consent fulfils three separate functions within the doctor–patient relationship – to secure the patient's trust and co-operation in using the doctor's medical expertise to assist them in accepting the mode of care deemed appropriate to their care; to ensure autonomous decision-making; and to provide a legal justification for intrusive interventions involved in diagnosis and treatment.[24] As the process of UCB collection involves the physical touching of the umbilical cord and insertion of a needle into the umbilical vein to withdraw the stem cells, it is just as important to secure

19 M Brazier, *Medicine, Patients and the Law* (3rd edn, London: Penguin, 2003) p 479.

20 S Boseley, 'Grotesque breach of trust at Alder Hey' *The Guardian Online* (London 29 January 2001) www.guardian.co.uk/society/2001/jan/29/health.alderhey/print accessed 30 November 2015.

21 M A Jones, 'Informed consent and other fairy stories' (1999a) 7 *Modern Law Review* 103.

22 For a further discussion on this point see: E Salvaterra and others, 'The ethics of cord blood banking in light of ownership, informed consent, and solidarity' (2006) 4 *Cell Preservation Technology* 2, 91–96.

23 Royal College of Obstetricians and Gynaecologists (RCOG), Scientific Impact Paper No. 2, 'Umbilical cord blood banking' (2006) www.rcog.org.uk/globalassets/documents/guidelines/scientific-impact-papers/sip_2.pdf accessed 10 February 2009.

24 J Montgomery, *Health Care Law* (2nd edn, Oxford: Oxford University Press, 2003) p 346.

valid consent from the pregnant woman as it is with any other medical procedure; and as discussed in Chapter 2, to interfere with a person without their consent would be to undermine their personal autonomy and may invoke a number of possible legal consequences, namely trespass to the person torts in a civil action and even criminal liability in assault and battery.[25]

Since the introduction of the Human Tissue Act in 2004, the primacy of consent with regard to the removal, storage and use of bodily material has been reinforced and the threat of criminal penalties for failure to comply now exists.[26] However, it is rare for medical professionals to face criminal prosecution for acts carried out in the course of their professional duties,[27] and most medical malpractice litigation is claimed in negligence, which includes a breach of the duty to warn.[28] Post the organ retention scandals, the need to gain valid authorisation to retain bodily material once it has been removed from the body has never been more prevalent.

Consent and the Human Tissue Act 2004

The aftermath of the organ retention scandal of the late 1980s led to legislative change with regard to the removal and storage of human tissue. The Human Tissue Act, which received Royal Assent on 15 November 2004, repeals and replaces the Human Tissue Act 1961, the Anatomy Act 1984 and the Human Organ Transplants Act 1989 and sets out a legislative framework for whole body donation, and the taking, storage and use of all human organs and tissues throughout England, Wales and Northern Ireland.[29] The Act extends its provisions relating to the use of DNA to Scotland, but most of the law in Scotland is governed by the Human Tissue (Scotland) Act 2006. Under the terms of the 2004 Act, the Human Tissue Authority (HTA) was introduced to regulate activities involving human tissue, which include UCB stem cells. The HTA is also the Competent Authority for the purposes of the EUTCD across the UK and includes Scotland in this remit.[30] As the Human Tissue (Scotland) Act 2006 largely mirrors that of the HT Act 2004, it is expected that the import and export of cells from Scotland meet the standards required of the rest of the UK and

25 J Herring, *Medical Law and Ethics* (5th edn, Oxford: Oxford University Press, 2014) 150.

26 Human Tissue Act 2004 s 25.

27 Notwithstanding the now notorious cases of serial murderers such as Dr Harold Shipman and Nurse Beverley Allitt.

28 *Chester v Afshar* [2004] UKHL 41; *Montgomery v Lanarkshire Health Board* [2015] UKSC 11.

29 For Ireland, the Act specifically repeals and replaces the Human Tissue (Northern Ireland) Act 1962, the Human Organ Transplant (Northern Ireland) Order 1989 and the Anatomy (Northern Ireland) Order 1992. For a general outline of the Act, see: M Brazier and S Fovargue, 'A brief guide to the Human Tissue Act 2004' (2006) 1 *Clinical Ethics* 26.

30 The equivalent body to the HTA in Scotland is the Scottish Executive Health Department.

therefore Scotland is not to be treated as a separate country for these purposes.[31]

UCB is classed as a 'relevant material' for the purposes of the Act because it 'consists of or includes human cells'[32] and therefore 'appropriate consent'[33] must be obtained before it can be lawfully stored for private or public use. Consent is required for the purpose of its storage and use if it is carried out for the purpose of a Schedule 1 Part 1 listed activity, which includes transplantation and research in connection with disorders or the functioning of the body. However, there are exceptions to the need to obtain consent for the storage and use of UCB, one of which relates to research. Section 1(7) provides that the Act does not apply to research programmes that have received Research Ethics Committee approval.[34] But as Herring points out, this 'permits the use of material for research, even where the patient positively objects'.[35]

Under Section 44, surplus material abandoned by the patient following an operation, for example an excised appendix, can also be kept, used or disposed of without consent and, in the same way, UCB from a discarded placenta could also be used without the mother's permission.[36] As long as consent to the original treatment had been given, neither scenario is likely to attract controversy.[37] What may prove problematic, however, is where a mother gives consent to the donation of UCB for the purposes of a research programme with ethics committee approval, but later changed her mind, instead preferring to bank it privately. Once procurement is complete, consent is no longer required under the Act; and true to the nature of giving

31 HTA, 'Code of Practice – import and export of human bodies, body parts and tissue' (May 2007, Code 8) www.tissuebank.it/publicazioni/docUfficiale/LegislazioniNazionali/LeggeInglese/CodeOfPracticeImportExportHumanBodies.pdf accessed 5 December 2015.

32 Section 53 of the Act governs 'relevant material', which is defined as tissue, cells and organs of human beings, excluding gametes and embryos outside the body (as these are governed by the Human Fertilisation and Embryology Act 1990 as amended by the Human Fertilisation and Embryology Act 2008) and hair and nails from a living person.

33 Human Tissue Act 2004 s 1(1) 'appropriate consent' is simply defined as 'his consent', which is taken to mean consent that is given voluntarily by the donor or an appropriate person.

34 Ibid., s 1(9)(a). There is an additional provision at s 1(9)(b) that material must be anonymised. See also: HTA, 'Code of Practice – research' (Code 9 July 2014 version 14.0) paras 51–53.

35 Herring, 2014 at 422. It should also be noted here that research ethics approval from the relevant Research Ethics Committee (REC) would need to be sought before research is carried out and consent provisions would certainly be closely scrutinised before approval was given, and the REC might impose stricter constraints than the HTA.

36 For example, where a pregnant woman has not requested UCB collection for her own private use or as a donation. Placentas are routinely discarded by the mother as biological waste and may be used for research, therapeutic and non-therapeutic purposes.

37 However, see ethical concerns about commercialisation raised in: P Sawyer, 'NHS hospital sells placentas for cosmetic use' *The Telegraph Online* (London 17 May 2008) www.telegraph.co.uk/news/1973229/NHS-hospital-sells-placentas-for-cosmetic-use.html accessed 30 November 2015.

up all rights to the UCB once voluntarily donated, as we saw in the previous chapter, the mother is left with no claim to the cells.

This would appear to be at odds with the provisions for other types of donations, such as gametes or embryos. Existing safeguards under the Human Fertilisation and Embryology (HFE) Act 1990 (as amended) include the ability for the donor to change or withdraw consent up to the point that the gametes or embryos are used in treatment or research.[38] Furthermore, both the egg and sperm donor involved in the creation of an embryo enjoy an additional post-storage 12-month 'cooling-off'[39] period prior to implantation, in the same way as can happen in a conventional contractual agreement. It would appear then that the Human Tissue Act fails to offer the same kind of protection to women who choose to donate their UCB as embryo donors because once the unit has been procured and stored for public use, all rights are relinquished and there is no turning back.[40]

Although the Act applies to the storage[41] and use[42] of UCB where derived from a living pregnant woman, Part One does not apply to the *removal* of bodily material from living humans and therefore appears to have little significance for consent to UCB collection, which is instead governed by the Human Tissue (Quality and Safety for Human Application) Regulations 2007 and the common law. However, their provisions remain useful in that they provide analogies for the application of the common law and indicate best practice. The following discussion regarding the essence of consent is therefore provided to contextualise the law of consent in the UK as a whole.

Controversially, the Act does not specifically define what is meant by the term 'consent' or what validates its presence. This has been criticised by some commentators[43] because of the criminal sanctions that a lack of consent may promulgate. Its meaning is instead explained in the HTA's Consent Code of Practice, which states that, akin to common law, consent is valid when voluntarily given by an appropriately informed person with capacity and the nature of what has been consented to, including its risks, has been communicated and understood.[44] The Code states:

38 HFE Act 1990 (as amended) Schedule 3 s 4(1)

39 Human Fertilisation and Embryology Authority (HFEA), Code of Practice (8th edn) (2009) 'Storage of gametes and embryos' Revised October 2015 Guidance Note 17E www.hfea.gov.uk/docs/ HFEA_Code_of_Practice_8th_Edtion_(Oct_2015).pdf accessed 4 December 2015.

40 NHS Choices website, 'Blood donation (giving blood) – cord blood donation' www.nhs.uk/Conditions/Blood-donation/Pages/Cordblooddonation.aspx accessed 30 November 2015.

41 Human Tissue Act 2004 s 1(1)(d).

42 Ibid., s 1(1)(f).

43 J Zimmern, 'Consent and autonomy in the Human Tissue Act 2004' (2007) 18 *King's Law Journal* 2, 313.

44 Human Tissue Authority (HTA), 'Code of Practice – consent' (Code 1 July 2014 Version 14.0) at para 35. www.hta.gov.uk/sites/default/files/Code_of_practice_1_-_Consent.pdf #page=24 accessed 4 December 2015.

> For consent to be valid, the person should understand what the activity involves and, where appropriate, what the risks are. When seeking consent, healthcare professionals or other suitably experienced people should ensure that it is appropriate for the intended purpose.[45]

The term 'appropriate consent' is defined by the Code in terms of who may give consent, which it describes as the person concerned, or where they lack capacity, their nominated representative[46] or someone they are in a qualifying relationship with.[47]

Whereas the language of the 2004 Act speaks in terms of 'consent', in Scotland, different wording is used. In line with the recommendations of the Scottish Independent Review Group into organ retention at post mortem, the Human Tissue (Scotland) Act 2006 refers to the concept of 'authorisation', which is taken to be a positive expression that the wishes of the living regarding the use of their bodily material will be adhered to after death, as opposed to the concept of a 'lack of objection' enshrined in the Human Tissue Act 1961, which the 2006 Act repeals for Scotland. Essentially, 'authorisation' is taken to be synonymous with 'consent' in the 2004 Act[48] but was adopted as its replacement to reflect the Review Group's concerns that 'consent' was an inappropriate word to use in the retention of organs following post mortem, particularly in cases involving children. They argued that parents and those in a qualifying relationship are afforded legal authority to consent to a decision only when the decision is deemed to be in the child's 'best interests' but this proposition is very difficult to play out in this context, and that to offer 'authorisation' to retain organs more adequately reflects the act of organ retention.[49]

In Wales, the law of consent has recently been re-examined in the context of organ donation. Following the introduction of the Human Transplantation (Wales) Act 2013, which came fully into force on 1 December 2015, two concepts now apply to transplantation – 'express consent' and 'deemed consent'. Express consent is interpreted as the same as 'appropriate consent' set out in the Human Tissue Act 2004,[50] which is taken to mean consent that is given voluntarily by the donor or an appropriate person. However, after death, the Act provides that a person's consent will be deemed to have been given (hence the term 'deemed consent'), unless

45 Ibid., at para 32.

46 Human Tissue Act 2004 s 4.

47 Ibid., s 27(4).

48 HTA,'Human Tissue (Scotland) Act 2006: a guide to its implications for NHS Scotland' (Undated) at para 8 www.hta.gov.uk/sites/default/files/Information_about_HT_(Scotland)_Act.pdf accessed 30 November 2015.

49 Scottish Government Health and Social Care Directorates, 'Independent Review Group on Retention of Organs at Post-Mortem: Final Report' (2001) www.sehd.scot.nhs.uk/scotorgrev/Final%20Report/ropm-01.htm accessed 30 November 2015.

50 Human Tissue Act 2004 s 1(1).

they had expressed a wish for or against donation, or appointed a representative to make the organ donation decision on their behalf. Three exceptions apply to deemed consent – they are when the consent applies to children,[51] the incompetent[52] and those who do not normally reside in Wales.[53]

As part of the provision, it is open for a member of the deceased's family or a long-standing friend to provide evidence that the deceased would have objected to donation and if this claim is upheld, deemed consent will be invalid. For this reason, deemed consent is described as a 'soft opt-out' system – that is, the system permits relevant others to object to the donation on the deceased's behalf. For our purposes, however, it should be remembered that 'deemed consent' in Wales applies only to organ donation, whereas consent to UCB banking remains confined to the provisions of Section 4 of the 2004 Act in Wales.

Information provision, knowledge and understanding

Consent to UCB collection in the UK is governed by the common law. It is a legal requirement that can only be met if the information provided has been fully understood and cannot be deemed valid if the patient has been ill-informed or misinformed. This is exactly the type of situation that Lord Templeman spoke of in his legal opinion in *Sidaway*[54] where he intimated that a patient might not have the necessary mental capability to appreciate what was in fact in his or her own 'best interests',[55] and concluded that the provision of information might cloud a patient's judgement when making the choice:

> A patient may make an unbalanced judgement if deprived of adequate information. A patient may also make an unbalanced judgement if he is provided with too much information and is made aware of possibilities, which he is not capable of assessing because of his lack of medical training, his prejudices or his personality.[56]

His Lordship appeared to place great importance on the medical professional's experience and wisdom, an attribute that the average layperson may fail to possess. This view was supported by Lord Bridge, who suggested that 'to educate the patient to his own standard of medical knowledge of all the relevant factors involved'[57] would be an impractical and unrealistic exercise.

51 Human Transplantation (Wales) Act 2013 s 6.
52 Ibid., s 5(3)(b).
53 Ibid., s 5(3)(a).
54 *Sidaway v Board of Governors of the Bethlem Royal Hospital* [1985] AC 871.
55 Ibid., at 904 (Lord Templeman).
56 Ibid.
57 Ibid., at 899 (Lord Bridge).

Whilst this may seem logical, he appears to have sidestepped any recognition of what the patient would want to know in order to make a decision. As a true expression of autonomous decision-making, the patient should not only be informed of their treatment procedure, but also its intended and possible consequences. For those anticipating UCB banking, this includes a conversation whereby both the benefits of public and private banking are discussed as well as the risks identified in Chapter 2. As with all forms of medical treatment, internet websites and information leaflets also provide a rich medium with which to carry out independent research into a particular procedure. This mode of 'self-awareness' can help to inform a prospective parent's decision of whether or not to even enquire about UCB banking and to seek a dialogue about the procedure with their healthcare professional. Alternatively, pregnant women delivering at specific hospitals may be approached directly to donate UCB. So what information do those contemplating UCB collections have available to them, and what specific information is then communicated prior to the collection procedure?

For those who wish to donate to a public bank, patient information leaflets can be obtained on request from certain NHS Trusts or through the NHSBT website. In addition, the RCOG provides an information leaflet, published in August 2006, for both public and private UCB collection, use and storage.[58] More recently, the Human Tissue Authority has produced a comprehensive and transparent guide for parents, which includes information on current uses of UCB, banking options, collection methods and statistical odds of usage.[59]

For private banking, internet websites, marketing brochures, online videos and pregnancy mobile apps offer a wealth of information for prospective clients, in addition to verbal information provided by an advisor, generally by an online 'chat' facility, telephone hotline, personal appointments or at external events such as baby shows. Marketing information provided by the commercial industry typically includes the company's background and directorship, generic stem cell information, specific information relating to UCB's current and possible future uses, collection kit instructions, storage facilities, contractual obligations and payment options.

While a plethora of advertising mediums are therefore available, the onus is on prospective clients to acquaint themselves with the available material. This mode of self-informing has a number of drawbacks. First, corporate brochures and website information is compiled by the industry and may be biased; and they are likely to use professional marketing specialists and public

58 RCOG, 'Cord blood banking: information for parents' (August 2006) www.nhs.uk/ipgmedia/national/royal%20college%20of%20obstetricians%20and%20gynaecologists/assets/cordbloodbanking-informationforparents.pdf accessed 8 December 2015.

59 HTA, 'Cord blood banking: a guide for parents' (February 2016) www.hta.gov.uk/sites/default/files/Cord%20Blood%20Guide%202016%20230316.pdf accessed 2 May 2016.

relations experts who deploy sophisticated sales and promotional techniques. Arguably, the use of such expertise promulgates the dissemination of 'selected information' carefully chosen to focus on the advantages of banking UCB rather than its transparency.

Internet parenting forums do provide a type of 'self-help' means of information-sharing amongst expectant families but these are generally set up by parents with little or no technical or medical knowledge, quoting statistics that may be either incomplete or out of date. The online *Parents' Guide to Cord Blood Foundation*,[60] however, attempts to present a more balanced view by enlisting notable experts in the UCB field to inform its website content. UCB transplant specialist Dr Joanne Kurtzberg, who was pivotal in the treatment of Matthew Farrow, referred to in Chapter 1, is one of the 15 experts that make up the group's advisory panel.

Whether those who consult the available literature and information actually understand what is presented, however, is quite another matter. Results of a study[61] carried out in the US, published in 2007, are interesting. The study began with the hypothesis that women were poorly informed about UCB and the results showed that not only was the hypothesis correct, but also that a fully informed decision for the purposes of valid consent to UCB collection may be difficult to obtain. Of the 724 questionnaires distributed over a six-month period from April to September 2006, 325 were completed. Results revealed that the women demonstrated a strikingly poor understanding with regard to the current uses for cord blood therapy. When asked whether stem cells derived from UCB had been successfully used in the treatment of Alzheimer's and Parkinson's disease, only 28 and 24 per cent respectively responded correctly that it had not.[62]

Furthermore, in response to the question, 'For most conditions requiring cord blood therapy, could a child use cord blood from his/her own placenta?', 26 per cent of women who had chosen to bank privately responded as 'Always', with 37 per cent as 'Usually' and 23 per cent as 'Sometimes'.[63] In contrast to the participants' beliefs, authoritative bodies such as the RCOG have argued that autologous UCB is unlikely to be used for clinical application. As we saw in Chapter 1, not only are the chances of using autologous cells particularly low, but patients also have access to the 600,000 UCB banked worldwide available for clinical use and an international database of more than 22 million bone marrow donors at their disposal. Clearly, these factors are not advertised by the industry.

60 Parents' Guide to Cord Blood Foundation and Charity, http://parentsguidecordblood.org/ accessed 8 December 2015.

61 N Fox, C Stevens and R Ciubotariu, 'Umbilical cord blood collection: do patients really understand?' (2007) 4 *Journal of Perinatal Medicine* 35.

62 Ibid., at 314

63 Ibid., at Table 3 Question 3.

What is interesting is that the participants of the study possessed a high educational status with over 60 per cent of those wishing to either donate or bank privately attaining a postgraduate degree. Whilst such qualifications indicate the necessary mental capability to understand the presented information, the results also indicate that they are likely to have been influenced by the private sector's advertising strategies and information. Given that, as we saw in Chapter 3, the private industry's advertising materials have been widely criticised as misleading,[64] it is possible that women involved in this study had been misinformed about the merits of UCB banking.

Variations in marketing techniques appear commonplace. A particularly popular method is to present the latest advancements in stem cell technology via an online 'rolling screen'. With headlines such as 'Damage to the brain caused by Parkinson's Disease can be healed using stem cells'[65] 'Wheelchair-bound MS patients given "miraculous" stem cell treatment'[66] and 'Stem cells help women regrow breasts after surgery',[67] it is little wonder that some parents are tempted to invest. What some of the headlines used do not make clear, however, is that the results may refer to experimental stages of medical research rather than a wide application of current clinical use. Moreover, they may not even relate specifically to stem cells derived from UCB and instead may refer to studies conducted using bone marrow, adult cells, peripheral blood stem cells or even induced pluripotent stem cells (iPSCs). Indeed, the generic use of the word 'stem cell' by UCB websites can in itself be misleading in its attempt to sell the misconception that one size fits all. Notably, the message from the critics is that, '[f]uture research should focus on strategies to educate women earlier in pregnancy so that they are prepared to make a truly informed decision at the appropriate time',[68] and for its part, the commercial UCB industry 'must provide clear, honest, and unambiguous information for their customers'.[69] After all, it is difficult for patients to act autonomously in their decision-making if they are ill-informed.

The effectiveness of written information in the form of leaflets has been tested by the courts in relation to the provision of information by a health professional, which can add some context to consent. In *Al Hamwi v Johnson and Another* [2005],[70] the claimant commenced legal proceedings following the birth of a child with chromosomal abnormalities against her consultant. She claimed that due to the consultant's over-emphasis on the risks

64 N M Fisk and others, 'Can routine commercial cord blood banking be scientifically and ethically justified?' (2005) 2 *Plos Medicine* 2. www.ncbi.nlm.nih.gov/pmc/articles/PMC549592/, accessed 20 October 2015.

65 Cells4Life online website, 'News' (10 November 2014) www.cells4life.co.uk/news-events/damage-brain-caused-parkinsons-disease-healed-stem-cells accessed 8 December 2015.

66 Ibid.

67 Ibid.

68 Fox, Stevens and Ciubotariu, 2007.

69 Fisk and others, 2005.

70 *Al Hamwi v Johnson and Another* [2005] EWHC 206.

associated with having an amniocentesis test, she decided not to take the test, which would have revealed the abnormality and she would then have opted for a termination. However, the trial judge held that there had been no breach of duty.[71] Despite Mrs Al Hamwi being of Syrian origin, she had 'an understanding of English'[72] and had been supplied with an interpreter. He accepted that the consultant had provided sufficient information by way of an information leaflet about amniocentesis and that the risks and benefits of the procedure had been adequately imparted during the consultation by following a 'checklist'.[73] The leaflet had sufficiently explained the nature and process of the procedure, its risk and likelihood of occurrence and under what circumstances the procedure is advised.[74]

Written information then – depending on the nature of that information – may go some way towards assisting the process of information provision. By adopting a 'checklist' method, UCB facilitators may be able to satisfy themselves (and a court) that the risks and benefits of the process have been sufficiently communicated and that they have no reason to believe that the information has been misunderstood. Indeed, the court in *Al Hamwi* held that, 'The checklist provides powerful evidence that the claimant was given appropriate counselling in amniocentesis'.[75] A checklist method for UCB could contain information such as available banking options, the risks and benefits presented by competing collection and clamping methods, the odds of ever using the cells, and current and possible future uses of UCB. By 'ticking off' relevant points on the list as they are discussed, the UCB facilitator is more likely to demonstrate that sufficient information had been communicated.

However, this method of communication can attract criticism. Although there is no legal requirement to *ensure* that a patient has understood presented information, health professionals have a duty to take 'reasonable and appropriate steps to satisfy themselves that the patient has understood'.[76] Simply conveying information in a mechanical 'tick-box' manner with no further thought to the responses of the patient may not be the most appropriate method in all situations and the specific circumstances would still need to be determined on a case-by-case analysis.

So, if a pregnant woman, based on her own self-assessment, decides to pursue private banking or to donate, what type of dialogue takes place between the woman and her health care professional? As already noted, for consent to a medical intervention to be deemed legally valid, all material risks and the benefits should be discussed and understood. Material risks are described as ones that, 'a reasonable person in the patient's position would be likely to attach significance to the risk, or the doctor is, or should

71 Ibid., at 76 (Simon, J).
72 Ibid., at 71.
73 Ibid., at 55–60.
74 Ibid., at 17.
75 Ibid., at 59.
76 Ibid., at 69.

reasonably be aware, that the particular patient would be likely to attach significance to it'.[77] In terms of UCB collection, the risks of personal injury to herself or her child are arguably of particular importance to the pregnant woman, especially where there is no current medical need or family history of disease to specifically warrant collection.

While there is a dearth of empirical evidence relating to the communication process that takes place prior to the signing of a consent form for private banking, Helen Busby has provided some evidence of how consent is negotiated in UCB donation. Interviews were conducted with 27 women six to eight weeks post donation to the KingsCord public banking programme in Nottingham, an initiative set up to address the shortfall in the number of publicly available UCB units from the BAME population. Although the information provision section of this project was part of a larger study, the collated evidence is illuminating.

The provision of information to the UCB donors involved in the study took two forms: an information leaflet (made available to patients during the course of general maternity services) and a verbal presentation by the midwife (given towards the later stages of pregnancy). The leaflet outlined the patient's ability to contribute to the KingsCord programme, the logistics involved in the collection procedure, and explained that the collected UCB would be used in treatment, cell therapy, or for use in an ethically approved research project. Further, it stated that the pregnant woman's consent would be sought prior to her participation. The leaflet also emphasised that approximately half of all donated units are given up to research projects because they fail to meet the necessary quality standards required for transplant purposes.

The presentation element delivered by the midwife consisted of a potted history of the rise of UCB as an accepted alternative to bone marrow in the treatment of blood disorders and diseases and its current uses, which was personalised by explicit reference to individual success stories of those whose lives had been saved by UCB and those who had died whilst waiting for a donor. The presentation continued by highlighting the 'wasteful' nature of failing to save such a valuable resource and espousing the programme's endeavours to boost UCB supplies from the BAME population. Busby notes the emotive nature of the presentation. She writes:

> The narrative that emerges is a powerful one that merges together the missing futures for the children who did not reach adulthood, the futures regained for children who were recipients of successful transplants and the future needs of unknown children and adults.[78]

77 *Montgomery v Lanarkshire Health Board* [2015] UKSC 11 at 87 (Lords Kerr and Reed).

78 H Busby, 'The meanings of consent to the donation of cord blood stem cells: perspectives from an interview-based study of a public cord blood bank in England' (2010) 5 *Empirical Ethics* 22–27.

Moreover, she records that the majority of the donor interviewees appear to have been influenced by the midwife's pitch into, 'doing something useful and helpful' and if the UCB is not collected, it is 'something that would go to waste'.[79] These types of statements sound strangely familiar. Akin to the commercial UCB companies that have been criticised for their emotive advertising tactics, it would appear that KingsCord have simply deployed similar techniques to attract donors to their programme. Certainly the recruitment leaflet and presentational material elicit the same type of responses from donors to the public bank as can be seen from those who bank privately. Arguably then, it is the UCB industry as a whole, rather than the private industry alone, that facilitates the conscription process by tapping into the inner psyche of the UCB consumer-base and manipulates the emotional vulnerabilities of pregnant women to attract those who act either altruistically or in a self-interested manner. In that respect, any criticism should be meted out equally and not just towards the commercial sector.

One of the programme's key aims is described as, 'to give thorough information to prospective mothers on the uses and potential benefits of cord blood banking, and to obtain their consent to collect the cells for the public bank'. However, as we saw earlier, should anything go wrong during the collection process that results in a legally recognised harm, the quality of that consent would be scrutinised by the courts. Although Busby is keen to point out that the collated qualitative research, 'focused on exploring donors' narratives, rather than scrutinising the effectiveness of information-giving or compliance with formal consent processes',[80] the persuasive language and methods to obtain consent used may be in question. It should also be noted that both the information leaflet and presentation appear to be silent on the risks involved in carrying out an additional procedure during the third stage of labour. However, this is perhaps not so surprising. Unlike collection for private use, there is less urgency to collect the maximum number of cells for public banks because they are simply collected to supplement a public pool of resources and any non-standard units would be used for research. That said, there would be less pressure to deploy the riskier in-utero collection and early cord clamping methods that optimise results.

The process of record-keeping is also key for health professionals as written notes provide documentation of the verbal exchange with the patient. This is especially important if personal harm materialises years later and the UCB collector is reliant upon his or her written notes to recall details of the communication that took place at the time. Even while working under pressure, clear records should be written up in the patient's notes within 24 hours.[81] As the Nursing and Midwifery Council (NMC) warn:

79 Ibid., as noted by interviewee number 24.

80 Busby, 2010.

81 B Dimond, *Legal Aspects of Midwifery* (4th edn, London: Quay Books, 2013) p 146.

> Good record keeping is an integral part of nursing and midwifery practice and is essential to the provision of safe and effective care. It is not an optional extra to be fitted in if circumstances allow.[82]

The UCB industry should also bear in mind that it is not only adults that have the ability to consent to the UCB collection procedure, but also the competent minor. As the private cord blood industry does not impose an age limit on those able to preserve UCB, young pregnant women are not excluded from UCB banking. Despite a continued decline in teenage conception rates in the UK since 1998, the number of pregnancies amongst young people in England remains high compared to their peers in other Western European countries.[83] That said, it is arguable that pregnant teenagers may now be categorised as a potential target audience[84] for the UCB industry due to their potential lack of maturity and may therefore be more open to exposure from emotive marketing.

Cord blood collection, consent and the competent minor

A patient's age and maturity may have an influential effect on their ability to fully comprehend presented information regardless of its quality or extent. While the Mental Capacity Act 2005 does not apply to children, it does provide a valuable insight into how the law deals with this issue in other areas of medical law. Part 1, Section 1(2) of the Act provides that '[a] person must be assumed to have capacity unless it is established that he lacks capacity' and Section 2(3)(a) provides that a lack of capacity cannot be established merely by reference to their age. While there is a presumption that everyone has capacity unless proven otherwise, the Act only applies to those aged 16 years and over, which is expressly stated in its Code of Practice:

> The Act's starting point is to confirm in legislation that it should be assumed that an adult (aged 16 or over) has full legal capacity to make decisions for themselves (the right to autonomy) unless it can be shown that they lack capacity to make a decision for themselves at the time the decision needs to be made.[85]

82 Nursing and Midwifery Council (NMC), 'Guidance on record keeping' (London: NMC, 2009).

83 UK Government website, 'Under 18 conception rate in England continues to fall' (24 February 2015) www.gov.uk/government/news/under-18-conception-rate-continues-to-fall-in-england accessed 8 December 2015.

84 However, it is acknowledged that as a target audience some teenagers are less likely to be in a financial position to consider private collection than working adults. That said, the lack of finances may simply contribute to any sense of 'guilt' experienced by young mothers who do not save the cells.

85 Department for Constitutional Affairs (DCA), 'Mental Capacity Act 2005 Code of Practice' (TSO, London 2007) at Chapter 12 www.dca.gov.uk/legal-policy/mental-capacity/mca-cp.pdf accessed 16 December 2015.

For the purposes of UCB collection, the Act therefore deems all pregnant women over 16 years of age to possess sufficient mental capacity to consent to the procedure *unless* it can be shown that they lack the capacity to do so. In addition, the Family Reform Act 1969 provides that a young person of 16 and 17 years is given a statutory right to consent to surgical, medical or dental treatment via Section 8(3), which is as effective as that of an adult.[86] For 'baby mums'[87] under 16 years of age who wish to preserve UCB, it is necessary to consult the common law. For issues of consent by minors, the courts have adopted the approach of the House of Lords in *Gillick v West Norfolk and Wisbech Area Health Authority*.[88]

The *Gillick* case concerned the lawfulness of a 1980 Department of Health and Social Security (DHSS) memorandum of guidance on family planning services. The guidance allowed, in exceptional circumstances, for a doctor to lawfully give contraceptive advice or treatment to a patient under 16 without their parents' knowledge or consent. Mrs Victoria Gillick, then mother of four daughters all under 16 years of age, objected to the memorandum and wrote to the local area Health Authority (HA) to seek assurance that no contraceptive advice or treatment would be given to any of her daughters without her involvement. The HA refused her request, reiterating that in accordance with its guidance, the final decision would be a matter for a doctor's clinical judgement.

Undeterred, Mrs Gillick made an application to the High Court[89] for a declaration that the circular was unlawful. The claim was dismissed and it subsequently went to the Court of Appeal[90] and then to the House of Lords[91] where a three–two majority deemed the circular to be lawful. Their Lordships held that a child's age alone did not determine capacity and that it was not unreasonable for a child to be able to give valid consent to contraceptive advice or treatment.[92] Moreover, consent can be taken as valid if in the exercise of their clinical judgement, the doctor 'satisfies himself that [the child] can understand his advice'.[93]

This common law ruling provides that if a child is mature enough to make his or her own decision with regard to medical treatment and the doctor is

86 Consent to organ donation and non-therapeutic research is not covered by this provision.

87 The term 'baby mums' was coined at the Centre for Bioethics and Medical Law Symposium, Lancaster University, 21–22 September 2007. Conference paper presented by Professor Hazel Biggs and Dr Sara Fovargue, 'Baby mums: who decides?'

88 *Gillick v West Norfolk and Wisbech Area Health Authority* [1986] AC 112.

89 *Gillick v West Norfolk and Wisbech Area Health Authority* [1984] QB 581.

90 *Gillick v West Norfolk and Wisbech Area Health Authority* [1985] 2 WLR 413. In the Court of Appeal, Mrs Gillick's claim was initially successful, but leave of appeal to the House of Lords was approved.

91 *Gillick v West Norfolk and Wisbech Area Health Authority* [1986] AC 112.

92 Ibid., at 169 (Lord Fraser).

93 Ibid., at 174. Although what is meant by the term 'clinical judgement' is not explained, Lord Scarman was keen to point out that there could be no compulsion in law for a government department to spell out to a doctor the terms of the phrase.

satisfied that they understand the information being given, consent is effective without the need for the parent or guardian's approval.[94] Such a minor is commonly known in medico-legal terms as a '*Gillick*-competent child'[95] and is interpreted as a child who has reached 'a sufficient understanding and intelligence to know what they [contraceptive advice, examination and treatment] involve'.[96]

It would therefore appear that competent minors under 16 can provide consent for UCB collection, and personal communication with commercial companies Cells4Life,[97] Future Health Biobank[98] and Smart Cells International[99] have confirmed that private companies impose no minimum age restriction. The situation for public donation, however, is quite different. NHS Blood and Transplant (NHSBT) claims that '[t]o donate cord blood you must be aged 17 or over',[100] but offers no explanation as to why reaching this particular age is deemed suitable. However, it is likely that this age restriction is stipulated to mirror that of whole blood, which is also set at 17 years.[101] While this is a feasible explanation, this differs from the minimum age for platelet donation (a component of whole blood), which is given as 18 years. This higher age threshold is imposed due to the invasive nature of the platelet procedure when compared to whole blood, which is relatively pain-free. Similarly, the donation of bone marrow attracts an 18-year minimum age requirement due to the procedure's invasiveness.

It would therefore appear that *Gillick*-competency is not recognised by the NHSBT in relation to the donation of whole blood, platelets, bone marrow or UCB. Yet in direct contrast, the Human Tissue Act 2004 makes express provision in Section 2 for the competent minor to consent to the donation of 'relevant material', which includes UCB for private and public storage and use. Appropriate consent within the Act can be given by a living competent minor – subject to *Gillick*-competency[102] – or an incompetent

94 As a point of interest, it should be noted that although '*Gillick*-competency' is a necessary condition for the consent to treatment, there is no similar capacity to refuse treatment as per Lord Donaldson's judgement in *Re R (a minor) (wardship: medical treatment)* [1992] Fam 11.

95 Herring, 2014 at 191.

96 *Gillick v West Norfolk and Wisbech Area Health Authority* [1986] AC 112 at 169–170 (Lord Fraser).

97 Cells4Life online customer support facility (Personal correspondence 8 December 2015).

98 Future Health Biobank Customer Care Manager (Personal email correspondence 8 December 2015).

99 Smart Cells International online customer support facility (Personal correspondence 8 December 2015).

100 NHS Cord Blood Bank, 'How to donate' www.nhsbt.nhs.uk/cordblood/howtodonate/canidonate/ accessed 8 December 2015.

101 'Whole blood' is the term given to blood donated at general blood donor sessions via the NHSBT. Whole blood consists of red blood cells, platelets, plasma and white blood cells.

102 Explanatory notes to the Human Tissue Act 2004 s 2(16) 'Appropriate consent – Children'.

minor, providing consent is sought from a person with parental responsibility.[103]

Clearly, the provisions of the Human Tissue Act regarding consent by a minor are at odds with the practical requirements of the NHSBT and leaves competent under-16s with an inconsistent UCB donor status and is an issue that should be revisited and clarified if consenting minors are to be included in the UCB donor pool. Given that some ethnic minority groups have been identified as being more vulnerable to becoming teenage parents,[104] competent minors may provide a suitable source for collection centres seeking to expand their stocks of ethnically diverse donor units for ethnic communities who remain under-represented in public banks.

Conclusion

This chapter has shown that since the organ retention scandals at Bristol and Alder Hey in the late 1980s, the issue of consent has been prioritised within healthcare and a doctor–patient partnership approach has been adopted to ensure that patients can make fully autonomous decisions about the type of health provision they receive based upon sufficient information communicated by an open dialogue. Indeed, with a wealth of guidelines now at their disposal, health professionals are better equipped to follow best practice and to place the patient more centrally within the decision-making process and to take reasonable steps to impart relevant information to ensure their consent to anything done to their body is valid.

In the context of UCB donation, greater care should be taken to ensure that the emotive techniques demonstrated by the private industry do not filter into the recruitment process. Although 'self-information techniques' are now commonplace in modern-day healthcare, this is no substitute for the legal requirement of a communication exchange between the pregnant woman and the UCB collector. Care should also be taken to ensure a clear set of notes are recorded in the pregnant woman's records relating to the communication and collection processes as they may later be relied on in court.

Although written information can enhance the provision of information, the UCB collector would need to take reasonable and appropriate steps to satisfy themselves that the imparted information has been understood. After all, pregnant women who are primarily self-informed about the pros and cons of the process may be found to be ill-informed or misinformed, putting

103 HT Act 2004 ss 27(4) and 54(9) provide a hierarchical list of 'Qualifying Relatives' who can be consulted where no other valid consent exists.

104 The Family Planning Association, 'Teenage pregnancy factsheet' (August 2010) www.fpa.org.uk/sites/default/files/teenage-pregnancy-factsheet-august-2010.pdf accessed 8 December 2015.

their consent into doubt. Such an observation applies to pregnant women of all age groups, but maybe more so for competent minors seeking to preserve UCB. Indeed, to gain valid consent to the procedure is imperative if a negligence claim is to be avoided.

5 Cord blood and the standards of care in negligence in the UK

> Medical paternalism has been dealt a clear and crucial blow by the Supreme Court. No longer tested by a responsible body of medical opinion, the law [on risk disclosure] now rests with 'a reasonable person in the patient's position'.[1]

Although it is an established principle in English law that a health professional has a duty to disclose information relevant to a proposed course of treatment,[2] as we saw in the previous chapter, the nature and content of that information may be scrutinised by the courts if the validity of a patient's consent is in doubt. Not only is consent a fundamental feature of law, it lies at the heart of the standard of care in negligence regarding the provision of information and the doctor's duty to warn. This chapter continues this exploration of consent by analysing the standards of care required of the medical profession in the context of UCB banking and maps the significant changes in the approach of the UK courts to risk disclosure in recent years.

The standard of care in negligence – *Bolam* examined

The existence of a duty of care between a doctor and a patient is widely accepted and rarely challenged.[3] Moreover, the duty is raised by the mere fact that all health professionals are deemed by the expertise in their relevant fields to foresee that their acts or omissions have the potential to cause harm

1 D J R Hutchon, 'Concerns about consent, the NICE guidelines regarding resuscitation and early cord clamping' (2015) 11 *Infant* 3.

2 M A Jones, 'Informed consent and other fairy stories' (1999a) 7 *Modern Law Review* 103.

3 Except when there is some dispute as to whether the individual concerned is an actual patient – for example, where a doctor carries out medical checks on an individual on behalf of a prospective employer, or for insurance purposes. Where there is no established precedent, the Caparo three-stage test is applied. In *Caparo Industries v Dickman* [1990] 2 AC 605, the House of Lords declared that a duty of care would arise in a novel situation when there was foreseeability of damage, sufficient proximity between the parties and when it was deemed fair, just and reasonable to impose a duty.

to those in their care.[4] This duty relates to treatment, diagnosis and the provision of information,[5] which extends to the midwifery profession. The standard of care for professionals is determined by the application of the '*Bolam* Test' and the appropriate standard for the midwifery profession is that of a reasonable midwife who acts in accordance with the particular practice accepted as proper by a professional body of opinion.[6] In order to comply with accepted practices, the midwife must demonstrate that (s)he had acted within the remit of protocols, policies and guidelines laid down by the profession both locally and nationally.[7] This standard can be achieved by the continuous updating of knowledge on clinical standards as they are changed and modernised within the profession. With regards to UCB banking, the Royal College of Midwives advise that '[a]ll midwives should be aware of the evidence and issues around stem cell harvesting so that they can discuss this with women and their partners as appropriate'.[8]

Since 2008, many hospital trusts have developed their own local policies in accordance with advice from the RCM and the RCOG, and while such policies tend to highlight the merits of delayed over early cord clamping, as highlighted in Chapter 2, for cord blood collection they do not *expressly* advise one clamping method over the other and instead simply recommend that midwives should not alter third stage practices (which presumably means delayed clamping as the preferred method) and to abandon collection if contraindications arise.[9] Yet this could put UCB collectors in a difficult position if they are pressurised by expectant mothers to maximise optimal UCB output and exacerbated by their desire to 'bend over backwards'[10] to

4 As per Lord Atkin's now famous dictum in *Donoghue v Stevenson* [1932] AC 562 15, which established 'the neighbour principle'. This principle dictates that a duty shall be owed to those who are so closely affected by what someone does or fails to do, that they should consider the consequences for that person when they carry out their act or omission.

5 *Sidaway v Board of Governors of the Bethlem Royal Hospital* [1985] AC 871.

6 And for the informal collector, the standard expected of a reasonably competent collector expressing to have that skill.

7 Nursing and Midwifery Council (NMC), 'The Code: professional standards of practice and behaviour for nurses and midwives' (January 2015). The Code should be read in conjunction with the Midwives Rules and Standards (2012).

8 Royal College of Midwives, (RCM) 'Position statement 1: umbilical cord blood collection' (2002) www.rcm.org.uk/news-views-and-analysis/analysis/position-statement-no-1-commercial-umbilical-cord-blood-collection accessed 11 January 2016. See also: RCM, 'Guidance paper 1a: commercial cord blood collection' (July 2008) www.rcm.org.uk/news-views-and-analysis/analysis/guidance-paper-1a-commercial-umbilical-cord-blood-collection accessed 11 January 2016.

9 For a recent Trust policy example see: Gloucestershire NHS Foundation Trust, 'Umbilical cord blood collection for storage of stem cells' (August 2015) Clinical policy A2005 www.gloshospitals.nhs.uk/SharePoint1/Clinical%20Policies/A2005.pdf accessed 27 January 2016.

10 L Machin, N Brown and D McLeod, '"Two's company – three's a crowd": the collection of umbilical cord blood for commercial stem cell banks in England and the midwifery profession' (2012) 28 *Midwifery* 358–365.

facilitate the birthing mother's wishes, as we saw in Chapter 3. Ultimately, this makes the *Bolam* test, in its strictest sense, difficult to apply. Its application, however, does not appear to be an exact science. Rather, decided cases will operate on questions of fact, which take into account 'all the circumstances'[11] of the case, such as errors of judgement,[12] conflicting expert evidence[13] and whether the argued standard is so totally removed from the whole of informed medical opinion.[14]

The use of *Bolam* has itself been met with criticism as it appears to bestow the upper hand to the medical profession. Seemingly, all a health professional need do to show that the required standard has been met is to find a comparable body that would have acted in the same way. To many, this test has proved too one-sided, reeks of medical paternalism and legitimises the internal policing of medical practices.[15] Montgomery further exemplifies this point by observing that the *Bolam* test precludes a detailed scrutiny of professional standards and 'leads to a form of self-regulation because the membership of those bodies is drawn almost exclusively from within the professions'.[16]

Montrose, writing in 1958, suggested that McNair J had erred on discussing the normative[17] nature of the test and, whilst he was keen to point out that any outdated modus operandi would not constitute a valid body of opinion for the purpose of litigation-avoidance, the judge had failed to look at whether there was any logical basis for following an accepted practice. In other words, instead of looking at what the doctor *should* do in order to satisfy an accepted standard of care, the ability to demonstrate that he *has followed* an accepted standard of care is prioritised.

Sheldon and Thomson offer an explanation as to how the normative element of the test had come to be omitted by McNair J.[18] They suggest that

11 *Bolam v Friern Hospital Management Committee* [1957] 1 WLR 582 at 587 (McNair, J).

12 *Whitehouse v Jordan* [1981] 1 WLR 246.

13 In *Maynard v West Midlands Regional Health Authority* [1985] 1 All ER 635, the House of Lords held that it is not for the courts to choose between the opinions of conflicting expert medical opinion. Moreover, it was enough to demonstrate that one professional body of opinion existed in support of the defendant's preferred method.

14 *Bolam v Friern Hospital Management Committee* [1957] 1 WLR 582 at 587 (McNair, J). It had already been established, however, in *Roe v Minister of Health* [1954] 2 QB 66 that the test of relevant knowledge at the time is one of foresight, not hindsight.

15 I Kennedy and A Grubb, *Medical Law Text with Materials* (2nd edn, London: Butterworths, 1994) pp 460–462. M Jones, 'Doctor knows best?' (1984) 100 *Law Quarterly Review* 355. For a feminist critique see: S Sheldon, 'A responsible body of medical men skilled in that particular art: rethinking the Bolam Test', in: S Sheldon and M Thomson (eds), *Feminist Perspectives on Health Care Law* (London: Cavendish Publishing, 1998) pp 15–32.

16 J Montgomery, 'Professional regulation: a gendered phenomenon?' in: S Sheldon and M Thomson (eds), *Feminist Perspectives on Health Care Law* (London: Cavendish Publishing, 1998) pp 33–51 at p 33.

17 A Montrose, 'Is negligence an ethical or sociological concept?' (1958) 21 *Modern Law Review* 259.

18 S Sheldon and M Thomson, *Feminist Perspectives on Health Care Law* (London: Cavendish Publishing, 1998) p 19.

the answer lies within the construction of the test's narrative. The words 'acted in accordance with a practice accepted as proper by a responsible body',[19] they say, indicate that the standard of a medical professional is one of 'accepted practice' as opposed to one that would be deemed 'acceptable' within society as a whole. The medical profession could therefore set its own standard and any practice that doctors, in their role of 'a responsible body of men', declared as 'proper' within their medical field of expertise, would not be deemed negligent.

It is unclear whether the omission of a normative quality to the '*Bolam* Test' was simply an oversight on the judge's part, or an attempt to preserve the doctrine of medical paternalism. For such a seminal judgment, one can only assume that the language used would have been chosen carefully. Brazier and Miola, however, have questioned whether McNair J actually appreciated how famous, or rather, infamous, the test he fashioned would become.[20] Regardless, the test has not survived untouched as it came under close scrutiny in *Bolitho v City and Hackney Health Authority* [1998],[21] where a significant qualification was developed. In a majority opinion, the House of Lords held that in spite of professional endorsement, there might be circumstances in which a doctor could still be held liable. Whilst this would occur only in a 'rare case',[22] nonetheless, liability in negligence could arise when the accepted practice was deemed unable to withstand logical analysis and would entitle the judge to declare the body of opinion as neither 'reasonable nor responsible'.[23] Furthermore, '[t]he use of these adjectives – responsible, reasonable and respectable – all show the court that the exponents of the body of opinion relied upon can demonstrate that such opinion has a logical basis.'[24]

The impetus behind the requirement for an opinion relied upon to be reasonable, responsible and respectable is perhaps founded in the court's acceptance that the *Bolam* test *does* in fact lack an objective approach. Prior to the *Bolitho* ruling, the courts were reluctant to interfere with a health professional's management of the case on the basis that 'the judge was insufficiently experienced to question clinical judgement'.[25] However, post-*Bolitho*, the medical profession could no longer rely on the 'find-any-supportive-expert standard'.[26] Rather, the claimant must show that their actions had failed to take into account the 'comparative risks and benefits'[27]

19 *Bolam v Friern Hospital Management Committee* [1957] 1 WLR 582 at 587 (McNair, J).
20 M Brazier and J Miola, 'Bye-bye Bolam: a medical litigation revolution?' (2000) 8 *Medical Law Review* 85.
21 *Bolitho v City and Hackney Health Authority* [1998] AC 232.
22 Ibid., at 233 and 243 (Lord Browne-Wilkinson).
23 Ibid., at 232 and 243 (Lord Browne-Wilkinson).
24 Ibid., at 241–242 (Lord Browne-Wilkinson).
25 N Castle, 'Applying Bolitho' (December 1998) *Journal of Personal Injury Law* 278.
26 S D Pattinson, *Medical Law and Ethics* (2nd edn, London: Sweet & Maxwell, 2014) p 113.
27 *Bolitho v City and Hackney Health Authority* [1998] AC 232 at 242 (Lord Browne-Wilkinson).

involved and that they had not reached a 'defensible conclusion'.[28] The *Bolitho* qualification has essentially supplemented the *Bolam* test in the respect that a defendant's conduct must accord with accepted medical practice *and* be able to withstand logical analysis, which for some[29] has been a welcome addition.[30]

How then do *Bolam* and *Bolitho* equate to UCB collection? Clearly, the method adopted by the UCB facilitator would need to be one that the midwifery profession (or private banks in the case of an informal collector) would accept as 'proper' but if the decision to adopt that method lacked any common sense, then the courts would still be entitled to declare a breach of duty. For example, if the potential risks of early cord clamping are ignored in order to procure an optimal UCB unit and harm results, the courts may deem this an illogical option, putting the collector in a legally precarious position.

However, while the *Bolam* test was held 'to apply to the informing of risks and to diagnosis and treatment',[31] Lord Browne-Wilkinson expressly *precluded* coherence from risk disclosure cases. He stated, 'I am not here considering questions of disclosure of risk'.[32] This revelation appears to imply that the decision-making process of the UCB collector does not necessitate an element of common sense or reasonability, which could leave the pregnant woman at greater risk of potential harm.

But was this in fact what his Lordship had attempted to infer? As his was the only substantive opinion in *Bolitho*,[33] it is difficult to determine exactly what was meant but some academics have indicated that his comment was merely a 'throwaway phrase'[34] or that he was simply pointing out that risk disclosure was not an issue for the courts to decide upon in the case before them.[35]

A more accepted version[36] is that Lord Browne-Wilkinson had the benefit of earlier deliberations of the House of Lords which had already clarified the position on the duty to warn 13 years earlier in *Sidaway v Board of Governors of the Bethlem Royal Hospital* [1985].[37] This case raised questions as to

28 Ibid., at 242 (Lord Browne-Wilkinson).

29 In particular see the Right Honourable Lord Woolf, 'Are the courts excessively deferential to the medical profession?' (2001) 9 *Medical Law Review* 1.

30 For an application of the *Bolitho* test logic to the *Bolam* Test, see *Smith v Tunbridge Wells Health Authority* [1994] 5 Med LR 334. In this case, the failure to warn a patient of the risk of impotence in an operation he consented to was deemed 'neither reasonable nor responsible' by the court.

31 *Bolam v Friern Hospital Management Committee* [1957] 1 WLR 582 at 583 (McNair, J).

32 *Bolitho v City and Hackney Health Authority* [1998] AC 232 at 242 (Lord Browne-Wilkinson). The statement was written in parenthesis.

33 Lord Browne-Wilkinson delivered the lead opinion. Lord Slynn of Hedley, Lord Nolan, Lord Hoffmann and Lord Clyde agreed with his reasoning without further discussion.

34 Brazier and Miola, 2000.

35 Pattinson, 2014 at 113.

36 Brazier and Miola, 2000.

37 *Sidaway v Board of Governors of the Bethlem Royal Hospital* [1985] AC 871.

whether the doctor's discretion should prevail over risk disclosure cases or whether the patient has an unfettered right to be consulted on all the risks involved in a treatment they consent to. Second, whether the American-style 'doctrine of informed consent', as seen in the landmark US case of *Canterbury v Spence* (1972),[38] should be adopted. The case determined that a doctor must disclose all material risks inherent in an operation that a reasonably prudent patient would want to be informed of in order to make an informed choice.[39] What was deemed a material risk was one that a reasonable patient would consider as significant enough to influence their decision whether or not to refuse or accept treatment.[40] The doctrine of informed consent is often referred to as 'The Prudent Patient Standard' or 'Canterbury Doctrine', and has been followed in various other countries.[41] *Sidaway* subsequently became the first House of Lords case to question whether the transatlantic doctrine of informed consent could apply to English law.

When *Sidaway* was heard in the mid-1980s, their Lordships did not feel that the time was ripe enough for change and the law of risk disclosure remained largely unchallenged – until very recently. In March 2015, the Supreme Court enshrined the importance of patient autonomy within the modern day doctor–patient relationship by expressly acknowledging that the US-style doctrine of informed consent was to be recognised by the English courts. Although *Sidaway* is now confined to discursive legal history, let us first track the process of the case that was discarded in favour of the biggest shake-up in the law on risk disclosure in the last 30 years.

Sidaway and the 'significance' of risk disclosure in cord blood collection

Sidaway was heard in the House of Lords[42] in December 1984, on appeal[43] by the claimant, Mrs Amy Doris Sidaway. Mr Falconer had been treating her for a trapped nerve, which culminated in an operation that carried two distinct risks: damage to the nerve root itself and damage to the spinal cord, the latter carrying a risk of less than 1 per cent. In spite of the operation being performed with all due care, this small risk *did* materialise and with catastrophic consequences. Counsel for Sidaway argued that she had not been informed of the risk to her spinal cord and that if she had, she would

38 *Canterbury v Spence* (1972) 464 F 2d 772.

39 An exception to this would be where the doctor has 'Therapeutic Privilege'.

40 *Canterbury v Spence* (1972) 464 F 2d 772 at 787.

41 See the Canadian case of *Reibl v Hughes* (1980) 114 DLR (3d) 1 and the Australian case *Rogers v Whitaker* (1992) 109 ALR 625. In the UK, the doctrine was examined in the lower English courts by Bristow J in *Chatterton v Gerson* [1981] QB 432 and Hirst J in *Hills v Potter* [1984] 1 WLR 641. In both instances, the '*Bolam* Test' was applied to determine the reasonableness of a failure to warn.

42 *Sidaway v Board of Governors of the Bethlem Royal Hospital* [1985] AC 871.

43 *Sidaway v Board of Governors of the Bethlem Royal Hospital* [1984] QB 493.

have declined the operation and thus avoided harm. However, after much deliberation, the court was satisfied that whilst he had communicated the general nature of the risks involved, the risks to the spine had been omitted.[44] There was no challenge to these findings.

The next question was therefore whether the failure to disclose constituted a breach of duty. There are a number of reasons why a medical professional may decide that it is not in 'the best interests'[45] of the patient to reveal the risks inherent in a particular procedure. Lord Scarman opined that disclosure may deter the patient from consenting to an operation deemed the most appropriate form of treatment, despite its risks. This view was concurred by Lord Diplock[46] with the added concern that volunteering unsought information about risks might have a detrimental effect on the patient's mental state. In such as situation, the medical professional can invoke 'therapeutic privilege' – the legal justification for withholding treatment when it is deemed to be in the patient's best interests to do so.[47] In the context of UCB collection, this type of scenario is only likely to arise in cases of directed donation (donations made on behalf of a known recipient) or where there is a familial history of disease. But what may be problematic here is that it is unclear whose 'best interests' are being protected, the recipient or the donor, as clearly, the interests of each often differ.

Despite the court acknowledging that there had been no breach of duty, the claimant's case now turned on whether the court would accept her second submission – that the doctrine of informed consent[48] could be invoked. While the House of Lords was not in the mid-1980s prepared to expand the common law to reflect a patient-centred approach as adopted in other jurisdictions, with Lord Scarman dissenting,[49] the majority declared

44 *Sidaway v Board of Governors of the Bethlem Royal Hospital* [1985] AC 871 at 880 (Lord Scarman quoting the trial judge, Skinner, J).

45 Ibid., at 877 and 883 (Lord Scarman).

46 Ibid., at 895 (Lord Diplock).

47 However, it has been noted that if an intervention is not medically necessary, for example some corrective cosmetic surgery or prophylactic treatment, then there is perhaps a greater need to consider the risks involved because the patient has more to lose. See, A J G M Janssen, 'Informing patients about small risks: a comparative approach' (2006) 13 *European Journal of Health Law* 159.

48 Until the 2015 Supreme Court ruling in *Montgomery*, the courts did not fully recognise the doctrine of informed consent, except in its very limited form as described by Bristow J in *Chatterton v Gerson* [1981] QB 432. Here it was held '[i]n my judgement, once the patient is informed *in broad terms of the nature of the procedure which is intended,* and gives her consent, her consent is real, and the cause of action on which to base a claim for failure to go into risks and implications is in negligence, not trespass' at 443 (Bristow, J). Author's emphasis.

49 It should also be noted that although Lord Scarman held that Mrs Sidaway *could* invoke the doctrine, her claim on this basis must still fail. The burden was on her to show that the risk to her spine was a material risk – one that Mr Falconer would have known that she, as a reasonably prudent patient, would have taken into account when making her decision on the operation. Clearly, on the facts, the claimant had failed to prove this point. As Lord Scarman points out at 890: '[l]ack of evidence was always her difficulty'.

that it 'regarded the doctrine as quite impractical in application'[50] for two key reasons. First, to give greater weight to the calculations of the patient over those of the medical professional would be detrimental to the doctor/patient relationship because it was assumed by the profession that the doctor knows best. Second, it would be 'unrealistic'[51] to restrict the evidence to issues of medical facts as this would deprive the court of the advantages to be gained from hearing an open discussion of accepted medical practices, which would make the outcome of medical negligence claims quite 'unpredictable'.[52]

However, the *Bolam* test was not completely left untouched by *Sidaway*. Recognising that there may be certain types of risk of which a patient *should* be informed, regardless of accepted medical opinion, Lord Bridge added an important qualification to the application of the test:

> I am of the opinion that the judge might in certain circumstances come to the conclusion that disclosure of a particular risk was so obviously necessary to an informed choice on the part of the patient that no reasonably prudent medical man would fail to make it.[53]

Ostensibly, Lord Bridge sought to clarify that a blanket application of *Bolam* could not be given to all cases of risk disclosure and held that there might be situations where the court could side-step the test to make its own assessment of the appropriate standard. These situations would typically arise where the nature of the risk in question so obviously justifies disclosure in order for the patient to make a considered decision, that failure to do so would warrant liability.[54] He envisaged such cases to be those that involve 'a substantial risk of grave adverse consequences',[55] which could constitute 'a 10 per cent risk'[56] of serious harm.[57]

On Lord Bridge's model then, a UCB collector may be deemed liable if (s)he failed to inform a pregnant woman of a substantial risk capable of causing serious harm to either herself or her newborn baby associated with the procurement of UCB, such as the effects of restricting up to 50 per cent of the baby's natural blood volume and that harm occurs. But is it realistic to expect a UCB collector to consider that the risk of such an occurrence is a 'substantial risk' and therefore significant enough to warrant disclosure,

50 *Sidaway v Board of Governors of the Bethlem Royal Hospital* [1985] AC 871 at 899 (Lord Bridge).

51 Ibid., at 899 (Lord Bridge).

52 Ibid.

53 Ibid., at 900 (Lord Bridge).

54 This was the same reasoning as applied in *Rogers v Whitaker* (1992) 109 ALR 625.

55 *Sidaway v Board of Governors of the Bethlem Royal Hospital* [1985] AC 871 at 900 (Lord Bridge).

56 Ibid., at 900 (Lord Bridge).

57 Ibid., Lord Bridge provided the example of a 10 per cent risk of a stroke from an operation to demonstrate what he considered a serious harm that required risk disclosure.

especially as the evidence remains equivocal? Despite the existence of children who have had their UCB collected at birth and are also suffering from harm – many of whom smile out from the advertising materials of private cord blood companies advocating the benefits of reinfusing their autologous UCB stem cells – the lack of any specific research that explores the connection between the two means that under *Sidaway*, the requirement of a 'substantial risk' of harm is unlikely to be fulfilled, which is good news for the health professionals facing litigation but unhelpful to parents left with a brain damaged child.

Lord Bridge's adaptation of the *Bolam* test certainly indicated a move towards acknowledging the rights of the patient to information. If a patient were to gamble with a relatively high risk of 'grave adverse consequence' he surmised, they have the right to be informed of it and make up their own minds whether to run that particular risk. The High Court of Australia in *Rogers v Whitaker* (1992)[58] also adopted this view. In this case, the Australian court highlighted the danger of a literal application of the *Bolam* test in the area of advice and information, and effectively endorsed the patient-centred approach. The court held that it was the doctor's duty to disclose all material risks inherent in the proposed treatment and that a material risk was one that:

> [i]n the circumstances of the particular case, a reasonable person in the patient's position, if warned of the risk, would be likely to attach significance to it or if the medical practitioner is, or should reasonably be aware that the particular patient, if warned of the risk, would be likely to attach significance to it.[59]

Here then we see evidence of the courts slowly beginning to acknowledge that the patient should have a greater say in what risks they wish to run in a proposed treatment and that only a full and frank disclosure of information will allow a fully autonomous decision to be made. It was this type of methodology that has been more recently evidenced by the House of Lords decision in *Chester v Afshar* [2004]. Recognising that even a small risk of paralysis inherent in a spinal operation was significant enough to warn the patient of, their Lordships found in favour of the claimant in the interests of autonomy.

The long road to *Chester*

In October 2004, the House of Lords recognised that the road to patient

58 In this case, the High Court determined that a small risk of loss of sight in the claimant's only 'good' eye was a 'material risk' worthy of disclosure.

59 *Rogers v Whitaker* (1992) HCA 58 (1992) 175 CLR 470 (19 November 1992) at 16.

autonomy had been well trodden[60] and that it now deserved to be placed on a more even footing. Set against a backdrop of human rights legislation and a cultural shift towards public policy considerations, the time was ripe for the judiciary to put the patient back in the driving seat – and Carole Ogilvy Chester was one such driver. At both first instance[61] and on appeal,[62] the court found in favour of the defendants. Undeterred, Chester brought her case before the House of Lords.[63] The facts of the case are as follows.

Mrs Chester suffered persistent pain from protrusions on her spinal discs that required surgery. Despite being extremely anxious to avoid an operation,[64] her consultant neurosurgeon, Mr Fari Afshar performed a microdiscectomy with her consent, after which she experienced both motor and sensory malfunction to the lower part of her body. The only explanation for her condition was that 'a small but unavoidable risk'[65] of cauda equina syndrome had materialised, leaving several areas on her left side severely paralysed.

As the operation had been performed without negligence,[66] what information had been imparted during the consultation between Afshar and Chester subsequently became the main focus of the legal dispute. Chester argued that she had not been informed of the small risk of cauda equina syndrome, a claim Afshar contested. He gave evidence that 'he *thought*'[67] he had informed her of this risk in addition to the risks of refusing surgery. However, the trial judge held that Chester's evidence was the true version of events,[68] and the Court of Appeal refused permission to challenge this finding.

Chester's account was that although she had not specifically asked about the risk of cauda equina syndrome, she had asked lots of questions about the risks involved in that particular operation. Indeed, there appears to be no logical reason for her to have enquired about the risk of a particular condition that she did not know existed. In response to her general enquiries, the surgeon's alleged reply was '[w]ell, I have never crippled anybody yet',[69] to which he later added, '[o]f course, you could be my first'.[70] Although this

60 As R Heywood observes in 'Informed consent through the back door? Case note: *Chester v Afshar* [2004] 41 All ER 587' (2005) 56 *Northern Ireland Legal Quarterly* 2, quoting M A Jones, 'The Bolam test and the reasonable expert' (1999b) 226 *Tort Law Review* 236: [i]n the previous six medical negligence actions to come before the House of Lords the scores stood at Claimants 0; Defendants 6'.

61 *Chester v Afshar* [2000] WL 33201379.

62 *Chester v Afshar* [2002] EWCA Civ 724.

63 *Chester v Afshar* [2004] UKHL 41.

64 Ibid., at 3 (Lord Bingham).

65 Ibid., at 900 (Lord Bingham).

66 *Chester v Afshar* [2000] WL 33201379 at 56 (Taylor, J).

67 Ibid., at 43 (Lord Hope of Craighead) (Author's emphasis).

68 *Chester v Afshar* [2000] WL 33201379 at 64 (Taylor, J).

69 Ibid., at 23 (Taylor, J).

70 Ibid., at 23 (Taylor, J).

response appears rather off-hand, the court accepted that as Chester was over-anxious the reply was merely intended to reassure her in a light-hearted way.

Finding for the claimant on the issue of breach, the court was satisfied that at no time during the conversation had the surgeon informed his patient of the risk of cauda equina syndrome or that the operation could result in paralysis, which he should have done in order for his patient to make a fully autonomous decision. Although the risk was small, it was a material risk – that is, significant enough to warrant disclosure. Instead, he had merely drawn her attention to his performance of over 300 operations of this kind per year and had made the operation sound 'simple and routine'.[71]

But where have we heard this type of dialogue before? This type of encouragement is reminiscent of that used by the private UCB industry who tout UCB collection as a 'simple, safe and painless procedure'[72] that can produce huge future health benefits. Just as Chester was informed of only the benefits of surgery and the potential consequences of refusing treatment,[73] those contemplating UCB collection are directed to its benefits rather than its risks.

While the court found for Chester on the issue of breach, they did not go as far as to declare the existence of a so-called 'doctrine of informed consent'. Yet, as advanced by Lord Scarman in *Sidaway* and American jurisprudence; elements of a 'reasonably prudent patient test' had begun to emerge. Rather than a rigid application of the 'professional standard', it had evolved to include consideration of what the patient would wish to know in order to make a fully autonomous decision.[74] Post *Chester* then, not only must the patient be informed in broad terms about the nature and purpose of the treatment being offered, but also all material risks inherent in it, in order to make an informed choice. The dissenting view of Lord Scarman in *Sidaway*[75] may have taken a long time to be acknowledged, but some progress towards a 'reasonably prudent patient standard' which he championed had at last been made.[76]

71 Ibid.

72 Biovault Family online website, 'How will my cord blood be collected?' http://biovault-family.com/the-knowledge-centre/cord-blood-banking/?gclid=CjwKEAiAoIK1BRCRiMqphvnlwlwSJAAOebPMZp8NsGFgw6HwwgwVY5-9rcQqMtGjdzsvADA9YLFakxoCwzbw_wcB accessed 21 January 2016.

73 *Chester v Afshar* [2004] UKHL 41 at 43 (Lord Hope of Craighead).

74 For a discussion on the differences between these two approaches, see: J Miola, 'On the materiality of risk: paper tigers and panaceas' (2009) 17 *Medical Law Review* 63.

75 *Sidaway v Board of Governors of the Bethlem Royal Hospital* [1985] AC 871 at 889–890 (Lord Scarman).

76 I Kennedy suggests that Lord Scarman 'paints a picture of himself forging ahead while his brother judges trod more carefully'. See: I Kennedy, *Treat Me Right: Essays in Medical Law and Ethics* (Oxford: Clarendon Press, 1988) p 211.

What then was the influence behind such a 'wind of change'[77] and how is a shift towards patients' rights in risk disclosure cases relevant to UCB collection? In the years that have elapsed since *Sidaway*, it would appear that the medical profession itself has sought to redress the imbalance of power within the doctor–patient relationship in the informing of risks.[78] As Lord Steyn pointed out in his judgment in *Chester*:

> The result ought to come as no surprise to the medical profession, which has to its credit subscribed to the fundamental importance of a surgeon's duty to warn a patient in general terms of significant risks: Royal College of Surgeons: Good Surgical Practice (2002): Chapter 4, Guidelines on Consent.[79]

What his Lordship appeared to infer by this observation was that members of each area of medical expertise, such as neurosurgery, have in modern day practice already endorsed the need for greater patient autonomy as evidenced by their profession's practice directions and guidelines.[80] Moreover, acknowledgement that decision-making should be made by doctors and patients in partnership has been evidenced by the GMC's policy document *Consent: Patients and Doctors Making Decisions Together* (2008),[81] which prioritises the need for more autonomous decision-making. In addition, a wealth of medical literature[82] has demonstrated that from within the profession itself, there is a common understanding that, 'Effective communication and clarity of information exchange is essential for quality of care and patient safety'.[83]

In addition to breach of duty, the final hurdle for any claim in the tort of negligence is for the claimant to prove that the defendant(s) had, on the balance of probability, caused the resultant harm. However, in certain situations, the courts have used public policy considerations to justify modifying the rules of causation in order to effect a remedy, examples of which can be seen in both *Chester* and *Fairchild v Glenhaven* [2003].[84]

77 S Mclean and J K Mason, *Legal and Ethical Aspects of Healthcare* (London: Cromwell Press, 2003) p 51.

78 Heywood, 2005.

79 *Chester v Afshar* [2004] UKHL 41 at 26 (Lord Steyn).

80 The Royal College of Surgeons, *Good Surgical Practice Guidelines* (2002) to which Lord Steyn refers has now been replaced by *Good Surgical Practice* (2014) www.rcseng.ac.uk/standards-and-research/gsp accessed 27 January 2016.

81 GMC, 'Consent: patients and doctors making decisions together' (June 2008) www.gmc-uk.org/guidance/ethical_guidance/consent_guidance_index.asp accessed 29 October 2015.

82 For some examples, see: GMC, 'Good medical practice: working with doctors, working for patients' (April 2013) paras 31–34 www.gmc-uk.org/static/documents/content/GMP_.pdf See also Department of Health (DH), 'Guidelines on consent: reference guide to consent for examination or treatment' (2009) 2nd edn www.gov.uk/government/uploads/system/uploads/attachment_data/file/138296/dh_103653__1_.pdf accessed 27 January 2016.

83 The Royal College of Surgeons, 2014 at para. 3.1.

84 *Fairchild v Glenhaven Funeral Services Ltd* [2003] 1 AC 32.

Causation, public policy and the 'fairness' of *Fairchild*

Although Carole Chester had established breach, she still had to prove cause in fact[85] and law;[86] that is, she had to prove that had she been properly informed of the risks of surgery, she would not have had the operation and therefore avoided paralysis.[87] However, her evidence was that she may still have gone ahead with the operation, albeit on another day, and after a thorough consideration of all her options. On orthodox principles then, causation had not been made out[88] – but the story did not end there. Lord Steyn held that where 'policy and corrective justice pull powerfully in favour of vindicating the patient's right to know',[89] then the 'but for' test can, in exceptional circumstances, be modified. Public policy required that, in the interests of patient autonomy, the duty to warn must be adhered to; and where it was not, the principles of justice and fairness demand recompense for the claimant by a certain degree of 'manipulation'[90] of causal principles, as to find otherwise would render the duty to warn meaningless. Thus, Chester won her case and in spite of dissentions from Lords Bingham and Hoffmann, Hoffmann did concede that Chester's right to choose had been impinged and a 'modest solatium'[91] should be awarded in recognition of the harm.[92]

85 For a full discussion on the application of the 'but for' test see: S Deakin, A Johnston and B Markesinis, *Markesinis and Deakin's Tort Law* (7th edn, Oxford: Oxford University Press, 2013) Chapter 5, pp 223–238.

86 Cause in Law is comprised of two steps: First, the test of remoteness, which is measured by the foresight of the reasonable person. If the reasonable person could foresee the kind of damage suffered by the claimant, then so too should the defendant. The test is laid down in *Overseas Tankship (UK) v Morts Dock & Engineering Co; The Wagon Mound 1* [1961] AC 388. The second is whether the resultant damage was caused by another's act, which occurred *after* the defendant's breach and therefore breaks the chain of causation, which either limits or extinguishes the defendant's liability.

87 In *Smith v Barking, Havering and Brentwood Health Authority* [1994] 5 Med LR 285 it was held that on the balance of probabilities, the claimant would have consented to the operation even if properly advised as to the risk of tetraplegia and therefore failed to establish cause in fact.

88 Although Lord Steyn in *Chester v Afshar* [2004] UKHL 41 at 19–20 suggests that the 'but for' test *had* been made out. On the balance of probabilities, the likelihood of the random risk of cauda equina syndrome materialising on a subsequent day would be at 98–99 per cent. In other words, the claimant would have run the same risk but, on balance, there would have been a different outcome. However, he appears to accept that Mr Afshar had not actually increased the risk of the injury occurring and thus did not satisfy the broader causal principles.

89 Ibid., at 22 (Lord Steyn).

90 Heywood, 2005.

91 A 'modest solatium' is a symbolic payment of a modest sum awarded by the courts in recognition of a harm.

92 *Chester v Afshar* [2004] UKHL 41 at 33 (Lord Hoffmann). Interestingly, despite his dissent, Lord Hoffmann appears to be acknowledging here that a 'loss of autonomy' is a 'harm'. In *Rees v Darlington Memorial Hospital NHS Trust* [2002] EWCA Civ 88, this was worth a £15,000 conventional award.

So what effect could such a departure from established causation principles have on a UCB-related claim? The enquiry will begin with Lord Steyn's reference to the case of *Fairchild v Glenhaven Ltd* [2003].[93] This case concerned a group of employees who had been negligently exposed to asbestos dust over a number of years resulting in mesothelioma, a fatal form of lung cancer. As the condition can be caused by one single fibre of asbestos entering the lining of the lung,[94] they were unable to prove *which* employer had been responsible, hence the 'but for' test could not be satisfied.[95] However, recognising that in certain circumstances justice required the claimants to recover,[96] the House of Lords modified causation, as it did later in *Chester*, to reach a fair outcome. To achieve this, they held that as each defendant had materially increased the *risk* of harm, then they should be deemed liable,[97] because, '[a]ny other outcome would be deeply offensive to instinctive notions of what justice requires and fairness demands'.[98] Clearly, in an era where the dangers of asbestos were known, as a matter of public policy, justice should warrant recovery for those harmed.

If justice and fairness is the key to recovery, could this also apply to the negligent procurement of UCB? The problem faced here is that the burden of proof would lie with the mother to show that the collection process was the cause of harm and not some other external factor – the precise difficulty that prevented the claimant in *Wilsher*[99] from recovering in 1988. Proving causation in a UCB collection claim is therefore likely to be extremely problematic, particularly as there may be other causative development and birth factors involved. Furthermore, it would appear that the *Fairchild* modification applies only to incidents that involve a single causative agent such as the asbestos in *Fairchild* and the operation in *Chester*, and would therefore be of little assistance to this type of claim.

93 Note, there is now some debate over whether *Fairchild* applies in medical negligence cases. For example, see: *Wootton v J Docter Ltd & Anor* [2008] EWCA Civ 136. In this case, the appellant had failed to establish that the prescribing of two Logynon pills had materially increased the risk of contraceptive failure. It was held that the appellant could not invoke the *Fairchild* principle because this was simply a matter of being unable to prove causation.

94 Unlike asbestosis, which is a cumulative condition, meaning that (a) increased exposure increases the likelihood of contracting the disease, and (b) the greater the exposure, the greater the risk that the condition will be more severe.

95 Both the High Court and the Court of Appeal upheld that as different employers had exposed the claimants at different times, they would need to prove on the balance of probabilities for each employer that but for his negligence, they would not have developed mesothelioma. As they could not prove this, none of the employers were held liable.

96 Although mesothelioma is a rare condition, it is 1,000 times more likely to occur to those occupationally exposed than the general public.

97 Previously used in *McGhee v National Coal Board* [1972] 3 All ER 1008, a case about the contracting of skin dermatitis and negligent exposure to brick dust.

98 *Fairchild v Glenhaven Funeral Services Ltd* [2003] 1 AC 32 at 36 (Lord Nicholls).

99 *Wilsher v Essex Area Health Authority* [1988] AC 1074.

But whilst difficult, it may not be impossible, as other *Wilsher*-type causation cases have shown. In *Bailey (by her father and litigant friend) v MOD and another* [2008],[100] a claimant's negligent treatment in a military hospital had materially contributed to hypoxia and eventual brain damage, even though she suffered from pre-existing serious health problems. The court held that because the negligence had materially contributed to the claimant's harm,[101] the hospital was liable for the resultant brain injury in spite of other existing causal factors. That said, it is at least arguable that *Bailey* could provide a basis for a UCB-related claim where harm results even where other birth-related causal factors may be present, and where the courts determine that it would be unjust for any resultant damage to go uncompensated.

What we have so far seen from cases such as *Fairchild* and *Chester* (and to a certain extent, *Bailey*) is the willingness of the modern day courts to use the function of the law not only to right wrongs and ensure justice but to effect a remedy that 'reflects the reasonable expectations of the public in contemporary society'.[102] In terms of communicating risks, the doctor–patient relationship can no longer withstand the force of a patient's right to make their own decisions in healthcare and there has been a judicial acceptance that autonomous decision-making can only be achieved after a full exchange of information between the patient and their health professional. Indeed, it is for the patient, and the patient alone, to decide what risks they should personally bear, and true consent will only be given if they are allowed that opportunity.

By the mid-2000s then, the law relating to risk disclosure in England and Wales had made huge in-roads in favour of patient autonomy and had effectively turned its back on medical paternalism, without expressly adopting the doctrine of informed consent. But by the beginning of 2015, this was about to be rectified. In a landmark Scottish pregnancy-related case that fundamentally altered the law on information provision throughout the UK, the 'prudent patient standard' came into its own.

The *Montgomery* milestone

Following the traumatic labour and birth of her son, Sam, at Bellshill Maternity Hospital, Lanarkshire on 1 October 1999, Nadine Montgomery sued the Health Board for the severe disabilities suffered by Sam, which she claimed were caused by the negligence of her consultant obstetrician, Dr Diane McLellan, on two distinct grounds. First, that she had not been warned of the risk of shoulder dystocia during vaginal birth, where the baby's shoulder becomes lodged within the pelvis; or been offered the alternative of

100 *Bailey (by her father and litigant friend) v MOD and another* [2008] EWCA Civ 883.

101 *Bonnington Castings v Wardlaw* [1956] AC 613. As opposed to materially increasing the *risk* of harm as evidenced in *McGhee v National Coal Board* [1972] 3 All ER 1008.

102 *Chester v Afshar* [2004] UKHL 41 at 25 (Lord Steyn).

having a Caesarean section to avoid that risk. This was important because she was carrying a large baby, and being a diabetic and extremely small in stature, the risk of shoulder dystocia was placed at 9–10 per cent.[103] Should this occur, further risks of the baby suffering a broken arm or nerve damage and an increased risk of an occluded umbilical cord resulting in cerebral palsy or death are present.[104] Second, that when these precise risks and other complications presented during labour, Dr McLellan negligently managed the labour and failed to act upon warning signs from the foetal monitor. As a result, Sam was deprived of oxygen for 12 minutes and was later diagnosed with dyskinetic cerebral palsy, caused by a lack of oxygen at birth, and a permanent disability to the affected arm.

Both grounds were rejected by the Outer Court (Scotland) in 2010[105] and their findings upheld by the Inner Court (Scotland) in 2013.[106] On the first ground they held that following Lord Bridge's majority decision in *Sidaway*, while the risk of shoulder dystocia could be classed as a 'substantial' risk, the chance that it could result in 'grave adverse consequences' to the baby was 'very small'[107] or even 'tiny';[108] and following the application of the 'Bolam Test',[109] the consultant had not breached her duty to warn. Moreover, the consultant's evidence was that if you mentioned this particular risk to every diabetic patient, or to point out to every pregnant woman that there is a small risk of neonatal death involved in vaginal labour, then all women would want a Caesarean section, a procedure that the consultant deemed was 'not in the maternal interests for women to have'.[110] They also determined as a finding of fact that had Montgomery been warned of the risks, she would still have accepted the advice of the consultant and consented to a vaginal delivery.[111]

While it was accepted that Mrs Montgomery had, like Mrs Chester, raised concerns about the proposed treatment to her consultant, she had only enquired about her ability to deliver a large baby vaginally and not about the specific risks associated with vaginal delivery. Following Lord Bridge's speech in *Sidaway*, the court held that although the doctor has a duty to answer truthfully and fully if the patient enquires about a risk,[112] like Sidaway

103 *Montgomery v Lanarkshire Health Board* [2015] UKSC 11 at 13 (Lords Kerr and Reed).
104 Ibid., at 12 (Lords Kerr and Reed).
105 *Montgomery v Lanarkshire Health Board* [2010] ScotCS CSHOH_104.
106 *Montgomery v Lanarkshire Health Board* [2013] ScotCS CSIH_3.
107 *Montgomery v Lanarkshire Health Board* [2015] UKSC 11 at 13 (Lords Kerr and Reed).
108 Ibid., at 28 (Lords Kerr and Reed).
109 The equivalent case in the Scottish courts is *Hunter v Hamley* 1955 SC 200, 206.
110 *Montgomery v Lanarkshire Health Board* [2015] UKSC 11 at 13 (Lords Kerr and Reed).
111 Ibid., at 3 and 35 (Lords Kerr and Reed). Mrs Montgomery gave evidence that she was 'not arrogant enough to demand a Caesarean section' if not offered to her.
112 *Sidaway v Board of Governors of the Bethlem Royal Hospital* [1985] AC 871 at 898 (Lord Bridge).

herself,[113] 'Mrs Montgomery would have had to have raised questions of specific risks involved in vaginal delivery'[114] for that duty to arise. Merely expressing concerns of a general nature about the ability to give birth, they opined, fell short of Lord Bridge's qualification.[115]

Such a requirement appears very harsh, effectively disadvantaging those who lack specific knowledge, and pertains that Montgomery would have had to have known about existing risks associated with vaginal delivery, particularly in women of small physique (and the chance of dystocia shoulder materialising specifically) in order to have enquired about them. To possess such knowledge is, indeed, a very big ask. Under the *Sidaway* model, those who choose to preserve UCB would also have to show that they had specifically requested information on the risks involved and of the type that had materialised, but again, this is to assume that parents have some kind of prior knowledge of the *specific* risks involved in the procedure, which is of course a big assumption to make.

In response to the second ground of Montgomery's claim, the consultant was able to demonstrate that her management of Montgomery's labour had complied with the opinion of a reasonably competent obstetrician and that the actions of the obstetric team was *Bolitho*-compliant.[116] Having therefore lost in both lower courts, but with the same determination as Carol Chester, Montgomery appealed the issue of risk disclosure to the Supreme Court. Their Lordships revisited the current law of risk disclosure in March 2015 and were urged by counsel for Montgomery to depart from the decision in *Sidaway*. On causation, they were invited to accept that either the Lord Ordinary had erred in his treatment of the evidence or that he should have followed the House of Lords' lead in *Chester* in its treatment of causation by modifying the approach in order to effect a remedy.

Commencing with the issue of the duty of disclosure, Lords Reed and Kerr first mapped the background to *Sidaway*'s demise. They espoused that in the years that had elapsed since the case first came before the courts, social and legal developments had pulled away from medical paternalism in response to the recognition of a paradigm shift in health provision and the doctor/patient relationship.[117] They opined that patients are no longer passive recipients of treatment,[118] a view enhanced by the stimulus of human rights[119] in an era where treatment information is readily accessible; and that

113 The requirements referred to by the court in *Sidaway* were for patients to ask for specific information and/or the risk to be in the region of 10 per cent to be deemed sufficient enough to be disclosed. Essentially, Mrs Sidaway did not ask about the risks and the risk itself was only in the region of 1 per cent.

114 *Montgomery v Lanarkshire Health Board* [2015] UKSC 11 at 29 (Lords Kerr and Reed).

115 Ibid., at 33.

116 Ibid., at 26–29.

117 Ibid., at 75.

118 Ibid., at 75.

119 Ibid., at 80.

it was now therefore 'manifestly untenable'[120] to regard patients as incapable of understanding medical matters and exclusively dependent upon the doctor's consideration.[121] In addition, although the use of therapeutic privilege remained intact,[122] it should not be used as a sword by which to drive through what the doctor deemed to be in the patient's best interests at the expense of the patient making an informed choice.[123] That said, it could not have been in the claimant's interests to deny her a Caesarean section as it was undisputed that had this been performed, the baby would have been delivered unharmed.[124]

Akin to the court in *Chester*, the Supreme Court was particularly persuaded by the subscription to current professional practice already present, in particular the GMC's *Good Medical Practice* guidance (2013), which expresses the doctor's duty as one that, 'Works in partnership with patients ... [and] respects patients' rights to reach decisions with you about their treatment.'[125] In their Lordships' view, it is the 'patient's entitlement to decide whether or not to incur [a] risk'[126] and their involvement in the decision-making process can, as the GMC identify, not only produce therapeutic benefits for the patient but is also 'regarded as an integral aspect of professionalism in treatment'.[127]

In a restatement of the law in relation to risk disclosure as it should apply in the twenty-first century, and drawing their influence from the Australian court in *Rogers v Whitaker* (1992) and the dissenting view of Lord Scarman in *Sidaway*, their Lordships decreed that, unless the patient chooses not to be availed of information regarding treatment, the 'correct position' is one where the doctor is:

> [u]nder a duty to take reasonable care to ensure that the patient is aware of any material risks involved in any recommended treatment, and of any reasonable alternative or variant treatments. The test of materiality is whether, in the circumstances of the particular case, be reasonable person in the patient's position would be likely to attach significance to the risk, or the doctor is or should reasonably aware that the particular patient would be likely to attach significance to it.[128]

Put simply, the Supreme Court held that as the consultant herself had given evidence that Montgomery (and indeed most pregnant women) would have

120 Ibid., at 81.
121 Ibid., at 13.
122 Ibid., at 85.
123 Ibid., at 91.
124 Ibid., at 104.
125 Ibid., at 77.
126 Ibid., at 82.
127 Ibid., at 78.
128 Ibid., at 87.

been likely to have requested a Caesarean had she been informed of the risk of harm to herself and/or her child, then those risks were 'material' to her. Essentially, knowledge of the risks would have made a fundamental difference to the decision she made about the type of birth she consented to. Subsequently, the consultant had breached her duty to warn and the omission had been the 'but-for' cause of the harm, which would have been avoided by performing the alternative option of a Caesarean section.[129] Furthermore, they determined that it was no longer necessary to assess whether a risk was 'material' enough to warrant disclosure based upon percentages and statistical evidence because information regarding the severity and frequency of risks are 'fact-sensitive' to each individual patient, the merits of which hold a different level of importance depending on the patient's personal circumstances.[130]

In contrast, in a case heard a few days following the *Montgomery* ruling, it was held that the small risk of chromosomal abnormality in a developing child, which had not been communicated to the claimant, was not a 'material risk' worthy of disclosure.[131] While the claimant, Ms A, gave evidence that she would have opted for a late termination if she had been aware of the possible defect and that it could result in having a disabled child, the court held that as she was prepared to accept the background risk of having a Down's Syndrome child, the knowledge of a chromosomal defect would not have affected Ms A's decision-making process, or anyone in Ms A's position.

As the essence of *Sidaway* was now on its knees, there still remained the issue of risk enquiry, a significant element of the duty to warn. On this the court in *Montgomery* slammed the 'profoundly unsatisfactory' nature of placing the onus on a patient to question the doctor about specific risks that they may not be aware of. Referring to the judgment of Sedley, LJ in *Wyatt v Curtis* [2003][132] the court declared that there was 'something unreal'[133] about leaving patients who lack knowledge to express their concerns about their treatment in general terms because, '[I]ronically, the ignorance with which such patients seek to have dispelled disqualifies them from obtaining the information they desire.'[134] The communication of concern, the court declared, should instead be interpreted as an expression of a patient's needs and it is the duty of the doctor to respond to those individual needs and circumstances.[135]

129 Ibid., at 104.

130 Ibid., at 46 and 89.

131 *A v East Kent Hospitals University NHS Foundation Trust* [2015] EWHC 1038 (QB).

132 *Wyatt v Curtis* [2003] EWCA Civ 1779. *Wyatt* concerned the communication of a 1 per cent risk of brain damage following chicken pox in pregnancy. Applying *Pearce v United Bristol Healthcare NHS Trust* [1999] PIQR 53, the court noted that, 'what is substantial and what is grave are questions on which the doctor's and the patient's perception may differ'. Moreover, what a doctor may class as an 'insubstantial chance', to the patient the risk may be 'sufficiently real for her to want to make an informed decision about it'.

133 *Montgomery v Lanarkshire Health Board* [2015] UKSC 11 at 58 (Lords Kerr and Reed).

134 Ibid., at 58.

135 Ibid., at 73.

As *Sidaway* drew its last breath, it was left to Lady Hale to drive the 'prudent patient standard' home. Adding a footnote to the comprehensive judgment of Lords Reed and Kerr, her words resonated with an air of satisfaction. Citing academic literature, professional regulation and recent case law as a means to signpost with a degree of certainty that informed consent was already present in all but name within UK law, she held that, 'This case [*Montgomery*] has provided us with the opportunity not only to confirm that confident statement, but also to make it clear that the same principles apply in Scotland'.[136] The doctrine of informed consent had finally been expressly recognised in full force within the UK and elevated the patient's right to act autonomously.

What then does all this mean for those involved in UCB banking? Modern day health jurisprudence has prioritised the need for a meaningful dialogue between health providers and their patients and using 'high-risk-only' standards of disclosure imposed by the House of Lords in *Sidaway* has been swept away in favour of patients' rights and more closely reflects the expectations of current healthcare policies. For example, the 2008 GMC Guidance on Consent advises that health professionals should 'explain the options to the patient, setting out the potential benefits, risk, burdens and side-effects of each option, including the option to have no treatment'.[137] Moreover, the GMC speaks of a need for the doctor to 'give patients the information they want or need'[138] and that they 'should explore these matters with patients, listen to their concerns [and] ask for and respect their views'.[139] This advice post *Montgomery* can be read as highlighting the need for meaningful communication before any medical treatment takes place, and one that places the patient as final arbiter of their own destiny.[140]

While UCB collection will undoubtedly be viewed as a rather trivial medical intervention when compared to more invasive types of treatment such as surgical operations and Caesarean sections, it is none the less a treatment procedure that can attract the same level of legal implications in the event of a medical mishap because the same set of legal principles apply. That said, as the current potential benefits and risks of preserving UCB remains equivocal, a full discussion process needs to be conducted if patient autonomy and choice is to be upheld. Put another way, any outcome that the reasonable patient would want to be aware of in order to make an informed decision is now necessary after *Montgomery*.[141] As we saw in Chapter 2, there a number of health risks associated with the collection

136 Ibid., at 107.
137 GMC, 2008 at para 5(b) accessed 25 January 2016.
138 Ibid., at para 9.
139 Ibid., at para 10.
140 It should also be noted that in *Jones v Royal Wolverhampton Hospitals NHS Trust* [2015] EWHC 2154 (QB), *Montgomery* has since been applied retrospectively.
141 The legal principles set out in *Montgomery* were also successfully applied in *Spencer v Hillingdon* [2015] 1058 (QB).

process, such as early cord clamping, which can have negative effects on a child's neural development, cognitive abilities and may increase behavioural problems in later life; and the in-utero collection method, which poses increased health risks to the pregnant woman. It is argued that these are factors that those contemplating UCB banking would want to be made aware of before choosing those methods.

Conclusion

Having traced the current law as it relates to the standard of care in negligence and risk disclosure, it is clear that all healthcare professionals should take note of the latest judicial developments in appraising the doctor/patient relationship. The last decade has certainly witnessed an increased awareness of patients' rights, an ideal perhaps jettisoned by the introduction of the Human Rights Act (HRA) (1998), which fully came into force on 2 October 2000, affecting both statutory legislation and the common law; and incorporates the majority of the provisions of the European Convention on Human Rights (ECHR).[142] With the notion of 'rights' at the forefront of the Act's jurisprudence, both policy-makers and the courts have since been more inclined to take cognisance of a respect for a patient's autonomy. In a marked shift from a society pre-occupied with the *duties* owed between citizens to one concerned with the *rights* of individuals, both the courts and the medical profession have certainly become more responsive to upholding the needs of a 'rights-based society'[143] and may explain why the anticipated influx of cases under the Act has been rather over-estimated, particularly with regard to risk disclosure.[144]

Yet while it would appear that patient autonomy is being taken seriously, it does place additional pressures on health professionals to ensure that their communication and documentation process is fully robust. Indeed, the thoroughness of this process is neatly captured by the RCOG who advise:

> To obtain informed consent the process of shared understanding and decision-making between patient and clinician must be approached diligently and robustly. Before seeking a woman's consent for a test, treatment or intervention or operation, you should ensure that she is fully informed, understands the nature of the condition for which it is being proposed, its prognosis, likely consequences and the risks of

142 There are a number of relevant convention rights that may apply to healthcare – namely; the right to life (Article 2), the right not to be subjected to inhumane or degrading treatment (Article 3), the right to liberty (Article 5), respect for private and family life (Article 8) and respect for religious views (Article 9).

143 The Right Honourable Lord Woolf, 2001.

144 J V McHale, 'Medical malpractice in England – current trends' (2003) 1 *European Journal of Health Law* 135.

receiving no treatment, as well as any reasonable or accepted alternative treatments.[145]

While *Bolam* remains at the cornerstone of professional standards, *Montgomery* has restated the law on risk disclosure. A risk should be communicated if a reasonable person in the same position as the patient would be likely to regard a particular risk as significant, or the doctor is (or should) reasonably be aware that the patient would be likely to attach significance to it, such as those involved in UCB collection. Communicating effectively for the UCB collector, however, can only be achieved if (s)he remains updated on both the risks and benefits involved in the procedure and is afforded adequate space during antenatal appointments to engage in a proper discussion with a pregnant woman seeking to participate in UCB banking.

While the pregnant woman cannot *demand* treatment,[146] if the request to collect UCB is acceded to, then full legal obligations apply. And if, in the exercise of choice, the pregnant woman requests a collection method that carries greater risks in order to procure an optimal UCB unit, as advocated by private banks, then such risks that the collector knows, or ought to know, would be 'material' to that particular woman's decision-making process and should be communicated to her to ensure her consent is valid.

What is relevant is that social and legal developments have pointed towards patients being able to comprehend that most medical treatments involve some element of risk, and patients act autonomously by 'accepting responsibility for the taking of risks affecting their own lives, and living with the consequences of their choices'.[147] This seems rather poignant in the context of UCB banking, not only in terms of information provision, but also because the exercise of choice 'does not depend exclusively on medical considerations'.[148] Making an informed choice about whether or not to preserve UCB either for private use or donation is an opportunity that only comes around once in a child's lifetime and it is therefore an important one that requires full consideration and when in possession of all material facts.

145 RCOG, Clinical Governance Advice No. 6, 'Obtaining valid consent' (January 2015) www.rcog.org.uk/globalassets/documents/guidelines/clinical-governance-advice/cga6.pdf accessed 25 January 2016.

146 *R (Burke) v GMC* [2005] EWCA Civ 1003 at 31 (Lord Phillips, MR).

147 *Montgomery v Lanarkshire Health Board* [2015] UKSC 11 at 81 (Lords Kerr and Reed).

148 Ibid., at 13 (Lords Kerr and Reed).

6 Cord blood ownership

> In this jurisdiction developments in medical science now require a re-analysis of the common law's treatment of, and approach to, the issue of ownership of parts or products of a living human body, whether for present purposes (namely an action in negligence) or otherwise.[1]

As we have so far seen throughout the preceding chapters, modern healthcare jurisprudence has witnessed a marked shift in favour of upholding patients' personal autonomy and choice. This change can be noted from within the profession's own professional regulations and has been acknowledged by the judiciary as cases such as *Chester* and *Montgomery* demonstrate. Respect for a patient's autonomy is underpinned by the law on consent, a key ethical imperative that has been more fully recognised post the *Bristol* and *Alder Hey* organ retention scandals, and one that seeks to maintain a patient's right to make their own decisions based on their own needs and values; and in addition, to a negative right not to be subject to arbitrary restrictions. In this sense we speak of patients holding certain 'rights' to their bodily integrity, situated as the ultimate decision-makers in their own destiny. Certainly, the legislative effect of acknowledging 'consent'[2] and 'authorisation'[3] enshrined in the Human Tissue Acts places patients' and their guardians' wishes as being central to what is done to their bodies and its parts, even after death.

If we can exercise control over our bodies by consenting to the removal of body parts and tissue, what continued rights, if any, do we have over that excised bodily material? We often speak in possessory terms in relation to the body – phrases such as '*his* body was donated to medical science', 'she donated *her* kidney to her sister' and 'I donated *my* blood to help others' – but these are likely to be simple linguistics used to describe the notion of control that we have over our bodies and body parts, and possessory nouns used in conjunction with actions that the law permits us to do. For example,

1 *Yearworth v North Bristol NHS Trust* [2009] EWCA Civ 37 at 30 (Lord Judge, CJ).
2 Human Tissue Act 2004.
3 Human Tissue (Scotland) Act 2006.

the law allows us to donate blood and body tissue to save or enhance life,[4] donate gametes or embryos via IVF technology to create new life,[5] we can sell and use human hair to make wigs,[6] preserve a deceased foetus for scientific interest[7] or even display human blood in artworks.[8] However, the law also imposes restrictions on that individual freedom, such as prohibiting the commercial sale of organs for fear of exploiting the vulnerable and offending society's moral compass;[9] gametes and embryos may not be used in a way not directed by the given consent;[10] a woman cannot use her body to profit from surrogacy agreements;[11] and we cannot enjoy personal financial gain from cell lines created from bodily material consensually removed if it later transpires that the material is of commercial value.[12] The law's starting point to enquiries regarding ownership in the body is that there is no property in the living human body or corpses, subject to certain exceptions. Until recently, the law relating to parts or products of the living human body has received little attention, probably due to their perceived lack of value. However, as we have seen with UCB, advancements in medical science and our knowledge of certain biological materials' potential invite us to view bodily material very differently, particularly in terms of asserting rights over them.[13]

With property rights come certain duties and responsibilities, which have been colloquially referred to as rights within a bundle of sticks, or 'bundle of rights'. The concept of a 'bundle of rights' is viewed as 'a legal construct that has evolved to describe the rights as well as the responsibilities that attend ownership quite independently of whatever "thing" is owned'.[14] The term 'property' denotes a set of 'entitlements' bestowed in law over a particular object to the 'owner' – entitlements or 'rights' that the owner has a better claim to than all others. 'Possession', which is often used interchangeably with the term 'ownership', can be distinguished in that it is a lesser right to ownership and is achieved by obtaining physical control over the object

4 For example, UCB donation and as seen in the case of 'saviour siblings'.

5 Human Fertilisation and Embryology Act 1990, as amended 2008.

6 Human Tissue Act 2004 s 53(2)(b).

7 *Doodeward v Spence* (1908) 6 CLR 406.

8 National Portrait Gallery, 'National Portrait Gallery shows Mark Quinn's frozen "blood head"' *News Release* (10 September 2009) www.npg.org.uk/about/press/marc-quinn-press.php accessed 3 March 2016.

9 Human Tissue Act 2004 s 32.

10 *Evans v United Kingdom* (2006) 43 EHRR 21 Application 6339/05.

11 Surrogacy Agreements Act 1985 s 2(3). For recent calls for reform to surrogacy arrangements, see: K Horsey, 'Surrogacy in the UK: Myth busting and reform'. Report of the Surrogacy UK working group on surrogacy law reform (Surrogacy UK, November 2015) www.surrogacyuk.org/Downloads/Surrogacy%20in%20the%20UK%20Report%20FINAL.pdf, accessed 3 March 2016.

12 *Moore v Regents of the University of California* 793 P 2d 479 (Cal, 1990).

13 *Yearworth v North Bristol NHS Trust* [2009] EWCA Civ 37 at 29 (Lord Judge, CJ).

14 D R Johnson, 'Reflections on the bundle of rights' (2007) 32 *Vermont Law Review* 247–272.

without being granted greater entitlements than the owner.[15] An example of this can be seen in the relationship between a landlord and tenant. The landlord rents the property he owns to a tenant and in doing so confers possessory rights to the tenant, who 'takes possession' of the property. The tenant can now physically control the property and exclude all others from it, including the landlord, with full ownership rights reverting back to the landlord at the end of the tenancy. This principle has been used by the courts to test the possessory nature of a body part. In the criminal case of *R v Bentham* [2005], the defendant was prosecuted for possession of an imitation firearm after concealing his fingers behind his back in the shape of a gun. The House of Lords held that, 'One cannot possess something which is not separate and distinct from oneself. An unsevered hand or finger is part of oneself. Therefore, one cannot possess it.'[16] If one cannot possess one's own body parts, it follows that they cannot own them. It is also well established that since the abolition of slavery[17] one cannot own another person. However, as Harris notes, just because we cannot be made a slave of, this does not necessarily mean that we own ourselves.[18] Exceptions to the no property rule, however, appear to have been made for bodily material such as hair,[19] urine[20] and peripheral blood[21] external to the body and were the subject of theft. In each of the criminal cases, the bodily material was held to be property belonging to another that had been appropriated without their permission.

Is it possible then to extend these limited exceptions outside of the criminal realm? Those who lay claim to materials external to the body would argue that they wish to retain control over them and to seek a remedy should those rights be interfered with. As has been advocated so far in this book, women who participate in UCB banking may wish to seek compensation for property damage should the cells they preserve later become damaged, but this can only be achieved if UCB is deemed property capable of giving rise to damages. Furthermore, in the event of a dispute over the use of the stored cells by competing parties, it is currently unclear who actually 'owns' the cells, if anyone. There have been many powerful arguments made that disputes over property status and ownership rights to bodily material can be more adequately addressed by using property-based models, particularly

15 It is accepted that these are very basic definitional offerings and do not do justice to the complexity of these concepts. For a fuller exploration of the terminology, see: N Hoppe, *Bioequity – Property and the Human Body* (Farnham: Ashgate, 2009) Chapter 4.
16 *R v Bentham* [2005] 1 UKHL 18 at 8 (Lord Bingham).
17 Abolition of Slavery Act 1833.
18 J W Harris, 'Who owns my body?' (1996a) 16 *Oxford Journal of Legal Studies* 1, 55–84.
19 *R v Herbert* (1961) 25 JCL 163; *Director of Public Prosecutions v Smith* [2006] EWHC 94 (Admin).
20 *R v Welsh* [1974] RTR 478.
21 *R v Rothery* [1976] 63 Cr App R 231.

with regard to UCB.[22] This chapter examines the basic principles of property rights – or 'bundles of rights' – and investigates the merits of applying a property law approach to establish the status of UCB for the purposes of a claim in tort; and by analysing existing case law, questions whether UCB can be a bodily material capable of being 'owned' and if so, by whom.

The property law model and rights over cord blood

The law relating to property has been derived from the common law, equity and statute, with the common law being the primary source of property law. Property rights – also known as 'rights in *rem*' – are traditionally distinguished from personal rights, or 'rights in *personam*'. The main difference between the two is that property rights are enforceable against all other parties, often referred to as being held 'against the whole world'. For example, a landowner can exert his property rights over a piece of land that he has full ownership of, preventing anyone else from entering the land without his consent. In contrast, personal rights arise only in situations typically involving two parties, for example, in contractual agreements or duty situations in tort. Unlike the property right, a personal right is only enforceable against parties to the legal relationship.

With regards to the body, Munzer argues that all bodily rights can be divided into personal and property rights. Personal rights respect the right to protect our personal interests and choices, a protection evidenced in the rise of a patient's autonomous decision-making. In contrast, property rights, he advocates, permit the transfer of that property to another gratuitously, such as through donation; or by economic transfer, for example, the right to sell semen. Emily Jackson notes that our notion of rights over our bodies, 'look very much like property rights: a right to use them, to exclude others, and to be compensated for negligently inflicted damage are all rights that also commonly exist in relation to things that we own.'[23]

Honoré[24] provides an account of what the duties and responsibilities of ownership consist of, and in effect make up the key 'sticks' in the rights bundle. He expresses these rights as the right to possess (to take physical control of) a 'thing', the right to use, manage and the power to bequeath it to another, a right to the income from it (to benefit financially or to allow others to derive benefit), a right to its security and a duty to prevent it

22 Notably, see: S R Munzer, 'The special case of property rights in umbilical cord blood for transplantation' (1999) 51 *Rutgers Law Review* 3, 493–568 and S R Munzer and F O Smith, 'Limited property rights in umbilical cord blood for transplantation' (2001) 23 *Journal of Pediatric Hematology* 207–211.

23 E Jackson, *Medical Law: Text, Cases and Materials* (3rd edn, Oxford: Oxford University Press, 2013) p 32.

24 A M Honoré, *Making Law Bind: Essays Legal and Philosophical* (Oxford: Clarendon Press, 1987) p 165. Originally published in A G Guest, *Oxford Essays in Jurisprudence* (Oxford: Oxford University Press, 1961) pp 107–147.

harming others, the right to capital (to sell, give it away, amend or destroy it), to be liable to execution (to have the thing seized to repay a debt) and ownership's residual character in that rights to the thing can expire (such as after death) and those rights transfer to another, including the State.

It should be noted that not *all* of these rights need to exist in order for full ownership to be recognised, only *most* of them.[25] Indeed, Goold notes that, 'few commentators have presented a case for according tissue the status of "property" in the sense that all or most of the rights generally associated with ownership should be exercisable in relation to it'.[26] While it is therefore possible to afford ownership rights without encompassing every essence of ownership, it would appear that some rights are more important than others; for example, the right to possession, from which many of the relevant duties and responsibilities for possessing and controlling that 'thing' then follow. However, Brownsword suggests that the most proprietary rights are those of an exclusionary nature – those that give us the right to exclude others from interfering with or dispossessing us of our property, which is particularly poignant with respect to how we view our bodies (*my* body, *your* body) and exert rights over its protection.[27] As we have seen throughout the chapters on consent (Chapter 4) and standards of care (Chapter 5), these exclusionary rights are also ones that have been prioritised in modern day healthcare jurisprudence. With a shift towards recognising patients as fully autonomous beings, capable of making decisions about their own treatment and having a right to make that choice by working in partnership with healthcare professionals rather than as passive bystanders, autonomy of the body has been afforded greater credence. That said, the body as seen by the judiciary and professionals is one that should not be interfered with without consent, thus *in this sense*, demonstrating the same 'exclusionary rights' in character as property capable of being owned.

Quigley powerfully argues that if the body can demonstrate most of the 'sticks' that constitute ownership, then we as individuals can be viewed as self-owners of our bodies. She states:

> If it can be shown that the body satisfies the criteria for property, anybody who believes in private property ought to be committed to treating it as such. In addition, if we start from a position of self-ownership, this at least raises the presumption of property in the separated parts and products.[28]

25 M Quigley, 'Property and the body: applying Honoré' (2007) 33 *Journal of Medical Ethics* 11, 631–634.

26 I Goold, 'Property or not property? The spectrum of approaches to regulating the use of human bodily material' (2013) 21 *Journal of Law and Medicine* 299.

27 R Brownsword, 'Stem cells, superman, and the report of the select committee' (2002) 65 *Modern Law Review* 568.

28 Quigley, 2007.

However, as our enquiry centres upon whether extracted UCB can be owned, we need not debate the merits of full body ownership as this lies outside the confines of our investigation.[29] Rather, it shall be argued here that the presumption of property arises in UCB because it is a body product that once collected from the umbilical cord at birth, is separate to the birthing mother's body, and in itself, contains most of the elements of ownership. If correct, then it is open for us to determine that UCB is capable of being owned by someone.

So, what can be said of using the bundle of rights as a basis for applying property law to UCB? A mother exerts the right to consent to UCB's procurement and retains exclusive physical control over its storage, donation and use via her informed consent (the right to possession); she has the right to use the UCB in treatment and to determine the terms of that usage, for example who can be granted access to it and whether that be for treatment or research, in addition to being able to withdraw the unit from storage at any time or order that it be used or discarded (the right to manage,[30] to capital and transfer to another). She also has the right to 'give the UCB away' as demonstrated in both directed and general donations. Arguably, her duty to ensure that UCB (as 'property') does not cause harm to its recipient is likely to be discharged via the extensive screening process that the unit endures prior to transplantation. Furthermore, should the mother fail to fulfil her contractual obligations to the storage company then that company holds the rights to recover the debt by extinguishing her right to store the unit and discard it, as indicated by the storage company's terms and conditions of storage. Similarly, in the event of the mother's death, these obligations would be passed to a third party, presumably a family member, who would either meet the financial commitments, withdraw or abandon the stored unit.

It would appear, however, that the right to sell and profit from UCB is absent from Honoré's 'bundle of rights'. Commercialising and commodification are of course common concerns associated with affording property rights in the body and its parts, but should this one missing element prevent UCB from being deemed property for our purposes? It has been suggested that the right to control is distinct from the right to profit.[31] While we may instinctively feel uncomfortable about regarding excised body parts and materials as 'property' for fear of exploiting the body through commodification, Herring

29 It is also worth noting that Harris has argued that there is no need to seek bodily protection via property rights because the law already affords adequate protection via protection to the person torts and the criminal law.

30 As an aside, for publicly donated UCB, the unit may also be 'managed' but only in a very restricted sense because while the unit may be returned to the donor, this remains subject to its availability. Furthermore, once donated, the unit is likely to be regarded as a 'gift', which extinguishes the donor's rights.

31 M S Dorney, '*Moore v. the Regents of the University of California*: balancing the need for biotechnology innovation against the right of informed consent' (1990) 5 *Berkeley Technology Law Journal* 2, 4.

reminds us that, 'it is possible to describe something as property, but then restrict the property rights that can be exercised. A national park is property, but there are severe limitations on how people can use it'.[32] Similarly, in *Yearworth v North Bristol NHS Trust* [2009], Lord Judge, CJ opined that although a pharmaceutical company has ownership rights over their products, their sale is restricted.[33] With this is mind, it is perhaps possible to class UCB as property giving rise to compensation for damage done to it, or as property capable of giving rise to ownership rights in cases involving disputes over its use, without going as far as recognising the right to financially profit from it.

Increasingly then, it appears that UCB demonstrates the requisite 'sticks', but there is one final hurdle. Honoré speaks of possession and control to be taken of a 'thing' – but what attributes does a 'thing' have, and does UCB have it? Douglas offers a property-based model that may elicit some guidance.[34] He argues that a property right against the whole world cannot exist in isolation, rather those rights must attach to something tangible – a physical 'thing'[35] – with the 'thing' being a separate physical entity to the rights-holder. Douglas notes that while we may be tempted to class intellectual property as 'property',[36] he argues that one cannot take physical possession of a person's ideas and it is the 'tangible thing' that he proposes best encapsulates the elements of ownership. What is essential to Douglas' model is that the 'thing' subject to ownership must be a physical, rather than an abstract entity, and must be external to the rights-holder. Arguably, procured UCB is capable of fulfilling this definition – the UCB unit is essentially a vial full of stem cells, which is a physical, tangible 'thing' that is a separate entity to the mother, capable of being physically moved, placed and cryopreserved within a storage unit. As with other everyday examples such as freehold houses, cars, clothing, jewellery, as a rights-holder, the mother can use, exclude others from, store, give away, transfer or destroy that property. Thus, if UCB is a physical, tangible, separate 'thing' that possesses the majority of the element of ownership under Honoré's definition, then UCB is capable of being 'owned'.

32 J Herring, *Medical Law and Ethics* (5th edn, Oxford: Oxford University Press, 2014) p 466.

33 *Yearworth v North Bristol NHS Trust* [2009] EWCA Civ 37 at 45(f)(ii).

34 S Douglas, 'Property rights in human biological material' in: I Goold and others (eds), *Persons, Parts and Property: How Should We Regulate Human Tissue in the 21st Century?* (Oxford: Hart Publishing, 2014a) Chapter 7. See also S Douglas, 'The argument for property rights in body parts: scarcity of resources' (2014b) 40 *Journal of Medical Ethics* 23–26.

35 A commonly used example is the right to reputation. This abstract right can be exerted against the whole world to ensure that one's good name and character are not violated but few would argue that something this non-tangible is a property right.

36 A Rahmatian, 'Intellectual property and the concept of dematerialised property' in: S Bright (ed.), *Modern Studies in Property Law* Vol. 6 (Oxford: Hart Publishing, 2011) pp 361–383 at 362.

If UCB can be owned, who then owns it and can assert property rights over it? Douglas further advocates the importance of the rules of acquisition to his model, expressed as a property right being acquired to a physical thing by taking physical possession of it and being able to transfer it by physically delivering it to another. As discussed above, and as Douglas claims, these acts are only made possible when applied to a physical, tangible thing and make no sense to abstract entities. An example of acquisition by transfer of title can be seen in the American case of *Washington University v Catalona* (2006).[37] Catalona, a university researcher, had built up a valuable database of tissue samples donated by a large number of participants for a cancer research project that he was conducting. When Catalona was offered a position at another university he sought to move the samples with him and gained consent from over 6,000 of his participants to do so. However, he was blocked by the university who argued that as his employer, they retained control over the samples, and consequently sought declaratory relief from the courts on the issue of ownership.

The university won their case. The court held that exclusive possession and control had been acquired by the university on receipt of the donated samples because the donors had transferred all their rights to the samples to the university when they agreed to donate. In spite of the claim that the participants' intention had been to donate the samples to Catalona and not the university, the signed consent form emblazoned with the university's logo suggested otherwise. The court also held that the samples had been donated to the research project as a gift to the university, and although the participants had a right to withdraw their continued participation, this did not equate to a right to continued control;[38] and in the interests of advancing rather than curtailing medical research, it would be contrary to public policy to have research participants calling the shots.[39]

There are some interesting points to be made here. First, the donated samples were excised tissues procured from the participant's body and physically delivered to the university. On receipt, and in recognition that the tissues were not intended to be returned, the transfer of title was made and the university acquired ownership rights of what could be considered either a gift or abandoned by the participants. Regardless, the samples must have been originally 'owned' by the participants for the transfer of title to have been transferred to the university, to have been 'given away' as a gift or simply abandoned. In order words, to transfer, give away or abandon bodily material only makes sense if some form of property rights existed in the first

37 *Washington University v Catalona* 437 F Supp 2d 985 (US Dist 2006).

38 The claim for bailment (that is, the expectation that the samples be at some point returned to them) failed due to lack of evidence that that was the expectation plus the unreasonableness of returning the samples post testing.

39 All points were later upheld in the appeal courts, *Catalona v Washington University* 128 S Ct 1122, 169 L Ed 2d 949 (2008).

place.[40] If this is correct, then likewise, UCB procured from the body of the mother is 'owned' by the mother.[41]

Second, there is the issue of bailment. The five classes of transaction that have been categorised as falling within the definition of bailment were set out in *TRM Copy Centres v Lanwall Services* [2008],[42] one of which being 'the gratuitous deposit of a chattel with the bailee, who is simply to keep it for the bailor'.[43] While the research participants' bailment claim in *Catalona* failed because they were unable to show that they expected the research centre (the bailee) to take possession of their (the bailors') tissue samples, to keep them safe and then return them, the UCB depositor's expectation is different – for them, the stored unit is to be exclusively held until it is returned for their personal use. Clearly, privately stored UCB (which I have argued is property capable of being owned) echoes the nuances of bailment, a breach of which could give rise to damages, and for our purposes, demonstrates that the mother retains ownership of the unit even when deposited with a bailee for safe-keeping.[44]

Few would disagree with the proposition that bodily material and tissue removed from the body during medical treatment, such as an appendix, a cyst or an ingrown toenail are items that patients would not especially want to preserve following removal. In fact, the Nuffield Council on Bioethics have suggested that it is implied in the nature of consent to medical treatment which involves tissue removal that it is abandoned by the person from whom it was removed.[45] UCB, however, is arguably different as rather than retaining its status as a 'waste product', current knowledge of its potential therapeutic utility adds value to it, and one that the mother may want to claim rights to in order to place protection over. As Mason and Laurie point out, 'Value exists in a variety of forms'[46] – this can be a therapeutic

40 For an alternative view, see: J W Harris, *Property and Justice* (Oxford: Oxford University Press, 1996b) p 59.

41 Given that the UCB is obtained from the umbilical cord, we shall consider later in this chapter the ownership rights, if any, of the child.

42 In *TRM Copy Centres v Lanwall Services* [2008] EWCA Civ 382, the five classifications of bailment were set out as: '(1) the gratuitous deposit of a chattel with the bailee, who is simply to keep it for the bailor; (2) the delivery of a chattel to the bailee, who is to do something without reward for the bailee to or with the chattel; (3) the gratuitous loan of a chattel by the bailor to the bailee for the bailee to use; (4) the pawn or pledge of a chattel by the bailor to the bailee, who is to hold it as a security for a loan or debt or the fulfilment of an obligation; and (5) the hire of a chattel or services by the bailor to the bailee for reward' at 10 (Thomas, LJ).

43 *TRM Copy Centres v Lanwall Services* [2008] EWCA Civ 382 at 10 (Thomas, LJ).

44 We shall return to this point later in the chapter via the prism of *Yearworth v North Bristol NHS Trust* [2009] EWCA Civ 37.

45 Nuffield Council on Bioethics, 'Human tissue: ethical and legal issues' (1995) para 9.14 (1).

46 J K Mason and G T Laurie, *Mason and McCall Smith's Law and Medical Ethics* (9th edn, Oxford: Oxford University Press, 2013) p 480.

value, an emotional value (as we saw in the organ retention scandals) or even an artistic value.[47] Perhaps the most controversial, however, is economic value – especially when, in a biotechnological age, vast sums of money can be made from biological products derived from human material. Arguably, the most famous case involving a dispute over the ownership rights of excised bodily material is *Moore v Regents of the University of California* (Cal, 1990).

The curious case of John Moore's spleen

In 1976, John Moore was diagnosed with hairy cell leukaemia. With his consent, he had his spleen and other tissues and blood samples removed by Dr Golde at the Medical School of the University of California at Los Angeles. At a very early stage in his treatment, Golde discovered that Moore's spleen displayed extremely unusual properties from which he could create an immortal cell-line that might commercially be very valuable, a fact that he kept from Moore. Desperate to develop the cell-line further, Golde and a number of researchers at the university proceeded to remove further tissue and blood samples from Moore on 12 different occasions for what he was led to believe was continued treatment for the leukaemia, when in fact the tests were therapeutically unnecessary and were made in an attempt to commercially exploit the cells. At no stage was Moore informed that the additional testing was for research on the excised tissue. After becoming suspicious, he later discovered that Golde and his researcher, Shirley Quan, had obtained a patent over the cell-line and sold it to a drug company for US$15 million and is reported to now be worth US$3bn in related drugs and therapies.[48] Moore filed 13 causes of action against the doctor, the researchers, the university and the drug company in the Californian Superior Court in 1984. The property-based actions were in conversion (that is, as the alleged 'owner' of the cells, the defendants had interfered with his property rights without his consent), a breach of fiduciary duty and lack of informed consent.

At first his claims were unsuccessful, but in his appeal to the California Court of Appeals,[49] the court held that it would be mere 'subterfuge'[50] to call rights and interests in one's own body anything other than 'property', and to not recognise rights in the body would be a violation of human dignity.[51] However, Moore's success in asserting rights over his excised bodily material was short-lived. On further appeal to the Supreme Court of California,[52] the

47 *R v Kelly* [1998] 3 All ER 714.

48 B Merz, 'Biotechnology: spleen-rights' *The Economist* (11 August 1990) p 30.

49 *Moore v Regents of University of California* 249 Cal. Rptr. 494 (Cal. Ct. App 1988)

50 Ibid., at 504–505.

51 Ibid., at 508.

52 *Moore v Regents of University of California* 793 P 2d 479 (Cal, 1990).

court took a completely different view. Taking a personal rights approach rather than property rights, the court held that there had been a breach of fiduciary duty and a lack of informed consent from the unauthorised taking of his cells and non-disclosure of their commercial value, but were reluctant to recognise property rights, especially where no precedent could be found.[53] They also held that as statutory rules relating to burial eroded the ability to resist disposal of excised body parts and material, this further restricted ownership rights. Finally, they declared that it was the job of the legislature to re-address the issue of rights in that material, if it so thought it necessary. As we shall see later, the issue of statutory restrictions preventing property rights was re-addressed in *Yearworth v North Bristol NHS Trust* [2009].[54]

But perhaps more importantly, the court in *Moore* appears to have been persuaded by public policy considerations in that to afford property rights would hinder medical research.[55] They opined that if the use of cells in research was deemed a conversion, then access to much-needed raw materials would either be denied, would thwart medical progress, or researchers would be subject to a 'litigation lottery'. One can imagine a situation where lawyers are frantically trying to unravel the origins of tissue samples used in biotechnology that have produced commercially valuable products in order to track down claimants and pursue claims.[56]

There are two competing views here. To recognise full ownership by the originator of the tissue may 'over-compensate' because it would fail to acknowledge the immense work and skill that researchers and pharmaceutical developers have put into creating a workable product. On the other hand, it is arguably unreasonable to deny the person who made it all possible any stake in the proceeds of his or her body.[57] Mason and Laurie suggest that this dichotomy could be resolved by acknowledging rights according to the level of contribution made to the resultant product. They claim, 'It is entirely reasonable to hold that some financial reward should also be given to the source of the valuable sample while, at the same time, accepting that the majority of the spoils should return to those who have done the work in creating a patentable invention.'[58] The 'source' referred to here is the natural creator of the now 'valuable' biological material – Mr Moore himself (and others like him) – with the researchers adding their own labour and expertise to convert the sample into a commercially viable commodity. That said, if

53 Ibid., at 493.
54 *Yearworth v North Bristol NHS Trust* [2009] EWCA Civ 37.
55 *Moore v Regents of University of California* 793 P 2d 479 (Cal, 1990) at 494–496.
56 Herring, 2014 pp 466–467.
57 Justice Mosk, in his dissenting opinion at 488, expressed that Moore had just as much right to do with his tissue as the defendants had done and that it should have been up to him to negotiate with researchers and the pharmaceutical companies, retaining control over the use of the developed product(s).
58 Mason and Laurie, 2013 p 481.

property rights were recognised on behalf of the originator rather than just awarding compensation for an infringement of his or her personal rights, this need not be full proprietary rights, which could stifle medical research. Rather, a nominal monetary reward could be made in acknowledgement of the original contribution before transfer of the remaining property rights to those who invest time and labour in changing its attributes. Apportioning property rights over physical material in this way makes much more sense as it affords a more meaningful 'right' over what is essentially a 'tangible thing' (as opposed to something intangible such as an idea) without going so far as to recognise full ownership rights that would permit it being sold off to the highest bidder.[59] After all, *most* excised tissue is of little worth in its natural state. It is only the work and skill applied to it that makes it financially attractive – skills unlikely to bestow your average patient undergoing medical treatment.[60]

So how could all this apply to UCB? The 'no property' rule would exclude ownership over the collected UCB unit by anyone, unless, like *Moore*, human intervention had changed its attributes to produce an item of pecuniary value; and in that situation it could only afford rights to those who had input such skill rather than the mother herself. But if an apportionment of rights according to 'contribution' to the end product is workable, then likewise, her contribution of the toil of her labour (and possibly that of the child) in creating the original source could be recognised. However, this is unlikely to be useful for our purposes as it would not address the needs of the mother seeking full compensation for damaged UCB or ownership rights in dispute resolution. We therefore need to look closer at the ability to recognise property rights by means of the application of human skill and how this principle came to be part of the law relating to property in the body.

'Application of work and skill' and the use of cord blood

The notion of property rights flowing from the input of others – or labour theory – is not new and can be traced back to the Australian courts in a decision regarding ownership of a dead two-headed foetus preserved in spirit in a jar. In *Doodeward v Spence* (1908) the claimant sued for the return of a corpse that he had purchased from an auction, which had been originally preserved and kept by the attending doctor to a birth in 1868 and sold to the claimant on his death. The question for the court was whether the 'unique specimen of malfunction' was capable of being owned. Although the law was clear that a human corpse awaiting burial was *nullius in rebus*

59 However, for the purposes of the Theft Act 1968, Section 4(1) defines property as including 'money and all other property, real or personal, including things in action and other intangible property'.

60 For an alternative view, see discussion in: S R Munzer, 'An uneasy case of property rights in body parts' (1994) 11 *Social Philosophy and Policy* 2, 259–286.

(nobody's thing) and that legal authorities ensured a lawful and timely burial, they held:

> when a person has by lawful exercise of work or skill so dealt with a human body or part of a human body in his lawful possession that it has acquired some attributes differentiating it from a mere corpse awaiting burial, he acquires a right to retain possession of it, at least as against any person not entitled to have it delivered to him for the purpose of burial, but subject, of course, to any positive law which forbids its retention under the particular circumstances.[61]

So, the claimant won due to the 'work and skill' that had been originally undertaken upon the corpse.[62] The attending doctor had lawfully acquired an abandoned foetus, applied his technical skill to preserve 'a curiosity' that held 'valuable or interesting information' in the same way that collections of anatomical and pathological specimens are formed and maintained; and was later lawfully sold. According to the court, as displaying the corpse did not offend public health or decency, possessory rights could be afforded to the claimant.

Post *Doodeward* then, the 'no property' rule was no longer absolute. It had attracted a notable exception that has more recently been enshrined in the Human Tissue Act 2004. Section 32 of the Act illustrates the will of parliament by expressing the importance of recognising material that is 'the subject of property because of an application of human skill'.[63] However, the boundaries of 'application of skill' which could transform body parts into property was clarified in *R v Kelly*, a case that determined whether body parts removed by a junior technician at the Royal College of Surgeons on behalf of an artist who wished to use them as moulds for artwork could be 'stolen'. The court held that the College was the rightful owner and had property rights over any lawfully appropriated body part that had 'acquired different attributes by virtue of the application of skill, such as dissection or preservation techniques, for exhibition or teaching purposes'.[64] More recently, the 'production of blocks and slides' was added to the list of recognised human skills in *AB v Leeds Teaching Hospital NHS Trust* [2004], whereas the mere placing of an excised body part in paraffin without any additional preparation was deemed not sufficient.

61 *Doodeward v Spence* (1908) 6 CLR 406 at 414 (Griffith, CJ).

62 As a point of interest, Barton J doubted that given its physical appearance, which he referred to as a 'dead-born fetal monster', it could be considered a corpse that the laws relating to a decent, Christian burial would apply to. 'It had acquired, as the evidence showed, a considerable monetary value, not as a corpse, but as something so unlike an ordinary corpse as to be a curiosity – a well-preserved specimen of nature's freaks'. Clearly our modern day judiciary (and society itself) have come a long way since the 1900s!

63 Human Tissue Act 2004 s 32(9)(c).

64 *R v Kelly* [1998] 3 All ER 714 at 749–750 (Rose, LJ).

In *Dobson v North Tyneside Health Authority* [1996][65] the defendant hospital placed the brain of a deceased patient in paraffin in order to determine the cause of death, which was later discarded. The family sued for unlawful disposal of the brain following attempts to retrieve tissue samples to determine the hospital's negligence. The court held that preparing the brain for post mortem did not equate to attracting property rights and were more concerned with the purpose of the application of skill to the tissue, or rather, its 'intended use'. As the brain had not been preserved, embalmed or stuffed to create a specimen to be used as an exhibit or in teaching but merely held for diagnosis purposes under the coroner's jurisdiction, it was not transformed into property. It would therefore appear that the question over property rights in excised bodily material is influenced by the intended purposes of the end product that has undergone a process of work and skill, with those who exert those skills as having greater claim to property rights over it than either the original source or their family.[66]

If we examine the law in light of *Doodeward*, *Dobson* and *Kelly*, what might we deduce in relation to UCB? It goes without saying that in the creation of UCB, it is the work and skill of the mother's body that toils to feed and nourish the developing embryo, a labour that continues throughout the term of the pregnancy and childbirth. Clearly, the mother's body works hard to maintain the blood within the umbilical cord to sustain the healthy development of the foetus.[67] On Lockean grounds – that ownership rights are grounded by mixing labour with raw materials[68] – the pregnant woman performs exactly that kind of physical work before facing extra risks (as we saw in Chapter 2) to both herself and her baby when she undertakes UCB collection.[69] Indeed, as the Human Tissue Act 2004 includes the notion of 'work and skill', it is possible to conclude that parliament is prepared to recognise Lockean grounds for rights.[70] In terms of the collected UCB's 'intended use', like the tissue that is preserved for teaching, exhibition purposes and artworks, the mother makes the conscious decision to preserve it for future therapeutic use and continues to 'labour' while facing the risks posed to herself and the child.[71] On Lockean theory then, the mother's work involved in the pregnancy, birth and decision-making process places her as the UCB rights-holder.

65 *Dobson v North Tyneside Health Authority* [1996] 4 All ER 479.
66 Mason and Laurie, 2013 p 490.
67 D Dickenson, *Property in the Body – Feminist Perspectives* (Cambridge: Cambridge University Press, 2007) 99.
68 J Locke, *The Second Treatise on Civil Government* (New York: Prometheus Books, 1986) p 20.
69 See also: K Devine, 'Risky business? The risks and benefits of umbilical cord blood collection' (2010d) 18 *Medical Law Review* 330–362.
70 Human Tissue Act 2004 s 32.
71 D Dickenson, *Body Shopping: The Economy Fuelled by Flesh and Blood* (Oxford: Oneworld Publications, 2008) pp 46–49.

However, if we look purely to case law, it is difficult to proclaim the mother's ownership over the cells on these grounds when the cases suggest that the requisite work and skill must be applied *post* extraction from the umbilical cord, changing the unit's original attributes, in order to lay claim over them. With that in mind, can it be said those who *procure* the cells can assert property rights over them instead? As we saw in Chapter 3, the collection process must now be carried out by a qualified UCB collector, normally a midwife or obstetrician or an informal collector such as a phlebotomist. The skill they display in collecting the cells, which constitutes procurement during the third stage of labour, use of multiple needles and competent labelling and packing of the samples, is arguably enough to create 'property' as this certainly requires more human application than simply placing the UCB in a jar of preservative. If correct, then we could potentially argue that private banks (and their storage facilities) could also claim property rights over the cells in which they have input their skill. Storage companies carry out extensive testing on the procured unit to record its characteristics for tracing purposes and ensure the unit's viability for transplantation before subjecting the cells to the appropriate cryopreservation technique deployed by the facility. In the same way as the researchers in *Moore* and the original doctor in *Doodeward* they too have expended skill and expertise that have changed the attributes of the collected UCB.

Yet to suggest that anyone other than the mother could claim property rights over the collected UCB would of course be particularly controversial given that she financially invests in the unit's storage for private use. Unlike a donation made to public UCB banks, where the mother transfers any rights that she may have had in the cells, those who bank privately do not intend to forgo or transfer any rights when they entrust the unit to the private bank's care. On the contrary, the mother's intention is for the unit to be held until she wishes to retrieve and utilise it.

If, however, we look to the UCB's intended purpose or use, the bank and its facility are very unlikely to be able to use the 'application of skill' argument to assert property rights for the following reason. Although it may be possible in the future for a valuable cell-line to be created from the UCB unit by the first person to apply work to the cells, such as occurred in *Moore*, for privately collected UCB, the additional work required could only be done with the mother's consent for she neither abandons the cells (unlike John Moore) nor donates them (as the participants in *Catalona* had done). In other words, the privately collected UCB is procured at the mother's request for an intended purpose and remains under the mother's control and upon whose consent must be sought to deal with the cells in any way other than she proscribes. Furthermore, as the privately held unit is preserved for future use, it cannot be argued that the mother has consented to it being transformed into a specimen for 'exhibition or teaching purposes' as seen in *Kelly*. That said, the *Doodeward* exception of 'work and skill' is unlikely to present the mother with a challenge from others to any rights she may have over the collected and stored cells.

More importantly, as we saw with the law relating to informed consent in the previous chapter, the twenty-first century saw yet another major shift towards placing the patient centre stage – this time in relation to property rights in the body. In *Yearworth v North Bristol NHS Trust* [2009] the Court of Appeal was to bring about a fundamental change in the way that bodily material, excised and stored on behalf of six cancer patients for their own exclusive use was, viewed as 'property'.

Yearworth, 'the right to use' and the generation of cord blood

Six men being treated for cancer accepted Southmead Hospital's offer to store samples of their sperm prior to receiving chemotherapy treatment on the advice of the medical team. On 28/29 June 2008, a malfunction at the storage facility due to the hospital's negligence meant that the men's sperm had 'perished irretrievably'.[72] Each of the men sued in negligence for damage to property and personal injury for the mental harm they suffered of varying degrees and length of time upon realising that unless their fertility recovered naturally, their chances of conceiving a biologically related child were nil. Although the hospital's NHS Trust admitted breach of duty, they argued that the men had not suffered a legally recognised harm. A claim for psychiatric injury of this type must be premised on either foreseeability of physical injury[73] or property damage,[74] neither of which, the Trust argued, applied to the men. They contended that as the damaged sperm was separate to the men's bodies, the men had not suffered any physical harm to themselves; and in light of the common law on property in the body, the men could not claim continued rights over the frozen sperm. Judge Griggs in the trial court agreed with the Trust, holding that the men had not suffered personal injury. In relation to property, and relying on Lord Brandon's judgment in *Leigh and Sillavan Ltd v Aliakmon Shipping Co Ltd* [1996],[75] the Judge held that to claim for property damage in negligence, the claimant must have had legal ownership or possessory title at the time of the loss; before surmising whether sperm was capable at common law of being owned. However, he simply side-stepped this question by declaring that as the provisions of the HFE Act 1990 (as amended 2008) restricted the men's control of the sperm and therefore their ability to use them as they wished, they could not assert

72 *Yearworth v North Bristol NHS Trust* [2009] EWCA Civ 37 at 8 (Lord Judge, CJ).

73 *Page v Smith* [1996] AC 155; *Rothwell v Chemical and Insulating Co Ltd* [2007] UKHL 39.

74 *Attia v British Gas* [1998] 1 QB 304.

75 *Leigh and Sillavan Ltd v Aliakmon Shipping Co Ltd* [1996] AC 785 at 809F (Lord Brandon).

sufficient property rights over them even if they were classed as property[76] and thus their claim must fail – so the men appealed.

In the absence of any precedent from domestic law or legal authority from the Commonwealth or United States relating to damaged bodily material being as extension of physical injury to the body,[77] the Court of Appeal (CA) upheld the Judge's decision that there had been no personal injury. That said, it would be difficult to argue that damage to procured UCB would be construed as personal injury for the purposes of a psychiatric injury claim should such an incident occur. However, the CA took a different view with regards to property. They opined that a decision on whether something is capable of being owned should be reached in context; in this case, ownership should be viewed in light of the breach of duty to take care of the sperm. Within the 'different collections of rights'[78] that constitute ownership, their Lordships drew importance to the men's right to use the sperm. Despite the restrictions on use imposed by statute, the sperm had been ejaculated by the men for a specific purpose – the purpose of fathering a biologically related child, which had now been denied them by the Trust's negligence. Drawing on Honoré's interpretation of the 'Bundle of Rights', the court was clear that 'the right to use' was of fundamental importance to ownership, declaring that, 'The right (liberty) to use at one's discretion has rightly been recognised as a cardinal feature of ownership and the fact that ... certain limitations on use also fall within the standard incidents of ownership does not detract from its importance.'[79]

With the right to use one's property as a 'cardinal feature of ownership' and the restrictions on use imposed by statute foremost in their minds, their Lordships drew upon both *Moore* and a Californian case involving ownership rights over stored sperm. In *Hecht v Superior Court of Los Angeles County* (1993)[80] the claimant argued that her deceased husband's frozen sperm had been bequeathed to her within his Will for her use, a fact disputed by the deceased's children from a previous relationship. Distinguishing *Moore* on the grounds that the claimant had not intended to exert control over his spleen post operation, the court held in favour of Ms Hecht, recognising the purpose of directing the sperm's use and in doing so acknowledged that parts

76 *Yearworth v North Bristol NHS Trust* [2009] EWCA Civ 37 at 25–27 (Lord Judge, CJ).

77 Counsel for the claimants attempted to invoke the German case of *Walkin v South Manchester Health Authority* [1995] 1 WLR 1543 in which a negligent sterilisation resulted in the birth of a child. The claimant successfully argued that the unwanted pregnancy was a physical injury to her body within the meaning of the Limitation Act 1980 on which she relied. The Court of Appeal in *Yearworth*, however, did not accept that the term 'physical injury' could so be extended to the men's sperm because unlike the unwanted child, the sperm was external to their physical bodies.

78 *Yearworth v North Bristol NHS Trust* [2009] EWCA Civ 37 at 28 (Lord Judge, CJ).

79 Ibid. (Lord Judge, CJ quoting Professor Honoré).

80 *Hecht v Superior Court of Los Angeles County* (1993) 20 Cal. Rptr. 2d 275.

or products of a living body could be owned.[81] That said, their Lordships in *Yearworth* stated, 'Indeed, it is hard to regard ownership of stored sperm for the purpose of directing its use following death as other than a step further than that which the men invite us to take in the present case'.[82] Persuaded by American jurisprudence, their Lordships were about to take the first tentative steps towards recognising the ownership of sperm property rights in sperm, but first sought to examine the argument accepted by the trial judge, and again advanced by counsel for the Trust in the CA, that *restrictions* imposed on the use of bodily material prevented its ownership, a factor that had also influenced the denial of ownership rights to John Moore.

Counsel for the Trust had argued that, 'the effect of the [HFE Act 1990, as amended 2008] was to eliminate any rights of ownership of the sperm otherwise vested in the men for the purposes of an action in negligence'.[83] In other words, as only licence holders were authorised to offer fertility services, store or prepare sperm for human application, the men alone could not have directed its use in any particular way, thus the Act constrained the men's control. Furthermore, the 'twin pillars' of the Act, namely welfare and consent, dictate that any request to use the sperm for reproductive purposes would be fettered by the need to consider the welfare of the prospective child and any other child affected by the birth; and in addition, the Act proscribes that sperm cannot be stored indefinitely, further restricting control.[84] However, the CA rejected this contention. The negative control that the men held through the Act's rigorous consent provisions were of equal importance, and were deemed by the court to be 'a fundamental feature of ownership'.[85] In light of the importance of 'the right to use' and on considering that the storage facility was unable to store, use or to treat anyone other than the men without their permission, and that only the men could consent to its withdrawal and set the terms of that consent, their Lordships were unpersuaded by the restrictions argument and expressed that this did not prevent sperm being classed as property.[86]

Pausing for a moment to consider UCB, what analogies might be drawn from the equivalent statute, the Human Tissue Act 2004 and its associated Regulations? Like those who engage the services of a clinic offering assisted reproductive technologies (ART), women who wish to store[87] and use[88] UCB

81 The Supreme Court in *Yearworth* noted that in the UK, future use of stored sperm by a co-habitant would be provided for by the consent provisions of the HFE Act 1990, as amended 2008.

82 *Yearworth v North Bristol NHS Trust* [2009] EWCA Civ 37 at 40 (Lord Judge, CJ).

83 Ibid., at 41 (Judge, CJ).

84 Ibid., at 42(a)–(f).

85 Ibid., at 45(f) (iii).

86 Ibid., at 44(a)–(f).

87 Human Tissue Act 2004 s 1(d) for storage for use for a purpose specified in Part 1 of Schedule 1 of any relevant material which has come from a human body.

88 Human Tissue Act 2004 s 1(f) for use for a purpose specified in Part 1 of Schedule 1 of any relevant material which has come from a human body.

can only do so with the assistance of a licence-holder who is themselves confined to carry out activities for scheduled purposes only. Akin to the restrictions argument, the women's ability to direct the use of privately stored UCB is, like sperm, subject to constraints. However, those who store UCB are also afforded the same negative controls identified in the *Yearworth* claimants – the ability to exclude all others from assessing and using the unit without their consent and having sole control over the unit's withdrawal or destruction.[89] Moreover, as the court in *Yearworth* has declared consent and 'the right to use' to be fundamental features of ownership, it could be argued that privately held UCB demonstrates the same characteristics. First, the purpose of its collection and storage is for the future treatment of the child or sibling should it be needed, and second, the ability to direct its use is at the bequest of the mother via the stringent consent provisions of the 2004 Act. Indeed, consent is an overarching feature of the Human Tissue Act 2004, even more so than the HFE Act 1990 (as amended 2008). Clearly then, UCB exudes the same hallmarks of ownership as the claimants' sperm.

But what of the application of human skill to excised bodily material? Although the court in *Yearworth* accepted that the 'work and skill' applied to cryopreserving the men's sperm could be encompassed by the *Doodeward* exception, it held that they 'were not content to see this area founded upon the principle'.[90] Despite the principle being incorporated within Section 32 (9) of the Human Tissue Act 2004, the CA noted that the section's wording did not preclude property being recognised on some other basis,[91] especially as the distinction between recognising property in tissues that had been subject to work and skill, and those that had not was 'not entirely logical'[92] and the principle itself lacked 'a solid foundation'.[93] Looking outside of this principle, they found that for the purposes of negligence, the sperm was to be treated as property for the following reasons: the men alone had generated and ejaculated the sperm;[94] their negative control over its use remained absolute;[95] the ability to sanction destruction of the sperm was a fundamental feature of ownership[96] and the 'right to use' the sperm was of primary importance;[97] and whilst a licence-holder has duties that arise in relation to storage and use, 'no person, whether human or corporate, other than each man has any rights in relation to the sperm which he has produced'.[98] On these principles, it is clearly arguable that negligently damaged UCB

89 Subject to the terms of the storage contract being fulfilled.
90 *Yearworth v North Bristol NHS Trust* [2009] EWCA Civ 37 at 45(d) (Lord Judge, CJ).
91 Ibid., at 38.
92 Ibid., at 45.
93 Ibid., at 45(c) and (d).
94 Ibid., at 45(f)(i).
95 Ibid., at 45(f)(ii).
96 Ibid., at 45(f)(iii).
97 Ibid., at 45(f)(v).
98 Ibid., at 45(f)(iv).

intended for private use can in the same way be classed as property. But can it be said that like the men's sperm, the UCB has been generated by the mother's body alone? After all, the CA clearly placed some importance on this feature when stating, 'By their bodies, they alone generated and ejaculated the sperm'[99] as it was the first factor referred to in their judgment.[100]

So, how is UCB generated? The starting point would have to be the pregnant woman's body in that it is from her body that the child, placenta and birthing tissue emerges. The UCB is retrieved from the umbilical cord, which provides an uninterrupted flow of blood from the placenta to the foetus during its development. The placenta is comprised of two parts – the basal plate, which is of maternal origin and has tissues and cells that are immunologically and genetically identical to the mother; and likewise, the chorion plate, which is of embryonic origin. The umbilical cord is a conduit comprised of two umbilical arteries and an umbilical vein surrounded by Wharton's jelly, with the arteries coiled around the vein in a helical fashion.[101] The maternal and foetal blood is separated by the placental membrane, and while they come into very close proximity, they do not mix. Rather, the vital maternal–foetal exchange of nutrients and gases are provided by villi within the placenta.[102]

While the mother toils to sustain the pregnancy and development of the child, there does appear to be a process that requires an element of labour from the foetus: the foetus sends oxygen-deficient blood via the umbilical arteries within the umbilical cord to the mother who receives it and then through her own respiratory function oxygenates the blood and returns it to the foetus via the umbilical vein. The respiratory function in oxygenating the blood within the umbilical cord looks very much like a two-way process – the foetus mixes its labour with the deoxygenated blood to send it to the mother for oxygenation. Viewed in this sense, is it possible to argue that the mother and child 'generate it' together on a developmental basis with the mother tasked with providing oxygen to the deoxygenated blood cells up until the moment of birth? Possibly so. And if we take a step back, it could also be said that the process of pregnancy is in itself a two-way street that generates or 'produces' a full-term child – without the mother there would be no child, and without the developing foetus, there would be no pregnancy. Without either, there would be no UCB, and on this basis, it would therefore be difficult to argue that the mother had, like the *Yearworth* men, 'generated it alone'.

99 Ibid., at 45(f)(i).

100 An alternative view is that despite being the first factor mentioned by the court, this does not necessarily mean that any special weight was given to it. I am grateful to Professor Donna Dickenson for this observation.

101 V L Ferguson and R B Dobson, 'Bioengineering aspects of the umbilical cord' (2009) 144S *European Journal of Obstetrics & Gynecology and Reproductive Biology* S108–S113.

102 N M Gude and others, 'Growth and function of the normal human placenta' (2004) 114 *Thrombosis Research* 397–407.

As an alternative to the proposition that UCB belongs solely to the mother, it may therefore be possible to argue that the child also has rights by virtue of its own labour in UCB's development. However, the second part of the CA's reasoning – that the men themselves procured the sperm by the process of ejaculation – may present as a stumbling block in the context of UCB because statutory requirements prohibit collections by non-qualified personnel, which includes most birthing women,[103] thus the analogy in the procurement of both sperm and UCB falls short. However, there are two things to be said here. First, when the men ejaculated for the purposes of sperm preservation for future use in treatment (as opposed to for pleasure), they would have done so under certain clinical restrictions.[104] Following the implementation of the European Union Tissues and Cells Directive (EUTCD) the procurement of gametes intended for human use must be licensed by the Human Fertilisation and Embryology Authority (HFEA) or be subject to an agreement with a licensed service to ensure its quality, safety and traceability. That said, the ejaculation of sperm intended for human application is just as much regulated as the collection of UCB. Second, although the men physically ejaculated the sperm themselves without third party assistance, it is very impractical to suggest that a pregnant woman in the third stage of labour would be sufficiently capable of halting the birthing process to collect the cord blood herself, especially when having undergone hours of physical labour and whilst heavily medicated.

It is therefore arguable that as an alternative to the mother as rights owner, any property rights are jointly owned by the mother and child as the child plays its part in producing the blood that is procured. Furthermore, although the UCB is always collected from the mother's side of the clamped cord, it makes no difference to the volume or viability of the unit whether the UCB is taken from the arteries (the foetal deoxygenated blood) or the umbilical vein (the maternal oxygenated blood). Moreover, in practice, both the artery and vein is cannulated separately if insufficient blood volume is anticipated.[105] That said, it is both oxygenated and deoxygenated blood that is collected and stored for future use, and by their joint generation it is possible to argue that both are afforded property rights in the same way as the claimant's in *Yearworth*.

Disputed cord blood rights and 'best interests'

What is now difficult for the child, however, is that as a newborn and minor, they are unable to assert any of the rights over the UCB and instead are

103 Notwithstanding the possibility of a birthing mother also being professionally qualified, such as a midwife or phlebotomist.

104 HFE Act 1990, as amended 2008 s 14.

105 I am very grateful to Dr Kouroush Saeb-Parsy, University lecturer and Honorary Consultant in Transplant Surgery, Addenbrooke's Hospital, Cambridge for his detailed explanation of the UCB collection process.

reliant upon the parents to make decisions on their behalf in their best interests. In this respect, their corresponding right in property law to procure, store, direct its use and withdraw or destroy would likely fall to the mother as 'joint owner' and as a person with parental responsibility. While it could be argued that by their biological input into the creation of the embryo, the father might also accrue rights over the UCB, the ability to consent to the collection procedure – which involves the physical touching of the woman's body – falls squarely within the mother's remit, and akin to abortion law, the father is powerless to exert control over her body. Indeed, following the judgments in *Re MB (An adult: Medical Treatment)*[106] and *St Georges Healthcare NHS Trust v S*[107] it is clear that it is the competent pregnant woman alone who can consent to anything done to her body, even if medical intervention would be in her or her unborn child's best interests.[108]

Following consent to the procurement, the mother then consents to the storage of the UCB via a contractual arrangement where it is held in a private account until it is withdrawn or the child reaches the age of 18, an age stipulation made by most private banks. In this respect, the private industry recognises ownership rights in the child upon reaching the age of maturity, which in itself implies that the mother simply acts as trustee of the UCB on the child's behalf until such an age and the bank's function is to act as a Trust.[109] Given our discussion on *Gillick*-competency in Chapter 4, setting such an age restriction may appear at odds with the *Gillick* test. Indeed, Salvaterra and others have argued that such a stipulation is controversial and that the child should have the ability to decide upon the disposition of the UCB on achieving competency.[110] However, if viewed in terms of a Trust, this is no different from other forms of 'investments' held until the age of maturity.

106 *Re MB (An adult: Medical Treatment)* [1997] 2 FLR 426.

107 *St George's Healthcare NHS Trust v S* [1998] 3 All ER 673.

108 It should also be noted that if the child suffers harm, and it is proven that collecting their UCB in case of a future need was not in their 'best interests', it is possible to envisage a claim being made against the mother on the child's behalf. As Levy and Blickstein have observed, 'obtaining cord blood for future autologous transplantation of stem cells needs early cord clamping and seems to conflict with the infant's best interests'. See T Levy and I Blickstein, 'Timing of cord clamp revisited' (2006) 34 *Journal of Perinatal Medicine* 4. Conversely, a court can authorise medical treatment under Section 8 of the Children Act 1989, but will only do so where it promotes the welfare of the child and is therefore in the child's 'best interests'.

109 In terms of public cord blood banking, Stewart and others provide a very powerful argument for these banks to be regarded as Charitable Trusts. See C Stewart and others, 'Public umbilical cord blood banking and Charitable Trusts' in: I Goold and others (eds), *Persons, Parts and Property: How Should We Regulate Human Tissue in the 21st Century?* (Oxford: Hart Publishing, 2014) Chapter 5.

110 E Salvaterra and others, 'The ethics of cord blood banking in light of ownership, informed consent and solidarity' (2006) 4 *Cell Preservation Technology* 2, 91–96.

Once UCB is stored, it is conceivable that an inter-parental dispute could arise over its future use. For example, conflict may arise over which family (or extended family) member should utilise the cells should someone within the familial group fall ill. Whereas one parent may wish to keep the UCB stored for the intended child, the other may wish to withdraw it from storage to treat another family member. In such a situation, a father may seek to side-step any potential claim in property and simply assert rights via an alternative route. First, if he has parental responsibility for the child, he may attempt to assert his legal rights to ensure what he believes to be in the child's best interests. But, as Herring points out, the 'best interests' concept is 'no more than a reflection of one person's view'[111] and often the courts are called upon to act as adjudicator in the case of disputes.

Whilst the Mental Capacity Act 2005 does not apply to children, the courts may look to the Act by way of analogy when determining the welfare of the child. With regards to 'best interests', Section 4 of the Act provides that all 'relevant circumstances'[112] must be taken into account to determine whether an act is performed for the benefit of the child – the circumstances of which are defined as those 'which it would be reasonable to regard as relevant'.[113] An issue that may be regarded as relevant in this type of scenario is whether a child whose UCB has been stored for its future use would suffer a benefit or detriment if it were released to treat another. For example, in *Re Y (Adult Patient) transplant: Bone Marrow* [1997][114] the sister of a mentally and physically disabled woman required a bone marrow transplant and Y was a potential donor. Despite being unable to consent, the court declared that her bone marrow could be harvested. The court reasoned that Y would gain an emotional, psychological and social benefit by donating to her sister, enhanced by the benefit that it would give Y's mother, her main carer.

In an American case, the court gave judgment in order to avoid a detriment. In *Strunk v Strunk* (1969)[115] the court approved the donation of an incompetent adult's kidney to his brother on the grounds that if the brother died, this would cause greater physiological and emotional harm to the donor than would arise from having the operation. Unlike these cases, however, the use of a stored UCB unit would not involve an invasive procedure or pose any additional risks to the donor child.

Second, if the father has jointly engaged in contractual obligations with the mother and the private bank, he may simply seek his rights within the contract. In this situation, the terms of the contract and whether any

111 Herring, 2014 at p 208.
112 Mental Capacity Act 2005 s 4(11).
113 Ibid., s 4(11)(b).
114 *Re Y (Adult Patient) transplant: Bone Marrow* [1997] Fam 110.
115 *Strunk v Strunk* 445 SW 2d 145 (1969).

contingency arrangements were built into the contract[116] would be at the heart of any resolution. However, personal communications with two UK commercial UCB companies regarding contractual obligations in the event of an inter-parental dispute have revealed that the issue of the father's or extended family's 'rights' are a moot point. Smart Cells regard the mother to be the legal donor of the cells and upon whose authority they seek to store cells; and upon whose consent is sought to release the UCB until the child turns 18.[117] Similarly, Biovault Family would seek consent of the mother before the unit is released as they regard her to be the 'legal guardian' of the cells until the child reaches 18.[118] It would therefore appear that the commercial industry itself recognises the child as the owner of the cells, with the mother acting as a trustee on his or her behalf retaining control over the stored UCB until the child reached the age of maturity, and the father falling outside the equation.[119]

As we saw earlier, consent was deemed in *Yearworth* as a 'fundamental feature of ownership', a view supported by the Nuffield Council on Bioethics who suggest that a preferable approach to disputes over collected material should be resolved according to the nature of consent given to the initial procedure for removal.[120] If we follow this reasoning, the mother's rights clearly trump all others in the race to claim ownership in UCB, which would also place her in a strong position to assert ownership rights in the event of a dispute over the stored cells. It would therefore appear that should damage to, or disputes over, stored UCB occur, the outcome in *Yearworth* certainly lends itself to UCB being capable of being owned, and the mother would be best placed to assert property rights over the cells on behalf of herself and the child.

116 In *Evans v Amicus Healthcare* [2004] EWCA Civ 727, one party to a contractual agreement to store a frozen embryo was able to veto its use by withdrawing consent prior to the embryo's implantation, which the court upheld. As a direct consequence of this case, consent forms now allow participants to specify certain mutually agreed arrangements for stored embryos. Furthermore, amendments to HFE Act 1990 in 2008 (Schedule 3 para. 4A) now provides a 12-month 'cooling-off period', a time span within which embryos cannot be used or destroyed but in which couples are encouraged to reach an amicable agreement.

117 Personal communication with Smart Cells customer advisor by email, 13 March 2016.

118 Personal communication with Biovault Family customer advisor by email, 13 March 2016.

119 It should be noted, however, that an alternative view on consent has been advanced. Stewart and others have argued that the consent process should, 'be inclusive and representative of the different family interests in the cord blood', see C Stewart and others, 'Ethical and legal issues raised by cord blood banking – the challenges of the new bioeconomy' (2013) 199 *The Medical Journal of Australia* 4, 290–292. This view is supported by Pertini who highly recommends the involvement of the father in the consent process due to his shared parental authority with the mother. See C Petrini, 'Umbilical cord blood collection, storage and use, ethical issues' (2010) 8 *Blood Transfusion* 3, 139–148.

120 Nuffield Council on Bioethics, 1995 para 9.14 (2).

While the tort of negligence could therefore provide a cause of action, there is perhaps a more lucrative option for negligently damaged UCB and/or the mental distress caused by their loss – an action in either contract or bailment.

Contract and bailment – an alternative course of action for damaged UCB?

As the claimants in *Yearworth* discovered, suing for mental harm in the tort of negligence presents many hurdles[121] as the claim must be framed within personal injury or property damage, and is only available to those suffering from a legally recognised harm.[122] Furthermore, they were unable to claim in contract because the NHS Trust had stored the sperm gratuitously as part of their treatment, which meant that they were unable to claim for mental distress, which would have been available to them for breach of contract.[123] Case law in this area has indicated that a claim for mental distress can be recovered in contracts where 'the very object of a contract is to provide pleasure, relaxation, peace of mind or freedom from molestation',[124] a provision that should be regarded by the courts as 'a major or important object'[125] of the contract. Indeed, it would be open for a mother who contracts with a private storage company to claim in this manner for breach of a term within the contractual agreement because storage of UCB is undertaken in order to provide 'peace of mind' for the future and is 'the very object'[126] of the agreement. This view is further supported by *Johnson v Unisys Ltd* [2001],[127] a case in which the House of Lords defined the categories of contract in which mental distress could be claimed as, 'contracts which are not purely commercial but which have as their object the provision of enjoyment, comfort, peace of mind or other non-pecuniary personal or family benefits'. Few would argue that this does not fit the category of a contract for private UCB banking.

Although the CA in *Yearworth* found in the claimants' favour with regards to property of the sperm, they were invited, notwithstanding their claim in tort, to advance arguments for a distinct cause of action against the Trust in the law of bailment. They reasoned that as the men had ownership of the sperm in tort, then it followed that they would hold the lesser possessory

121 Primarily, the claimant must be classed as either a primary victim (in the zone of danger to the original incident) or as a secondary victim (as a witness to the event).

122 Examples such as clinical depression, post-traumatic stress disorder (PTSD), myalgic encephalomyelitis (ME) to name a few.

123 *Jarvis v Swan Tours Ltd* [1973] 1 QB 233; *Watts v Marrow* [1991] 1 WLR 1421; *Farley v Skinner* [2001] UKHL 49.

124 *Watts v Marrow* [1991] 1 WLR 1421 at 1445G (Bingham, LJ).

125 *Farley v Skinner* [2001] UKHL 49 at 24 (Lord Steyn).

126 Ibid., at 24 (Lord Steyn).

127 *Johnson v Unisys Ltd* [2001] UKHL 13 at 70 (Lord Millett).

rights as bailors of it,[128] but that a claim in bailment would produce a more favourable measure of damages than in tort.[129] They described bailment as arising when the bailee acquires exclusive possession or a right to a chattel, even on a temporary basis, and a duty to take reasonable care of the chattel will fall to the bailee.[130] Counsel for the Trust relied upon the earlier examined case of *Washington University v Catalona* (2006)[131] arguing that as the research participants had failed in their bailment claim because they had abandoned any possessory rights to their tissue once they donated it to the university, then likewise, the claimants had also abandoned any rights to the sperm. However, the CA rejected this argument on the grounds that, in their view, the university was not a bailee of the sperm but were simply donees who had received bodily tissue as an unconditional gift from donors that had no intention of retaining any possessory rights in.[132] That said, the men's sperm was in a different category. Although no contractual bailment existed, the men had entered into a gratuitous bailment with the Trust, which attracted a duty of responsibility to take care of the sperm.[133] This was especially so as the NHS Trust held themselves out to deploy special skill in the sperm's cryopreservation, a promise that they had breached.[134] Accordingly, the men's sperm was declared property for the purposes of tort and bailment; and in bailment, both psychiatric harm and a modest recovery for mental distress[135] could be claimed against a gratuitous bailee.

So, could the law of bailment provide an alternative remedy in a UCB context? If we look to the outcome of the American case *York v Jones* (1989),[136] the law of bailment has successfully been argued in relation to frozen embryos. However, Quigley expresses some doubts about its usefulness outside of a gamete-related claim. She states,

> While it seems likely that similar reasoning [to *Yearworth*] would obtain in other cases involving gametes (and probably embryos), it is not clear that it would hold in cases involving other tissues. This is because great

128 *Yearworth v North Bristol NHS Trust* [2009] EWCA Civ 37 at 47 (Lord Judge, CJ).

129 Ibid., at 47 (Lord Judge, CJ).

130 Ibid., 48(a)–(i).

131 *Washington University v Catalona* 437 F Supp 2d 985 (US Dist 2006) and later upheld in the appeal court, *Catalona v Washington University* 128 S Ct 1122, 169 L Ed 2d 949 (2008).

132 *Yearworth v North Bristol NHS Trust* [2009] EWCA Civ 37 at 48(e) (Lord Judge, CJ).

133 A gratuitous bailment is one that exists without consideration passing from the bailor to the bailee, see *Coggs v Bernard* (1703) 92 E.R. 107.

134 *Yearworth v North Bristol NHS Trust* [2009] EWCA Civ 37 at 58 (Lord Judge, CJ).

135 Their Lordships were persuaded by the Australian bailment case of *Graham v Voigt* (1989) 95 FLR 146 and the Ontario case of *Mason v Westside Cemeteries Ltd* (1996) 135 DLR (4th) 361 that recovery for mental distress could be awarded for breach of a gratuitous bailment.

136 *York v Jones* (1989) 717 F. Supp. 421 (E.D. Va. 1989).

> emphasis was placed on the mental distress/psychiatric injury suffered by the men due to the implication of the loss of the sperm for their future chances of fatherhood. While cases involving other tissues may well be actionable in bailment, they are unlikely to attract the same level of damages as those involving gametes or embryos.[137]

It is arguably true that denying the chance of parenthood is likely to provoke a traumatic mental reaction in someone who has been denied the opportunity to become a parent to a biological *future* child due to a breach of duty – a loss so unimaginable that mental distress is at least a likely consequence of a storage company's failings. But it is also at least arguable that a parent who is denied the opportunity to utilise privately stored UCB – a biological resource that could potentially save the child's life – when faced with an *existing* sick child would also suffer the same level of mental distress. Of course, there is no guarantee that a UCB-transplant would be successful, but neither is there a guarantee that utilising frozen gametes would result in the birth of a live child. Similarly, while parenthood may be achieved by the natural restoration of a claimant's sperm or via other means such the use of donor sperm, adoption or fostering, there may be alternative methods of treatment available to a sick child outside of UCB use; but regardless, the foreseeable mental anguish experienced by the news that the much-needed biological resource has been damaged or lost would be all too real. After all, by its perceived value and intended use, and unlike other abandoned post-operative body tissue such as a spleen or appendix, privately stored UCB has been stored for an exacting purpose, just as the men's sperm in *Yearworth* had been.

With UCB being presented here as property capable of actionable damage, one further type of claim might be available for the mother who loses the opportunity to privately store and/or use UCB. In cases where the UCB has been negligently procured or stored, it may be possible to claim for a 'loss of chance' to utilise the cells.

'Loss of chance' claims in property-based cord blood claims

While a claim for 'loss of a chance' has been recognised in contract law[138] and in economic loss claims,[139] recent clinical negligence cases involving personal injury have failed, primarily due to the claimant being unable to demonstrate

137 M Quigley, 'Property: the future of human tissue. *Jonathan Yearworth and Others v North Bristol NHS Trust* [2009] EWCA Civ 37' (2009) 17 *Medical Law Review* 457–466.

138 *Chaplin v Hicks* [1911] 2 KB 786. However, any damages in contract for UCB are likely to be nominal.

139 *Allied Maples Group v Simmons and Simmons* [1995] 1 WLR 1602; *Dixon v Clement Jones Solicitors* [2004] EWCA Civ 1005; *Kitchen v Royal Air Force Association* [1958] 2 All ER 241.

on conventional causal principles (that is, on the balance of probabilities) an *actual* loss of a chance to achieve a better outcome.[140] In *Gregg v Scott* [2005],[141] the negligent diagnosis of cancer led to a delay in treatment, which reduced Gregg's chance of a full recovery from 42 to 25 per cent. The term 'full recovery' was couched in terms of loss of the prospect of survival for more than ten years from the date of his initial treatment. However, as he only had a 42 per cent chance of a full recovery before the negligent diagnosis (rather than a 50+ per cent), causation was not made out – moreover, when the case reached the House of Lords eight years later,[142] the claimant was still alive and the chance of losing a 'disease free ten-year survival'[143] had not yet been demonstrated and the 'adverse outcome'[144] was therefore very much like a tossed coin that was still in the air.[145] Further, the complexities involved in attempting to introduce liability for the loss of a chance in personal injury claims led Baroness Hale to declare that it should not be done,[146] a view later confirmed in the personal injury case, *Wright (a Child) v Cambridge Medical Group* [2011] EWCA Civ 669. As I have argued above, and akin to *Yearworth*, damage to procured UCB cannot give rise to a personal injury claim per se; and on this basis, precludes a claim for a lost chance to use the cells.

Yet while liability for a lost opportunity should therefore not be entertained in these types of cases, Hale did not preclude other types of damage and instead argued that, 'some kinds of negligence do result in liability for loss of chance'.[147] This perhaps opens the door for a UCB-related claim based on property just as the courts have allowed an action for loss of chance in financial situations.[148] Indeed, the door also appears to remain open in situations 'where the lost chance claimed has *literally* been lost',[149] which could apply to cases where negligence has denied the UCB account holder the opportunity to use the cells.[150]

But arguably, the lost chance to use procured UCB is not the same as losing a chance to prolong life (as Gregg was attempting to do) because the loss of the UCB unit first faces another set of variables – the claimant must

140 *Hotson v East Berkshire Area Health Authority* [1985] 3 All ER 167.
141 *Gregg v Scott* [2005] 2 AC 176.
142 Their Lordships deliberated over the decision for an unusually long time and Mr Gregg was a few months short of the ten-year 'survival' term when the judgment was eventually handed down.
143 *Gregg v Scott* [2005] 2 AC 176 at 197 (Baroness Hale).
144 Ibid., at 190 (Lord Phillips).
145 Ibid., at 211 (Baroness Hale).
146 Ibid., at 226 (Baroness Hale).
147 Ibid., at 218 (Baroness Hale). It should also be noted that *Gregg* included two powerful dissenting arguments and one weak decision in the majority judgment.
148 *Allied Maples Group v Simmons and Simmons* [1995] 1 WLR 1602.
149 K Horsey and E Rackley, *Tort Law* (4th edn, Oxford: Oxford University Press, 2015) p 264.
150 A claim for 'loss of chance' could also apply in cases of negligent storage of a private bank – however, it is more likely that a claim in contract and/or bailment would be pursued.

first show that but-for the negligent procurement, a unit of sufficient quality and quantity would have been obtained for transplant purposes *and* that the unit would have been needed for future treatment, before espousing the clinical odds of the treatment's success for that particular recipient. Rather, this would be classed as a hypothetical future loss, and akin to Gregg, the 'adverse outcome' would not yet have materialised.

However, this may not preclude a claim for damage to a UCB unit collected for a directed sibling-related transplant where the UCB is the recipient's only hope of a cure. As there is a 75–90 per cent chance of a one-year survival rate in sibling HLA-type matched UCB transplants,[151] if the UCB unit had been procured non-negligently, it would more likely than not have provided a 'cure' for the recipient. That said, such a claim is likely to reach the causation threshold that eluded Gregg. Moreover, if we consider other non-personal injury 'loss of chance' claims that were successful, such as the case of Mrs Chaplin who successfully sued for the loss of her chance to win an employment contract in a chorus line,[152] and that of Mr Kitchen who successfully sued his solicitor for the lost chance of bringing a civil action for damages,[153] a UCB-related claim may not be out of the question. After all, it is arguably no more speculative that Mrs Chaplin would have actually won the beauty contest she entered or that Mr Kitchen would have won his civil claim had he been given the opportunity to have the case heard than it is to argue that a UCB-transplant would not be successful.

Conclusion

This chapter has sought to unravel whether UCB is capable of being classed as property for the purposes of a claim in negligence and to determine on a property-based analysis whether UCB is capable of being owned, and if so, who has greater rights over it. By examining Honoré's 'bundle of rights' and case law involving property in the body in relation to excised body parts and materials, it has been argued here that it is possible for the mother and child to jointly hold property rights in the cells along similar reasoning as those adopted by the Court of Appeal in *Yearworth*. By her body the mother generates UCB – and as an alternative, this is a joint enterprise with the child who inputs labour into the process. The UCB is extracted from the umbilical cord with the mother's consent and is stored for the intended purpose of its future use. Subject to the contractual arrangements of the private bank, the mother alone retains control over the cells on her child's behalf, including retaining, withdrawing or destroying the cells; and her consent is sought before release of the unit is authorised by the storage company. Any

151 B H Lubin and others, 'Cord blood banking for potential future transplantation' (2007) 119 *Pediatrics* 1.

152 *Chaplin v Hicks* [1911] 2 KB 786.

153 *Kitchen v Royal Air Force Association* [1958] 2 All ER 241.

restrictions to the mother's control imposed by statute are no greater than those faced by the men in *Yearworth* and therefore do not present as a bar to recognising ownership rights in UCB. As the 'right to use' and consent have been declared 'fundamental features' of ownership by the judiciary, UCB is capable of being owned.

So whose cord blood it? Academic literature relating to the use, regulation and banking of UCB has tended to raise the question of its ownership without addressing it head-on. However, a few notable scholars have attempted to do so. Witte surmises that, 'In theory, because the cord blood once belonged to the infant, it would be property of that infant',[154] but does not explain how this conclusion has been reached. Similarly, Munzer determines that it is the child's property but his reasoning is a little unclear. Contrary to my assertion that UCB is collected from both the maternal vein and foetal arteries within the umbilical cord, Munzer claims that there is an ambiguity between whether UCB is harvested from the placenta or umbilical cord and further proclaims that, '[t]he ambiguity hinders a precise description of the harvesting procedure, but otherwise is of no consequence, for it is always the blood of the newborn that is at issue'.[155] While this process of deduction is hard to make out, his adoption of the newborn as owner is likely founded upon the claim that umbilical cord's tissues and cells 'are genetically and immunologically the same as those of the foetus'.[156] But as Dickenson points out, this argument is flawed because, '[i]n genetic and immunological terms, placenta and cord blood contain traits of both the mother and the fetus'.[157] Indeed, even the Royal College of Obstetricians and Gynaecologists (RCOG) have declared that 'legal rights of property are not generally founded on genetic identity'.[158] Added to this, Stewart and others have argued that to base ownership on genetics is to logically go one step further and afford the father and siblings (both past and present) rights in the UCB given the shared nature of the genetic information.[159]

If genetics and immunologies make it difficult to assert ownership, does viewing UCB in physiological terms fare any better? Petrini points to the umbilical cord itself – he believes that UCB belongs to the baby because, in his view, the umbilical cord originates from the allantois in the chorion plate,

154 C Witte, 'Cord blood storage, property and liability issues' (2005) 26 *Journal of Legal Medicine* 2, 275–292.

155 S R Munzer, 'The special case of property rights in umbilical cord blood for transplantation' (1999) 51 *Rutgers Law Review* 3, 493–568.

156 Ibid., at 499.

157 D Dickenson, *Property in the Body: Feminist Perspectives* (Cambridge: Cambridge University Press, 2007) p 98.

158 Royal College of Obstetricians and Gynaecologists (RCOG), (2006) 'Umbilical cord blood banking' (Scientific Impact Paper No. 2) www.rcog.org.uk/globalassets/documents/guidelines/scientific-impact-papers/sip_2.pdf

159 Stewart and others, 2013.

the foetal section of the placenta.[160] However, this fails to acknowledge the generation of the blood within the cord. In contrast, Dickenson offers an alternative physiological view, favouring UCB as the mother's property. She states:

> The placenta is part of the mother's body throughout the third stage of labour, remaining attached to the wall of her uterus. When the cord blood produced by the placenta is extracted during that stage, then clearly that blood also comes from the mother and is hers.[161]

While championing the mother as owner when adopting the in-utero method of collection, Dickenson accepts that if UCB is collected via the ex-utero method – that is, after the placenta is expelled from the uterus – then it is arguably abandoned and therefore open to the acquirer to proclaim ownership rights. However, post *Yearworth*, Dickenson's concerns are now likely to be addressed in that like the men's sperm, privately stored UCB is preserved for a specific purpose and is in no way viewed as being abandoned at birth.

In its opinion paper on UCB banking in 2006, the RCOG dedicates section 6.2 to the question, 'Whose blood is it?'[162] They appear emphatic in that this is a question that has not yet been legally answered. In fact, they begin by stating, 'The issue of whose [*sic*] owns cord blood has yet to be tested in the courts' and end the section with, 'Whether or not the child at majority has any rights over their cord blood … stored in a bank by their parent has not been tested.' While the jury is therefore still out on UCB ownership, the College does go as far as to opine that the storage of UCB 'may be the subject of a gift from the mother to her child' and that, '[I]f it is declared to be stored for the child's use', then it will be held on trust for the child and the trustee, 'will probably be the mother'. Taken together, these statements appear to nod towards the mother as owner who gifts it to the child and retains control over it on the child's behalf, acting 'in the best interests of the child'.[163] However, as the opinion of the RCOG is now over ten years old – and their joint statement with the RCM in August 2011 was silent on ownership[164] – only time will tell as to whether their view post *Yearworth* remains the same.

160 Petrini, 2010.
161 Dickenson, 2008 p 58.
162 RCOG, 2006.
163 It should also be noted that rather confusingly, the RCOG (2006) opinion paper also states, 'it seems likely that [the UCB] will be taken to have been the subject of a gift from the mother ***to the bank*** at the time of harvesting' [author's emphasis]. It is assumed here that the RCOG mean this to be read as a 'gift to the child' that is stored within a bank on their behalf rather than a 'gift to the bank' itself.
164 RCOG and RCM, 'RCOG/RCM statement on umbilical cord blood collection and banking' (August 2011) www.rcm.org.uk/sites/default/files/Joint%20Statement%20-%20UCB%20-%20aug%2011%20(6)%20v2.pdf, accessed 12 March 2016.

If the courts should ever need to adjudicate over the disputed use of stored UCB, their role would be to establish with as greater accuracy as possible what the child's wishes would be if they could express them. Taking all the circumstances into account, the courts are likely to take a holistic approach as to whether the unit should remain in storage for the child's future benefit or whether the child would benefit from donating the UCB to another family member, including the fact that the child would not be undergoing an invasive procedure, unlike bone marrow donation. Ultimately, what the courts would deem to be in the child's best interests would be decided on a case-by-case analysis.

I have argued throughout this chapter that in using a property-based model, viewed through the prism of the jurisprudence in *Yearworth*, UCB is capable of being owned by the mother who generates the blood – or as an alternative, produces it alongside the foetus on a developmental basis, which is saved on behalf of the child for the family's intended future use. That said, it is at least arguable that UCB is property for the purposes of a claim for its damage in either negligence, contract or bailment. Akin to the loss of sperm, it is also argued that a claim for mental harm or distress is also possible as a foreseeable consequence of damage to what could potentially be a life-saving resource. Whilst Quigley asserts that a claim for mental harm resulting from the loss of human tissue is unlikely to resonate with the judiciary in the same way as the loss of gametes or attract the same level of damages, it has been argued here that the loss of UCB intended for future private use would be just as mentally damaging, especially for those with an existing sick child or a family history of disease. After all, John Moore only sought rights over his excised spleen once he later became aware of its financial value and could not convincingly claim that he intended to retain the post-operative tissue. In contrast, a mother who saves UCB is acutely aware of its worth and has communicated her intention on contracting with a private bank to ensure her 'peace of mind'.[165]

Essentially, property rights in the body remains a thorny issue and until a UCB-related claim reaches the courts, whether anyone can legally own or assert rights over these valuable cells will continue to be a hypothetical question reserved for those who hold a keen interest. But until such time, it is healthy to engage in academic debate, and as Jordens and others suggest,

> Given that the commentaries arrive at conclusions on this question – and given also that ownership of umbilical cord blood remains an open question in law and that it will be impossible to avoid where it becomes a matter of legal dispute – it would be useful to open up discussion on the

165 Cells4Life online website, 'Searching for peace of mind: one couple's decision to bank cord blood' (6 February 2015) http://cellsforlife.com/searching-peace-mind-one-couples-decision-cord-blood-bank/, accessed 12 March 2016.

> different ways in which the question of property relations *can* be addressed in law.[166]

It is hoped that this chapter's exploration has contributed to the debate and goes some way towards presenting potential arguments in the context of ownership rights over negligently damaged autologous UCB and/or future disputes over its use for pregnant women and their offspring should the need ever arise.

166 C F C Jordens and others, 'Religious perspectives on umbilical cord blood banking' (2012) 19 *Journal of Law, Medicine and Ethics* 497–511.

Concluding remarks

As a strong believer in fate, when my daughter, aged 14, was diagnosed with an aggressive form of thyroid cancer in 2012, I did for one very brief moment think that the reason behind my extremely unlikely 'obsession' with stem cell treatment had just manifested itself. Yet, unlike other blood-forming stem cell resources such as bone marrow and cord blood, her treatment resource was readily available in the form of radioactive iodine (and a rather scary looking isolation unit); and we remain indebted to the pioneers of that particular treatment option and to those who continue to provide her care at the Royal Marsden Hospital today. As a child presenting with a rare adult cancer, she was classed as a 'multi-discipline patient' – a status that commanded a whole host of specialists from different disciplines, all sharing a common interest in an unusual case. As the surgeon removed the offending tumour and her complete thyroid, I did for a fleeting second think of John Moore and his spleen, and then the family of Matthew Farrow as he underwent his life-saving UCB transplant, before re-focusing on the matter at hand and the surgeon's words: 'This is one of our favourite cancers because we have the means to treat it – she will live a long and happy life'. And he was right. Sadly, those in need of a UCB transplant may not be so lucky, particularly if they happen to be from the black or ethnic minority communities.

In spite of the public perception that not enough is being done to preserve UCB for its life-saving and life-enhancing qualities, a view born from the comparatively low number of public banking facilities in the UK compared to those overseas and from the limited number of collecting hospitals, the UK government has not only recognised the value of UCB but has responded to the need to increase its public stocks, demonstrated by its governmental prominence and funding commitment in recent years. We have seen how UCB advocates have fought hard to prove its worth, its remarkable success in treating patients over the past 28 years, and how future possibilities appear grounded in regenerative medicine. Indeed, the continued efforts of the All Party Parliamentary Group on Stem Cell Transplantation must be congratulated for their part in raising awareness about donation and use, and for keeping the topic of UCB on the political agenda. As UCB use continues to go from strength to strength, its role in the foreseeable future of healthcare appears secure.

However, what we have also seen is an even greater need to ensure the cost-effectiveness of its infrastructure and the effective processing of the collected units. Rather than diverting finances towards preserving all UCB, the UK's priority has been to secure quality over quantity by internalising its efforts, streamlining access to registries to decrease waiting times and enhancing the quality of its stocks. As Parliament's response to the e-petition, which gained more than 10,000 signatures in 2014, calling for a greater awareness and availability of UCB donation, shows:

> The Government is committed to improving UK stem cell services and has allocated a total of £12 million to help implement the recommendations of the UK stem cell strategic forum...While an increased cord blood bank size will result in better patient outcomes, the relative value of each added unit diminishes as the inventory expands. On this basis, balancing service quality with cost effectiveness, a bank of 50,000 units was determined as optimal ... there is no scientific or financial case for the routine collection of cord blood.[1]

On addressing the need for a greater number of under-represented HLA-type UCB units, the response stated:

> The Government knows that black, Asian and minority ethnic populations are less likely to find a matched adult stem cell donor. To try to alleviate this, cord blood collection centres have been sited at hospitals in areas of highest ethnic diversity.

Clearly, more needs to be done to encourage UCB donations from the BAME communities to ensure that the current shortfall of units to treat under-represented groups is met, and for the expansion of strategically located collecting hospitals to provide the appropriate means for them to donate.

Sustained efforts in this area as well as increasing our clinical research endeavours to unlock UCB's full potential will help to minimise costs and maximise utility. In July 2015, the Antony Nolan produced the *Destination: Cure* Report[2] calling on the government and NHS England to establish a national stem cell transplantation trials network to provide the infrastructure

1 Parliamentary response to e-petition, 'Petition to increase awareness and availability of umbilical cord donation' (2014) https://petition.parliament.uk/archived/petitions/45622 accessed 12 May 2016.

2 Antony Nolan, 'Destination: Cure – arriving at a better future for people with blood cancer' (2015) www.anthonynolan.org/sites/default/files/670CM_DesinationCureReport_Final_digital.pdf accessed 12 May 2016.

and a centralised knowledge base for research on life-saving new therapies to be shared. Continually improving and sharing our understanding of UCB and the results of clinical advances is of course pivotal to future health discoveries. However, the ability to exploit our ever increasing medical and scientific knowledge for the good of healthcare is rarely delivered in isolation. Rather, with that ability come social, ethical and legal considerations that cannot be ignored. When stem cell technology is used in the context of pregnancy and childbirth and then further blended with a fusion of public/private healthcare provisions – such as we see in UCB use and banking – it is never going to be a problem-free treatment option.

The use of UCB has brought with it a plethora of controversies that have been played out throughout the pages of this book. It has shown how access to UCB can be restricted, how limits on the choice of banking options are imposed, and how altruism and self-interest can be diametrically opposed. It has highlighted not only the benefits of saving this precious resource but also the types of risk factors that pregnant women and UCB facilitators may encounter; and whilst the introduction of regulation has gone some way towards protecting NHS midwives, I have argued that the use of third party agreements still leaves the NHS and its staff in a precarious position.

What then can be done to alleviate the controversies that beset UCB banking? In the interests of cost-effectiveness, both the public and private sectors should seek to further their efforts in driving down the costs of UCB processing and storage to allay public spending concerns, extend choice to a wider audience by making private banking a more affordable option, and expand the mixed-banking option in response to the public versus private debate.

For their part, UCB collection facilitators should continue to 'press for support and unambiguous guidance from their employers to be able to advise women appropriately and prevent commercial companies from using the scarce resources of the NHS',[3] including guidance on procedures that involve the use of third party agreements and to keep up-to-date with the latest advice on UCB banking from authoritative bodies. Post *Montgomery*, health professionals face the challenging task of anticipating what 'a reasonable person in the patient's position' would want to know about the risks they face in healthcare. Clearly, good communication and diligent record-keeping is the key to litigation-avoidance.

In terms of the collection process itself, it may be wise to promote the use of designated areas away from the birthing room for the collection process to take place, as advanced by the RCOG and NICE. This would encourage the use of ex-utero collections and minimise the involvement of the midwife

3 RCM, 'Routine commercial umbilical cord blood collection' (July 2006) *Midwives Magazine* www.rcm.org.uk/news-views-and-analysis/analysis/routine-commercial-umbilical-cord-blood-collection, accessed 12 May 2016.

in third party collection agreements. Moreover, in a rejection of methods advocated by most private banks, but in line with the recommendations of the RCM, delaying cord clamping would encourage greater placental transfer to take place naturally[4] and should be encouraged to ensure that the child is not subjected to potential neurodevelopment difficulties, impaired cognitive abilities or behavioural problems later in life,[5] especially where there is no clinical indication for saving the cells. Also, if early cord clamping is requested by the pregnant woman to obtain optimal UCB, the midwife (whose task it is to clamp the cord), must be confident that the woman is fully aware of the risks. Furthermore, as the choice of private banking is likely to remain an option, there is perhaps a moral obligation on the private industry to work more closely with the NHS to improve its relations with midwives working under a third party agreement with informal collectors. Greater efforts should be made to ensure that, as far as is practicable, midwives and the NHS are protected from litigation for providing a free service for the financial benefit of the private banks.

It would also be prudent for the private industry to continue to reflect upon the contents of its advertising literatures and to strive towards greater transparency of information in order to help potential clients make the right decision for them. In turn, prospective parents seeking UCB banking should look beyond the advertising material of the private banks to avail themselves of unbiased information and factors relevant to their specific needs; and with the help of their healthcare provider, consider their options carefully before reaching a decision. That way, the interests of all parties concerned are most likely to best be served.

4 J N Tolosa and others, 'Mankind's first natural stem cell transplant' (2010) 14 *Journal of Cell Molecular Medicine* 488–495.

5 H Rabe and others, 'Long term follow-up of placental transfusion in full term infants' (2015) 169 *JAMA Pediatrics* 7, 623–624.

Bibliography

Advertising Standards Authority (ASA) 'The CAP Code: The UK Code of Non-broadcast Advertising, Sales Promotion and Direct Marketing' (Edition 12, 2014a) www.cap.org.uk/Advertising-Codes/~/media/Files/CAP/Codes%20CAP%20pdf/The%20CAP%20Code.ashx

ASA, 'ASA ruling on Precious Cells International Ltd' (18 June 2014b) www.asa.org.uk/Rulings/Adjudications/2014/6/Precious-Cells-International-Ltd/SHP_ADJ_252000.aspx#.VjxilK9OeUk

ASA, 'ASA ruling on Smart Cells International' (18 June 2014c) www.asa.org.uk/Rulings/Adjudications/2014/6/Smart-Cells-International-Ltd/SHP_ADJ_258261.aspx#.Vjxkl69OeUk

ASA, 'ASA ruling on Precious Cells International Ltd' (18 February 2015) www.asa.org.uk/Rulings/Adjudications/2015/2/Cells4Life-Group-LLP/SHP_ADJ_259676.aspx#.VjxvPK9OeUk

Alberta Heritage Foundation for Medical Research, *Cord Blood Transplantation* (Canada: University of York, 1996) Technical Note TN3, 6.

J Aleccia, 'Cord blood choice: private fears v public good – parents-to-be must weigh merits amidst barrage of advertising' *MSNBC News* (New York 21 July 2008) www.msnbc.msn.com/id/25723984/

L Amat and others, 'Cord blood collection for banking and the risk of maternal haemorrhage' (2011) 90 *Acta Obstetricia et Gynecologica Scandinavica* 1043–1045.

American Academy of Pediatrics (AAP), 'Cord blood banking for potential future transplantations: subject review' (1999) 104 *Pediatrics* 1, 116.

American Congress of Obstetricians and Gynecologists (ACOG), 'Routine storage of umbilical cord blood for potential future transplantation' *ACOG Committee Opinion No. 183* (Washington DC, 1997).

ACOG, 'Umbilical cord blood banking' *ACOG Committee Opinion No. 399* (Washington DC, 2008).

O Andersson and others, 'Effect of delayed cord clamping on neurodevelopment at 4 months of age: a randomised clinical trial' (2011) 343 *British Medical Journal*.

O Andersson and others, 'Effect of delayed cord clamping on neurodevelopment at 4 years of age: a randomized clinical trial' (2015) 169 *JAMA Pediatrics* 7, 631–638.

Antony Nolan, '365 days. 1,000 chances of life' (28 September 2012) www.anthonynolan.org/news/2012/09/28/365-days-1000-chances-life

Antony Nolan, 'Destination: Cure – arriving at a better future for people with blood cancer' (2015) www.anthonynolan.org/sites/default/files/670CM_Desination CureReport_Final_digital.pdf

Anthony Nolan, 'Frequently asked questions' www.anthonynolan.org/8-ways-you-could-save-life/donate-your-umbilical-cord-blood/frequently-asked-questions

Antony Nolan, 'How we are funded' www.anthonynolan.org/clinicians-and-researchers/cord-blood-services

B A Armson, D S Allan and R F Casper, 'Umbilical cord blood: counselling, collection and banking' (2015) 27 *Journal of Obstetrics and Gynaecology Canada* 9, 832–844.

Audit Scotland, 'Organ Retention Validation Review' (March 2002) www.audit-scotland.gov.uk/docs/health/2001/nr_020314_organ_retention.pdf

J Aznar Lucea, 'Umbilical cord blood banks. Ethical aspects. Public versus private banks' (2012) 23 *Cuadernos de Bioetica* 269–285.

K K Ballen and others, 'Bigger is better: maternal and neonatal predictors of hematopoietic potential of umbilical cord blood units' (2001) 27 *Bone Marrow Transplant* 1, 7.

K K Ballen and others, 'Collection and preservation of cord blood for personal use' (2008) 14 *Biology of Blood Marrow Transplant* 356–363.

K K Ballen, E Gluckman and H E Broxmeyer, 'Umbilical cord blood transplantation: the first 25 years and beyond' (2013) 122 *Blood* 4, 491–498.

K K Ballen, F Verter and J Kurtzberg, 'Umbilical cord blood donation: public or private?' (2015) 50 *Bone Marrow Transplantation* 10, 1271–1278.

J N Barker and others, 'Transplantation of 2 partially HLA-matched umbilical cord blood units to enhance engraftment in adults with hematologic malignancy' (2005) 105 *Blood* 3, 1343.

J N Barker and others, 'Double-unit cord blood (CB) transplantation combined with haplo-identical CD34+ cell-selected PBSC results in 100% CB engraftment with enhanced myeloid recovery' (2013) 122 *Blood* 21.

BBC Science and Nature Documentary, 'Lifeblood' Horizon BBC Two 9pm, 11 October 2001.

J Beard, 'Recent evidence from human and animal studies regarding iron status and infant development' (2006) 137 *Journal of Nutrition* 524S–530S.

A Berger, 'Science commentary: HLA typing' (2001) 322 *British Medical Journal* 218.

F Bertolini and others, 'Placental blood collection: effects on newborns' (1995) 85 *Blood* 11, 3361.

P Bianco and others, 'The meaning, the sense and the significance: translating the science of mesenchymal stem cells into medicine' (2013) 13 *Nature Medicine* 1, 35–42.

H Biggs and S Fovargue, 'Baby mums: who decides?' Conference paper. The Centre for Bioethics and Medical Law Symposium, Lancaster University, 21–22 September 2007.

Biovault Family, 'How will my cord blood be collected?' http://biovaultfamily.com/the-knowledge-centre/cord-blood-banking/?gclid=CjwKEAiAoIK1BRCRiMqphvnlwlwSJAAOebPMZp8NsGFgw6HwwgwVY5-9rcQqMtGjdzsvADA9YLFakxoCwzbw_wcB

Biovault Family, 'Sky Sports F1's Natalie Pinkham chooses Biovault Family' http://biovaultfamily.com/news/sky-sports-f1s-natalie-pinkham-chooses-biovault-family/

P Blackburn, 'Antony Nolan Trust to cut cord on pioneering blood bank' *Nottingham Post* (Nottingham 1 January 2015) www.nottinghampost.com/Charity-cut-cord-pioneering-blood-banks/story-25791882-detail/story.html

H Blacklock and others, 'Volunteer cord blood banking and transplantation' (2005) 118 *New Zealand Medical Journal* 1208.

E Blair and F S Stanley, 'Intrapartum asphyxia: a rare cause of cerebral palsy' (1988) 112 *Journal of Pediatrics* 4, 515–519.

S Boseley, 'Grotesque breach of trust at Alder Hey' *The Guardian Online* (London 29 January 2001) www.guardian.co.uk/society/2001/jan/29/health.alderhey/print

R J Boyle and J Savulescu, 'Ethics of using pre-implantation genetic diagnosis to select a stem cell donor for an existing person' (2001) 323 *British Medical Journal* 1240.

M Brazier, *Medicine, Patients and the Law* (3rd edn, London: Penguin, 2003).

M Brazier and S Fovargue, 'A brief guide to the Human Tissue Act 2004' (2006) 1 *Clinical Ethics* 26.

M Brazier and J Miola, 'Bye-bye Bolam: a medical litigation revolution?' (2000) 8 *Medical Law Review* 85.

P Brice, 'Public-private partnerships for UK cord blood banking' (6 October 2014) *Phg Foundation* www.phgfoundation.org/blog/16332/

N Brown and A Kraft, 'Blood ties: banking the stem cell promise' (2006) 18 *Technology Analysis & Strategic Management* 3, 313–327.

A Browne, 'Six couples seek "ethical" designer babies' *The Guardian Online* (London 24 February 2002) www.theguardian.com/uk/2002/feb/24/medicalscience.genetics

R Brownsword, 'Stem cells, superman, and the report of the select committee' (2002) 65 *Modern Law Review* 568.

H E Broxmeyer and S Cooper, 'High efficiency recovery of immature haematopoietic progenitor cells with extensive proliferative capacity from human cord blood cryopreserved for 10 years' (1997) 107 *Clinical and Experimental Immunology* 107 (Suppl. 1), 45.

H Broxmeyer and others, 'Hematopoietic stem/progenitor cells, generation of induced pluripotent stem cells, and isolation of endothelial progenitors from 21- to 23.5-year cryopreserved cord blood' (2011) 117 *Blood* 18.

BubHub, www.bubhub.com.au/community/forums/showthread.php?453132-Has-anyone-used-their-babies-cord-blood-for-treatment-for-their-baby

G Burgio and F Locatelli (1997) 'Transplant of bone marrow and cord blood hematopoietic stem cells in pediatric practice, revisited according to the fundamental principles of bioethics' 19 *Bone Marrow Transplant* 12, 1163–1168.

D Burrowes (Enfield, Southgate) (Cons) Hansard HC Vol 470 Cols 157–158 (8 January 2008) 'Umbilical cord blood donation'.

D Burrowes (Enfield, Southgate) (Cons) Hansard HC Vol 1480 Cols 1101–1109 (17 October 2008).

H Busby, 'The meanings of consent to the donation of cord blood stem cells: perspectives from an interview-based study of a public cord blood bank in England' (2010) 5 *Empirical Ethics* 22–27.

D Campbell, 'Hospitals warned to delay cutting umbilical cords after birth' *The Guardian Online* (London 11 July 2013) www.theguardian.com/society/2013/jul/11/hospitals-nhs-umbilical-cords-babies-delay-cutting

D Campbell, 'Age UK sounds alarm over cuts to care for older people' *The Guardian* (London 6 March 2014) www.theguardian.com/society/2014/mar/06/age-uk-cuts-to-elderly-care

Careers Advisory Service, 'Phlebotomist' http://careersadvice.direct.gov.uk/helpwithyourcareer/jobprofiles/profiles/profile1472

J Carvel, 'With love at Christmas – a set of stem cells' *The Guardian Online* (London 6 December 2005) www.guardian.co.uk/news/2005/dec/06/topstories3.genetics

N Castle, 'Applying Bolitho' (December 1998) *Journal of Personal Injury Law* 278.

Cells4Life, 'Common misconceptions' www.cells4life.co.uk/common-misconceptions-faq

Cells4Life, 'News' (10 November 2014) www.cells4life.co.uk/news-events/damage-brain-caused-parkinsons-disease-healed-stem-cells

Cells4Life, 'Searching for peace of mind: one couple's decision to bank cord blood' (6 February 2015) http://cellsforlife.com/searching-peace-mind-one-couples-decision-cord-blood-bank/

H C Chang, 'The third way of umbilical cord blood banking' (2014) 12 *Nature Biotechnology* 4.

N J Chao, S G Emerson and K I Weinberg, 'Stem cell transplants (cord blood transplantation)' (2004) 1 *Hematology* 354.

Y Cohen and others, 'Umbilical cord blood collection carry increased maternal bleeding risk during cesarean section' (2012) 25 *The Journal of Maternal-Fetal and Neonatal Medicine* 9, 1549–1551.

H Colleran, 'Irish parents urged to sue HSE over right to cord blood harvesting' (15 June 2009) *Bionews* www.bionews.org.uk/page_46203.asp

Commons Select Committee, 'NHS midwives shortage remains despite increasing numbers' (31 January 2014) www.parliament.uk/business/committees/committees-a-z/commons-select/public-accounts-committee/news/maternity-services-report/

CorCell, 'What are the odds my child will use their cord blood?' www.corcell.com/blog/what-are-the-odds-my-children-will-use-their-cord-blood/

Cordbank, 'Celeb mums who have banked cord blood – Ana Ortiz' www.cordbank.co.nz/celeb-mums-ana-ortiz-cord-blood/

Cord Blood Bank of Canada, http://cordbloodbankofcanada.com/step-2-collect-your-familys-biological-insurance-2/

CorCell, 'The process' www.corcell.com/the-process/

CordLife, www.cordlife.com/news/pdf_articles/Singapore_First_Cerebral_Palsy_treatment.pdf

CORD:USE Foundation (28 February 2015) www.zoominfo.com/CachedPage/?archive_id=0&page_id=5097744653&page_url=//www.cordusefoundation.org/index.php&page_last_updated=2015-02-28T01:55:05&firstName=Matthew&lastName=Farrow

C M Cotton, 'Feasibility of autologous cord blood cells for infants with Hypoxic-ischemic encephalopathy' (2014) 164 *Journal of Pediatrics* 5, 973–979.

Council Directive (EC) 2001/20 on the approximation of the laws, regulations and administrative provisions of the Member States relating to the implementation of good clinical practice in the conduct of clinical trials on medicinal products for human use [2001] OJ L121/ 37–39.

Council Directive (EC) 2004/23 on setting standards of quality for the donation, procurement, testing, processing, preservation, storage and distribution of human tissues and cells [2004] OJ L102.

A Craft, 'What exactly happened in the hospital treating Aysha King?' *The Telegraph Online* (London 5 September 2014) www.telegraph.co.uk/news/health/11078199/What-exactly-happened-in-the-hospital-treating-Aysha-King.html

Cryo-Cell International, 'Cord blood banking' www.cryo-cell.com/cord-blood-banking

Cryo-Cell International,'Frequently asked questions' www.cryo-cell.com/cord-blood/frequently-asked-questions

Cryo-Cell International, 'The banking process' www.smartcells.com/en/list-of-faqs/ is-there-any-chance-of-harm-to-me-or-my-baby.htm

Cryo-Cell International, 'Banking menstrual stem cells' www.cryo-cell.com/menstrual/stem-cells

CryoSave, 'Our process' http://cryo-save.com/en/about-cryo-save/our-process

CryoSave, 'Why save stem cells?' http://cryo-save.com/en/what-are-stem-cells/why-save-stem-cells

CryoSave, www.cryo-save.co.ke/six-year-old-girl-with-cerebral-palsy-treated-with-own-stem-cells-from-cord-blood/

A Curtis and M Leitner, 'Are pregnant women really vulnerable?' *Geographic Information Systems and Public Health – Eliminating of Perinatal Disparity* (Hershey, PA: IRM Press, 2005).

E Danzer and others, 'Attitudes of Swiss mothers toward unrelated umbilical cord blood banking 6 months after donation' (2003) 43 *Transfusion* 604.

S Davey, 'Next generation sequencing – tissue (HLA) typing adult and cord blood stem cell donors for transplantation' (January 2015) 44 *Blood and Transplant Matters* 18–19.

E Davis, 'Cord blood: a weapon against cerebral palsy?' *Los Angeles Times* (Los Angeles 7 April 2008) http://articles.latimes.com/2008/apr/07/health/he-cpalsy7

S Deakin, A Johnston and B Markesinis, *Markesinis and Deakin's Tort Law* (7th edn, Oxford: Oxford University Press, 2013).

G Deal, 'Cord blood banking: charitable, clinical and commercial' (Cambridge 26 January 2012) *Global Regulatory Services* www.globalregulatoryservices.com/blog/cord-blood-banking-charitable-clinical-and-commercial

J DeFao, 'Is it worth banking your baby's cord blood? Doctors say hard sell of hope is deceptive' *San Francisco Chronicle* (San Francisco 20 June 2005) www.sfgate.com/cgi-bin/article.cgi?file=/c/a/2005/06/20/MNG9GDBBLS1.DTL

Department for Constitutional Affairs (DCA), 'Mental Capacity Act 2005 Code of Practice' (TSO, London 2007) www.dca.gov.uk/legal-policy/mental-capacity/mca-cp.pdf

Department of Health (DH), 'Guidelines on consent: reference guide to consent for examination or treatment' (2009) 2nd edn www.gov.uk/government/uploads/system/uploads/attachment_data/file/138296/dh_103653__1_.pdf

K Devine, 'The UK's HTA to regulate the collection of cord blood stem cells' *BioNews* (Progress Educational Trust, 6 May 2008) www.bionews.org.uk/page_13374.asp

K Devine, 'Cord blood collection and cerebral palsy – is there a connection?' *Bionews*

(22 November 2010a, Progress Educational Trust) www.bionews.org.uk/page_82436.asp
K Devine, 'Tying the cord around the midwife's neck: the problem with umbilical cord blood collection' (2010b) 26 *Professional Negligence* 2, 83–95.
K Devine, 'Cord blood in the car park: cord blood stem cells, contamination and DIY collection exposed' *BioNews* (Progress Educational Trust, 16 March 2010c) www.bionews.org.uk/page_55941.asp
K Devine, 'Risky business? The risks and benefits of umbilical cord blood collection' (2010d) 18 *Medical Law Review* 330–362.
K Devine, 'Ethics and choice in healthcare: the case of public v private cord blood banking' in: N Priaulx and A Wrigley (eds), *Ethics, Law and Society* Volume V (Surrey: Ashgate, 2013) pp 55–68.
D Dickenson, *Property in the Body – Feminist Perspectives* (Cambridge: Cambridge University Press, 2007).
D Dickenson, *Body Shopping: The Economy Fuelled by Flesh and Blood* (Oxford: Oneworld Publications, 2008).
D Dickenson, *Me Medicine vs We Medicine: Reclaiming Biotechnology for the Common Good* (New York: Columbia University Press, 2013).
D Dickenson and P Vineis, 'Evidence-based medicine and quality of care' (2002) 10 *Health Care Analysis* (2002) 10, 243.
B Dimond, *Legal Aspects of Midwifery* (4th edn, London: Quay Books, 2013).
H Dinç and N H Şahin, 'Pregnant women's knowledge and attitudes about stem cells and cord blood banking' (2009) 56 *International Nursing Review* 250–256.
M Dobbin, 'Children to receive umbilical cord blood in world first cerebral palsy trial' *The Sydney Morning Herald* (9 March 2016) www.smh.com.au/national/health/children-to-receive-umbilical-cord-blood-in-world-first-cerebral-palsy-trial-20160309-gney2t.html
C Donaldson and others, 'Impact of obstetric factors on cord blood donation for transplantation' (1999) 106 *British Journal of Haematology* 1, 128.
S Donn, 'Medico-legal implications of hypoxic–ischemic birth injury' (2014) 19 *Seminars in foetal and neonatal medicine* 5, 317–321.
M S Dorney, '*Moore v. the Regents of the University of California*: balancing the need for biotechnology innovation against the right of informed consent' (1990) 5 *Berkeley Technology Law Journal* 2, 4.
S Douglas, 'Property rights in human biological material' in: I Goold and others (eds), *Persons, Parts and Property: How Should We Regulate Human Tissue in the 21st Century?* (Oxford: Hart Publishing, 2014a) Chapter 7.
S Douglas, 'The argument for property rights in body parts: scarcity of resources' (2014b) 40 *Journal of Medical Ethics* 23–26.
J Doward, 'Hepatitis C patients in England denied lifesaving liver drug' *The Guardian Online* (London 16 August 2015) www.theguardian.com/society/2015/aug/16/hepatitis-c-patients-england-denied-liver-drug-regulator
J Dreaper, 'Concern over cord blood banking' *BBC News Online* (London 13 May 2005) http://news.bbc.co.uk/1/hi/health/4541515.stm
J Dulaney, 'Born to save her sister's life, Marissa Ayala, now 23, will graduate from CSULB' *Press-Telegram News* (London 21 May 2013) www.presstelegram.com/general-news/20130521/born-to-save-her-sisters-life-marissa-ayala-now-23-will-graduate-from-csulb
K Dutta and K Grant, 'Cuts mean more women denied IVF on the NHS' *The*

Independent (London 15 September 2015) www.independent.co.uk/life-style/health-and-families/health-news/cuts-mean-more-women-are-denied-ivf-on-the-nhs-9733538.html

J L Ecker and M F Greene, 'The case against private umbilical cord blood banking' (2005) 105 *Obstetrics and Gynaecology* 6, 1282–1284.

Editorial, 'New device may make cord blood transplants possible for more adults' (2000) 11 *Blood and Marrow Transplantation* 3 (Newsletter 51).

Editorial, 'Preimplantation donor selection' (2001) 358 *The Lancet* 9289, 1195.

Editorial, 'Designer baby ruling condemned' *BBC News Online* (London 21 July 2002) http://news.bbc.co.uk/1/hi/health/2134314.stm

Editorial, 'Bone marrow appeal' *BBC News Online* (London 10 March 2004) http://news.bbc.co.uk/1/hi/programmes/breakfast/3497042.stm

Editorial, 'The 2-minute treatment that could save my baby's life (20 years from now!)' *The Daily Mail* (London 25 May 2004).

Editorial, 'Pa-pa voom!' *FQ Magazine* (Nov–Dec 2005).

Editorial, 'Need a heart – bank a cell' *The Telegraph* (Calcutta 7 January 2007) www.telegraphindia.com/1070107/asp/insight/story_7215292.asp

Editorial, 'Branson to launch new stem-cell bank' *BBC News Online* (London 1 February 2007) http://news.bbc.co.uk/1/hi/health/6317855.stm

Editorial, 'Branson launches Virgin stem cell bank' (London 1 February 2007) *The Guardian Online* www.theguardian.com/uk/2007/feb/01/science.health

Editorial, 'Umbilical cord blood stem cell banking service – Richard Branson launches Virgin Health Bank' *Medical News Today* (International, 1 February 2007) www.medicalnewstoday.com/articles/62106.php

Editorial, 'Holly Branson quits medicine to work for her billionaire father' *The Mail Online* (London 28 July 2008) www.dailymail.co.uk/news/article-1039174/Holly-Branson-quits-medicine-work-billionaire-father.html

Editorial, 'Why is Kourtney Kardashian carrying around umbilical cord blood?' *Hollywood Life* (9 December 2009) http://hollywoodlife.com/2009/12/09/would-you-save-your-babys-umbilical-chord-blood-like-kourtney-kardashian-intends-to-do/

Editorial, 'Should you save your child's own cord blood?' *CNN News* (30 May 2011) http://edition.cnn.com/2011/HEALTH/05/30/saving.blood.cord.p/

Editorial, 'After our own health scares, it was a no-brainer: Guiliana and Bill Rancic have banked newborn Edward's cord blood' *The Mail Online* (26 September 2012) www.dailymail.co.uk/tvshowbiz/article-2208980/Giuliana-Bill-Rancic-banked-newborn-Edwards-cord-blood.html

Editorial, 'London siblings' bone marrow Twitter plea boosts Jewish donors' *BBC News Online* (London 19 January 2013) www.bbc.co.uk/news/uk-england-london-21089305

Editorial, 'Obese people in Wales "denied" lifesaving treatment' *BBC News Online* (London 25 February 2014) www.bbc.co.uk/news/uk-wales-26334460

Editorial, 'Cancer patients denied "too expensive" drugs' *Sky News Online* (London 15 August 2014) http://news.sky.com/story/1319051/cancer-patients-denied-too-expensive-drug

Editorial, 'Genetic causes of cerebral palsy trump birth causes' (2 June 2015) *Science Daily* www.sciencedaily.com/releases/2015/06/150602074725.htm

L C Edozien, 'NHS maternity units should not encourage commercial banking of umbilical cord blood' (2006) 333 *British Medical Journal* 801.

L Eleftheriou-Smith, 'NHS calls for rare blood donors as O and B negative stocks hit four-year low' *The Independent* (15 March 2014) www.independent.co.uk/life-style/health-and-families/health-news/nhs-calls-for-rare-blood-group-donors-at-o-and-b-negative-stocks-hit-four-year-low-9194378.html

N Ende, 'Cord blood collection: effects on newborns (Medical-Legal)' (1995) 86 *Blood* 12, 4699.

A Epstein and R Ellis, 'Hard labour: the maternity service in crisis' *The Mail Online* (London 11 September 2007) www.dailymail.co.uk/health/article-481102/Hard-labour-The-maternity-service-crisis.html

J L Erickson, D Barry and A Doyle, 'The moral hazards of neoliberalism: lessons from the private insurance industry' (2000) 29 *Economy and Society* 4, 532–558.

M Escobedo-Cousin and others, 'Natural killer cells improve hematopoietic stem cell engraftment by increasing stem cell clonogenicity in vitro and in a humanised mouse model' (2015) 10 *PLoS One* 10.

European Commission, 'Stem cells: therapies for the future?' *European Commission Research DG/Life Sciences Directorates Projects Catalogue* (Brussels 18–19 December 2001) http://ec.europa.eu/research/quality-of-life/stemcells/pdf/projects_en.pdf

European Group on Ethics in Science and New Technologies (EGE) to the European Commission, 'Ethical aspects of umbilical cord blood banking' (Opinion No. 19, March 2004).

EuroStemCell, Factsheet (20 June 2012) 'Mesenchymal stem cells: the "other" bone marrow stem cells' www.eurostemcell.org/factsheet/mesenchymal-stem-cells-other-bone-marrow-stem-cells

M J Evans and M H Kaufman, 'Establishment in culture of pluripotent stem cells from mouse embryos' (1981) 292 *Nature* 154–156.

Excalibur Group, 'Virgin Health Bank' http://excalibur-group.co.uk/portfolio-companies/virgin-health-bank/

D Farrar and others, 'Measuring placental transfusion for term babies: weighing babies with cord intact' (2011) 118 *British Journal of Obstetrics and Gynaecology* 70–75.

V L Ferguson and R B Dobson, 'Bioengineering aspects of the umbilical cord' (2009) 144S *European Journal of Obstetrics & Gynecology and Reproductive Biology* S108–S113.

C V Fernandez and others, 'Knowledge and attitudes of pregnant women with regard to testing, collection and banking of cord blood stem cells' (2003) 168 *Canadian Medical Association Journal* 6.

N M Fisk and others, 'Can routine commercial cord blood banking be scientifically and ethically justified?' (2005) 2 *Plos Medicine* 2 www.ncbi.nlm.nih.gov/pmc/articles/PMC549592/

N M Fisk and R Atun, 'Public-private partnership in cord blood banking' (2008) 336 *British Medical Journal* 642.

N Foraz and C P McGuckin, 'The umbilical cord: a rich and ethical stem cell source to advance regenerative medicine' (2011) 44 *Cell Proliferation* (Suppl 1) 60–69.

C Fox, 'The great clamping debate' (4 April 2013) *Bioscience Technology* www.biosciencetechnology.com/articles/2013/04/great-clamping-debate

N Fox, C Stevens and R Ciubotariu, 'Umbilical cord blood collection: do patients really understand?' (2007) 4 *Journal of Perinatal Medicine* 35.

French National Consultative Ethics Committee for Health and Life Sciences, 'Umbilical cord blood banks for autologous use or for research' (Opinion No. 74, 2002).

C Fung, 'Is altruism a vice?' (1988) 17 *Journal of American Medical Association* 2509.

J Gallagher, 'UK national sperm bank opens for business' *BBC News Online* (London 30 October 2014) www.bbc.co.uk/news/health-29815524

Gamida Cell, (Press Release 9 September 2013) www.gamida-cell.com/press_item.asp?ID=57&t=Gamida-Cell-Announces-the-Successful-Transplantation-of-the-First-Patient-in-The-Company%E2%80%99s-Phase-I/II-Study-of-NiCord%C2%AE-in-a-Single-Cord-Configuration

General Medical Council (GMC), *Good Medical Practice* (London: GMC, 1998).

GMC, 'Consent: patients and doctors making decisions together' (June 2008) www.gmc-uk.org/guidance/ethical_guidance/consent_guidance_index.asp

GMC, 'Supplementary guidance – confidentiality: disclosing information about serious communicable diseases' (September 2009) www.gmc-uk.org/Confidentiality_disclosing_info_serious_commun_diseases_2009.pdf_27493404.pdf

GMC, 'Good medical practice: working with doctors, working for patients' (April 2013) www.gmc-uk.org/static/documents/content/GMP_.pdf

J M Gilmour, 'Patient safety, medical error and tort law: an international comparison' (May 2006) *Health Policy Research Programme, Health Canada* No. 6795-15-203/5760003 www.hc-sc.gc.ca/hcs-sss/alt_formats/hpb-dgps/pdf/pubs/2001-patient-securit-rev-exam/2001-patient-securit-rev-exam-eng.pdf

Gloucestershire NHS Foundation Trust, 'Umbilical cord blood collection for storage of stem cells' (August 2015) Clinical policy A2005 www.gloshospitals.nhs.uk/SharePoint1/Clinical%20Policies/A2005.pdf

E Gluckman and others, 'Outcome of cord blood transplantation from related and unrelated donor: Eurocord Transplant Group and the European Blood and Marrow Transplantation Group' (1997) 337 *New England Journal of Medicine* 373.

I Goold, 'Property or not property? The spectrum of approaches to regulating the use of human bodily material' (2013) 21 *Journal of Law and Medicine* 299.

I Goold and others (eds), *Persons, Parts and Property: How Should We Regulate Human Tissue in the 21st Century?* (Oxford: Hart Publishing, 2014).

Government and Parliament, 'Petition to increase awareness and availability of umbilical cord donation' (February 2014) https://petition.parliament.uk/archived/petitions/45622

L Gragert and others, 'HLA match likelihoods for hematopoietic stem-cell grafts in the U.S. Registry' (2014) 371 *New England Journal of Medicine* 4, 339–348.

M F Grieves and J Wiemels, 'Origins of chromosome translocations in childhood leukaemia' (2003) 3 *Nature Reviews Cancer* 639.

N M Gude and others, 'Growth and function of the normal human placenta' (2004) 114 *Thrombosis Research* 397–407.

A G Guest, *Oxford Essays in Jurisprudence* (Oxford: Oxford University Press, 1961).

G M T Guilcher, C V Fernandez and S Joffe, 'Are hybrid umbilical cord blood banks really the best of both worlds?' (2015) 41 *Journal of Medical Ethics* 272–275.

S Hall, 'Elixir of life claims of cord cell storage firms speculative, mothers-to-be warned' *The Guardian Online* (London 14 June 2006) www.guardian.co.uk/uk/2006/jun/14/health.healthandwellbeing

A Hardie, 'Baby blood bank firms prey on the vulnerable' *The Scotsman* (Scotland 23 February 2005).

D T Harris and I Rogers, 'Umbilical cord blood: a unique source of pluripotent stem cells for regenerative medicine' (2007) 2 *Current Stem Cell Research and Therapy* 4, 301–309.

J W Harris, 'Who owns my body?' (1996a) 16 *Oxford Journal of Legal Studies* 1, 55–84.

J W Harris, *Property and Justice* (Oxford: Oxford University Press, 1996b).

D Hart, 'Supreme Court reverses informed consent ruling: *Sidaway* is dead' *UK Human Rights Blog* (London 13 March 2015) http://ukhumanrightsblog.com/2015/03/13/supreme-court-reverses-informed-consent-ruling-sidaway-is-dead/

HC Session 2006–7 Early Day Motions 'Stem cells and Virgin Health Bank' 797 (6 February 2007).

Health and Social Care (HSC) Board, Directorate of Commissioning (27 February 2015) www.hscboard.hscni.net/consult/Previous%20Consultations/Cord%20Blood%20Bank%20Services/Consultation%20Letter.pdf

J Herring, *Medical Law and Ethics* (5th edn, Oxford: Oxford University Press, 2014).

R Heywood, 'Informed consent through the back door? Case note: *Chester v Afshar* [2004] 41 All ER 587' (2005) 56 *Northern Ireland Legal Quarterly* 2.

R Highfield, 'Umbilical cord blood banks are exploiting parents' *The Telegraph* (London 22 February 2008).

G J Hofmeyr and others, 'Periventricular/intraventricular haemorrhage and umbilical cord clamping. Findings and hypothesis' (1988) 73 *South African Medical Journal* 2, 104.

S Holm, 'Time to reconsider stem cell ethics – the importance of induced pluripotent stem cells' (2008) 34 *Journal of Medical Ethics* 63.

A M Honoré, *Making Law Bind: Essays Legal and Philosophical* (Oxford: Clarendon Press, 1987).

N Hoppe, *Bioequity – Property and the Human Body* (Farnham: Ashgate, 2009)

K Horsey, 'Surrogacy in the UK: Myth busting and reform'. Report of the Surrogacy UK working group on surrogacy law reform (Surrogacy UK, November 2015) www.surrogacyuk.org/Downloads/Surrogacy%20in%20the%20UK%20Report%20FINAL.pdf

K Horsey and E Rackley, *Tort Law* (4th edn, Oxford: Oxford University Press, 2015).

D Howarth, *Textbook on Torts* (London: Butterworths, 2005).

A Hoyle, 'Bone marrow transplant teenager: "I feel angry that my community let me down"' *Telegraph Online* (London 20 October 2014) www.telegraph.co.uk/news/health/11172662/Bone-marrow-transplant-teenager-I-feel-angry-that-my-community-let-me-down.html

HSC Board, 'Consultation on future arrangements to cord blood bank services in Northern Ireland' (March 2015) www.hscboard.hscni.net/consult/Previous%20Consultations/Cord%20Blood%20Bank%20Services/Consultation%20document%20-Cord%20blood%20bank%20services.pdf

HSC Board, 'Minutes of HSC Board meeting' (10 September 2015) Item 127/15 at p 3, www.hscboard.hscni.net/board/meetings/September%202015/Minutes%20-%2010%20September%202015.pdf

A Hubel and others, 'Liquid storage, shipment, and cryopreservation of cord blood' (2004) 44 *Transfusion* 4, 518.

Human Fertilisation and Embryology Authority (HFEA), Code of Practice (8th edn) (2009, Revised April 2015) 'Embryo testing and sex selection' www.hfea.gov.uk/docs/HFEA_Code_of_Practice_8th_Edtion_(Apr_2015).pdf

HFEA, Code of Practice (8th edn) (2009, Revised October 2015) 'Storage of gametes and embryos' Guidance Note 17E www.hfea.gov.uk/docs/HFEA_Code_of_Practice_8th_Edtion_(Oct_2015).pdf

Human Tissue Authority (HTA), 'Directions given under the Human Tissue Act 2004 implementing the Human Tissue (Quality and Safety for Human Application) Regulations 2007' 003/2010 www.hta.gov.uk/sites/default/files/2010-11-12_General_Directions_November_2010.pdf

HTA, 'Code of Practice – import and export of human bodies, body parts and tissue' (May 2007, Code 8) www.tissuebank.it/publicazioni/docUfficiale/Legislazioni Nazionali/LeggeInglese/CodeOfPraticeImportExportHumanBodies.pdf

HTA, 'Guide to quality and safety assurance for human tissue and cells for patient treatment' (12 November 2010) www.hta.gov.uk/sites/default/files/Annex_-_Guide_to_Quality_and_Safety_Assurance_for_Tissues_and_Cells_for_Patient_Treatment.pdf

HTA, 'F&Qs' www.hta.gov.uk/faqs/cord-blood-procurement-faqs#sthash.87t2klqf.dpuf

HTA, 'Code of Practice – research' (Code 9 July 2014 version 14.0).

HTA, 'Code of Practice – consent' (Code 1 July 2014 Version 14.0) www.hta.gov.uk/sites/default/files/Code_of_practice_1_-_Consent.pdf#page=24

HTA, 'Cord blood banking: a guide for parents' (February 2016) www.hta.gov.uk/sites/default/files/Cord%20Blood%20Guide%202016%20230316.pdf

HTA, 'Human Tissue (Scotland) Act 2006: a guide to its implications for NHS Scotland' (Undated) www.hta.gov.uk/sites/default/files/Information_about_HT_(Scotland)_Act.pdf

B Hurwitz, 'How does evidence-based guidance influence determinations of medical negligence?' (2004) 329 *British Medical Journal* 1024

D J R Hutchon (Letter), 'Commercial cord blood banking – immediate cord clamping is not safe' (2006) 333 *British Medical Journal* 919.

D J R Hutchon, 'Concerns about consent, the NICE guidelines regarding resuscitation and early cord clamping' (2015) 11 *Infant* 3.

Insception Lifebank, 'Celebrities banking cord blood' www.insception.com/blog/celebrities-banking-cord-blood/

Insception Lifebank, 'Factsheet' http://parentsguidecordblood.org/docs/FactSheet_Insception.final.pdf

Institute of Medicine of the National Academies, *Establishing a National Hematopoietic Stem Cell Program* (Washington, DC: The National Academies Press, 2005).

C Irvine, 'Midwives deal with three births at once, says expert' *The Telegraph Online* (London 22 September 2008) www.telegraph.co.uk/news/health/3044749/Midwives-deal-with-three-births-at-once-says-expert.html

E Jackson, *Medical Law: Text, Cases and Materials* (3rd edn, Oxford: Oxford University Press, 2013).

T H Jaing, 'Umbilical cord blood: a trustworthy source of multipotent stem cells for regenerative medicine' (2014) 23 *Cell Transplant* 4, 493–496.

A J G M Janssen, 'Informing patients about small risks: a comparative approach' (2006) 13 *European Journal of Health Law* 159.

J Jaroscaka and others, 'Augmentation of umbilical cord blood (UCB) transplantation with ex-vivo expanded UCB cells: results of a phase 1 trial using the Aastrom Replicell system' (2003) 101 *Blood* 5061.

D R Johnson, 'Reflections on the bundle of rights' (2007) 32 *Vermont Law Review* 247–272.

M Johnson, 'Payments to gamete donors: position of the Human Fertilisation and Embryology Authority' (1997) 12 *Human Reproduction* 1839.

E A Jones and others, 'Isolation and characterization of bone marrow multipotential mesenchymal progenitor cells' (2002) 46 *Arthritis Rheumatology* 3349–3360.

M Jones, 'Doctor knows best?' (1984) 100 *Law Quarterly Review* 355.

M A Jones, 'Informed consent and other fairy stories' (1999a) 7 *Modern Law Review* 103.

M A Jones, 'The Bolam test and the reasonable expert' (1999b) 226 *Tort Law Review* 236.

C F C Jordens and others, 'Religious perspectives on umbilical cord blood banking' (2012) 19 *Journal of Law, Medicine and Ethics* 497–511.

D Josefson, 'Couple select healthy embryo to provide stems cells for sister' (2000) 321 *British Medical Journal* 917.

JSB Market Research, 'Complete 2015–16 global cord blood banking industry report' (4 August 2015) www.jsbmarketresearch.com/healthcare-medical/r-complete-global-cord-blood-banking-industry-report-65397

G Katz and others, 'Banking cord blood stem cells: attitude and knowledge of pregnant women in five European countries' (2010) 51 *Transfusion* 3.

I Kennedy, *Treat Me Right: Essays in Medical Law and Ethics* (Oxford: Clarendon Press, 1988).

I Kennedy and A Grubb, *Medical Law Text with Materials* (2nd edn, London: Butterworths, 1994).

N Ketheesan and others, 'Effect of cryopreservation on the immunogenicity of umbilical cord blood stem cells' (2004) 30 *Transfusion and Apheresis Science* 1, 47.

L Kharaboyan and others, 'Understanding umbilical cord blood banking – what women need to know before deciding' (2007) 17 *Women's Health Issues* 277.

S M Kim and others, 'Gene therapy using TRAIL-secreting human umbilical cord blood-derived mesenchymal stem cells against intracranial glioma' (2008) 68 *Cancer Research* 23.

King's College Hospital NHS Foundation Trust, 'Women who give birth at King's College Hospital can save lives by donating cord blood' (14 February 2008) www.kch.nhs.uk/news/archive/2008/women-who-give-birth-at-kings-college-hospital-can-help-save-lives-by-donating-cord-blood/

Z Kmietowicz, 'Couple seeks permission to select an embryo to save a son's life' (2001) 323 *British Medical Journal* 767.

J Kurtzberg and others, 'Placental blood as a source of haematopoietic stem cells for transplantation to unrelated recipients' (1996) 335 *New England Journal of Medicine* 157.

L Lasky and others, 'In utero or ex utero cord blood collection: which is better?' (2002) 42 *Transfusion* 10, 1261.

M J Laughlin and others, 'Hematopoietic engraftment and survival in adult recipients of umbilical-cord blood from unrelated donors' (2001) 344 *New England Journal of Medicine* 24, 1815.

M J Laughlin and others, 'Outcomes after transplantation of cord blood or bone marrow from unrelated donors in adults with leukaemia' (2004) 351 *New England Journal of Medicine* 22, 2265.

J Laurance, 'Branson moves into biotechnology with launch of Virgin stem cell storage bank' *The Independent Online* (London 2 February 2007) www.independent.co.uk/life-style/health-and-wellbeing/health-news/branson-moves-into-biotechnology-with-launch-of-virgin-stem-cell-storage-bank-434714.html

J H Lee and others, 'Percutaneous transplantation of human umbilical cord blood-derived multipotent stem cells in a canine model of spinal cord injury' (2009) 11 *Journal of Neurosurgery: Spine* 6, 749–757.

O K Lee and others, 'Isolation of multipotent mesenchymal stem cell from umbilical cord blood' (2004) 103 *Blood* 5, 1669–1675.

S Lee and others, 'High-resolution donor-recipient HLA matching contributes to the success of unrelated donor marrow transplantation' (2007) 110 *Blood* 13, 4576–4583.

T Levy and I Blickstein, 'Timing of cord clamping revisited' (2006) 34 *Journal of Perinatal Medicine* 4.

LifeCell International, 'Gift of life (umbilical cord blood banking)' on CNN-IBN (published 11 September 2014) *YouTube* www.youtube.com/watch?v=PFkkRs5PlSE

Lifeline, www.lifelinecordblood.com/cgibin/hweb?-A=1866&-V=media

J Liu and others, 'Clinical analysis of the treatment of spinal cord injury with umbilical cord mesenchymal stem cells' (2013) 15 *Cytotherapy* 2, 185–191.

J Locke, *The Second Treatise on Civil Government* (New York: Prometheus Books, 1986).

B Lozoff and others, 'Long-lasting neural and behavioural effects of iron deficiency in infancy' (2006) 64 *Nutrition Reviews* S34–S43.

B Lozoff and others, 'Dose-response relationships between iron deficiency with or without anemia and infant social-emotional behaviour' (2008) 152 *Journal of Pediatrics* 696–702.

B H Lubin and others, 'Cord blood banking for potential future transplantation' (2007) 119 *Pediatrics* 1.

L Machin, N Brown and D McLeod, 'Giving to receive? The right to donate in umbilical cord blood banking stem cell therapies' (2011) 104 *Health Policy* 296–303.

L Machin, N Brown and D McLeod, '"Two's company – three's a crowd": the collection of umbilical cord blood for commercial stem cell banks in England and the midwifery profession' (2012) 28 *Midwifery* 358–365.

K MacLeod and others, 'Pediatric sibling donors of successful and unsuccessful hematopoietic stem cell transplants: a qualitative study of their psychosocial experience' (2003) 28 *Journal of Pediatric Psychology* 4, 223–231.

G Manegold and others, 'Controversies in hybrid banking: attitudes of Swiss public umbilical cord blood donors toward private and public banking' (2011) 284 *Archives of Gynaecology and Obstetrics* 99–104.

W Manger, 'Eastenders star's twins will become life-savers as soon as they're born' *Daily Record* (London 4 August 2015) www.dailyrecord.co.uk/entertainment/celebrity/eastenders-stars-twins-become-life-6189916.

K Mareschi and others, 'Isolation of mesenchymal stem cells: bone marrow versus umbilical cord blood' (2001) 86 *Haematologica* 1099–1100.

D Marian, 'Ethical implications of a new application of pre-implantation diagnosis' (2001) 285 *The Journal of the American Medical Association* 24.

P Martin, N Brown and A Turner, 'Capitalizing hope: the commercial development

of umbilical cord blood stem cell banking' (2008) 27 *New Genetics and Society* 2, 127–143.
J K Mason and G T Laurie, *Mason and McCall Smith's Law and Medical Ethics* (9th edn, Oxford: Oxford University Press, 2013).
M Mauss, *The Gift* (London: Cohen & West, 1966).
S J McDonald and P Middleton, 'Effects of timing of umbilical cord clamping of term infants on maternal and neonatal outcomes (Protocol)' (2003) *Cochrane Database of Systematic Reviews* 1 Art No. CD0040747.
S J McDonald and others, 'Effect of timing of umbilical cord clamping of term infants on maternal and neonatal outcomes' (2013) *Cochrane Database of Systematic Reviews* Art No. CD004074.
C P McGuckin and others, 'Production of stem cells with embryonic characteristics from human umbilical cord blood' (2005) 38 *Cell Proliferation* 245.
C P McGuckin and others, 'Cord blood revelations – the importance of being a first-born girl, big, on time and to a young mother!' (2007) 83 *Early Human Development* 733.
J V McHale, 'Medical malpractice in England – current trends' (2003) 1 *European Journal of Health Law* 135.
C McIvor, *Third Party Liability in Tort* (Oxford: Hart Publishing, 2006).
S McLean and J K Mason, *Legal and Ethical Aspects of Healthcare* (London: Cromwell Press, 2003).
M McLeod, '1000th cord blood donation collected' *Birmingham Women's NHS Foundation Trust* (25 June 2013) www.bwnft.nhs.uk/news/born-lifesavers
J S Mercer, 'Current best evidence: a review of the literature on umbilical cord clamping' (2001) 46 *Journal of Midwifery and Women's Health* 6, 402.
J S Mercer and D A Erickson-Owens, 'Rethinking placental transfusion and cord clamping issues' (2012) 26 *Journal of Perinatal and Neonatal Nursing* 3, 202–217.
B Merz, 'Biotechnology: spleen-rights' *The Economist* (11 August 1990).
E Meyer, K Hanna and K Gebbie, *Cord Blood* (Washington, DC: National Academies Press, 2005).
J Miola, 'On the materiality of risk: paper tigers and panaceas' (2009) 17 *Medical Law Review* 63.
K J Moise, 'Umbilical cord blood stem cells' (2005) 106 *Obstetrics and Gynaecology* 6.
J Montgomery, 'Professional regulation: a gendered phenomenon?' in: S Sheldon and M Thomson (eds), *Feminist Perspectives on Health Care Law* (London: Cavendish Publishing, 1998) pp 33–51.
J Montgomery, *Health Care Law* (2nd edn, Oxford: Oxford University Press, 2003).
A Montrose, 'Is negligence an ethical or sociological concept?' (1958) 21 *Modern Law Review* 259.
G M Morley, 'Premature clamping of the umbilical cord may result in brain damage to newborns' *Mercola.com online website* (8 March 2013) http://articles.mercola.com/sites/articles/archive/2003/03/08/umbilical-cord-part-two.aspx
Mumsnet, www.mumsnet.com/qanda/anthony-nolan
Mumsnet, www.mumsnet.com/Talk/pregnancy/2173940-Cord-blood-donation
S R Munzer, 'An uneasy case of property rights in body parts' (1994) 11 *Social Philosophy and Policy* 2, 259–286.
S R Munzer, 'The special case of property rights in umbilical cord blood for transplantation' (1999) 51 *Rutgers Law Review* 3, 493–568.

S R Munzer and F O Smith, 'Limited property rights in umbilical cord blood for transplantation' (2001) 23 *Journal of Pediatric Hematology* 207–211.

National Institute for Health and Care Excellence (NICE) Guideline [CG190] 'Intrapartum care for healthy women and babies' (December 2014) www.nice.org.uk/guidance/cg190/chapter/1-recommendations

National Institutes of Health (NIH), 'What are induced pluripotent stem cells?' http://stemcells.nih.gov/info/basics/pages/basics10.aspx

National Marrow Donor Program, 'Engraftment: Days 0-30' *Be the Match* https://bethematch.org/for-patients-and-families/getting-a-transplant/engraftment—days-0-30/

National Portrait Gallery, 'National Portrait Gallery shows Mark Quinn's frozen "blood head"' *News Release* (10 September 2009) www.npg.org.uk/about/press/marc-quinn-press.php

D Nelkin, 'Banking on blood: the strange made familiar and the familiar made strange' (1998) 5 *Civilisation* 3, 24.

B Nelson, 'Stem cell banking: lifeline or sub-prime?' *Nature Reports Stem Cells* (13 March 2008) www.nature.com/stemcells/2008/0803/080313/full/stemcells.2008.48.html

K B Nelson and others, 'Neonatal cytokines and coagulation factors in children with cerebral palsy' (1998) 44 *Annals of Neurology* 4, 665.

Netcord-FACT, 'Sixth edition of Netcord-FACT international standards for cord blood collection, banking and release for administration' (2016) www.factweb.org/forms/store/ProductFormPublic/sixth-edition-netcord-fact-international-standards-for-cord-blood-collection-banking-and-release-accefor-administration-free-download

C Newdick, *Who Should We Treat?* (2nd edn, Oxford: Oxford University Press, 2005).

New England Cord Blood Bank, 'What is cord blood?' www.cordbloodbank.com/future_potential_of_stem_cells.html

M D Newman and others, 'Transplantation of human umbilical cord blood cells in the repair of CNS diseases' (2004) 4 *Expert Opinion on Biological Therapy* 2, 121.

NHS Blood and Transplant (NHSBT), 'The future of unrelated donor stem cell transplantation in the UK: a report from the UK stem cell strategic forum' (July 2010) www.nhsbt.nhs.uk/download/uk_stem_cell_strategic_forum_report.pdf

NHSBT, 'Unrelated donor stem cell transplantation in the UK: effective, affordable, sustainable. A report from the UK Stem Cell Strategic Oversight Committee' (November 2014) www.nhsbt.nhs.uk/download/unrelated_donor_stem_cell_transplantation_in_the_uk.pdf

NHSBT, 'Information for donors: tests on your blood' (December 2014) www.blood.co.uk/pdf/tests_on.pdf

NHSBT, 'NHS blood and transplant first in UK to use new generation sequencing for HLA tying bone marrow donors for the British Bone Marrow Registry' (16 February 2015) *NHS Blood and Transplant News* www.nhsbt.nhs.uk/news-and-media/news-articles/news_2015_02_16.asp

NHSBT,'Q&A' www.nhsbt.nhs.uk/bonemarrow/qa/

NHS Choices, 'Blood donation (giving blood) – cord blood donation' www.nhs.uk/Conditions/Blood-donation/Pages/Cordblooddonation.aspx

NHS Cord Blood Bank, 'What the professionals say' www.nhsbt.nhs.uk/cordblood/cordblood/professionals/cristinanavarette/

NHS Cord Blood Bank, 'Public versus private cord blood banks' www.nhsbt.nhs.uk/cordblood/about/publicvprivate/

NHS Cord Blood Bank, 'How to donate' www.nhsbt.nhs.uk/cordblood/howtodonate/canidonate/

NHS Support Federation, 'NHS for sale? Proving NHS privatisation' (undated) http://nhsforsale.info/private-providers/private-provider-profiles-2/virgin.html

H Nicholl, 'Baby tooth bank opens its doors' *Bionews* (Progress Educational Trust, 23 July 2006) www.bionews.org.uk/page_12799.asp

NMC, 'Midwives rules and standards' (2012).

NMC, 'The Code: professional standards of practice and behaviour for nurses and midwives' (January 2015).

Nuffield Council on Bioethics, 'Human tissue: ethical and legal issues' (1995).

Nursing and Midwifery Council (NMC), 'Guidance on record keeping' (London: NMC, 2009).

PacifiCord, http://pacificord.com/1_0_Stem-Cells-Family-Cord-Blood-Bank.php

Parents' Guide to Cord Blood Foundation and Charity, http://parentsguidecord-blood.org/

D Parfit, *Reasons and Persons* (Oxford: Clarendon Press, 1984).

G Parkes, 'Improving the UK stem cell supply chain to ensure better stem cell transplant patient outcomes' (2014) 43 *Blood and Transplant Matters* 5–6.

Parliamentary response to e-petition, 'Petition to increase awareness and availability of umbilical cord donation' (2014) https://petition.parliament.uk/archived/petitions/45622

S D Pattinson, *Medical Law and Ethics* (2nd edn, London: Sweet & Maxwell, 2014).

J M Perlow, 'Intrapartum hypoxic-ischemic cerebral palsy injury and subsequent cerebral palsy: medico-legal issues' (1997) 6 *Pediatrics* 851–859.

C Petrini, 'Umbilical cord blood collection, storage and use: ethical issues' (2010) 8 *Blood Transfusion* 3, 139–148.

L Petz, 'Cord blood transplantation for cure of HIV infections' (2013) 2 *Stem Cells Translational Medicine* 9, 635–637.

S J Pickering and others, 'Pre-implantation genetic diagnosis as a novel source of embryos for stem cell research' (2003) 7 *Reproductive Biomedicine Online* 3, 353–364.

M Porter and I H Kerridge, '"Good mothering" or "good citizenship"? Conflicting values in choosing whether to donate or store umbilical cord blood' (2012) 9 *Bioethical Enquiry* 41–47.

Precious Cells International, (1 March 2016) www.reed.co.uk/jobs/phlebotomist/29090705?utm_source=adzuna&utm_medium=aggregator&utm_campaign=health_medicine&cmpid=124

S J Proctor and others, 'Umbilical cord blood banks in the UK have proved their worth and now deserve a firmer foundation' (2001) 323 *British Medical Journal* 60.

C Propper, 'The demand for private health care in the UK' (2000) 19 *Journal of Health Economics* 6, 855.

ProteanCells, 'Benefits of banking cord blood' http://proteancells.com/why-bank-stem-cells/benefits-of-banking-cord-blood/

P Pushpanathan and J James, 'NHS Blood and Transplant Cord Blood Bank: an update for 2013' (2013) 18 *Blood and Transplant Matters* 17 www.blood.co.uk/pdf/ publications/blood_matters_38.pdf

M Pyrnne, 'Bone marrow donor found for girl, 8, after #pantsonyourhead social media campaign' *The Telegraph Online* (London 14 July 2014) www.guardian.co.uk/technology/2008/dec/15/facebook-transplant-donor-campaign

S Querol and M Torrabadella, 'Session 13: Debate: is umbilical cord blood banking for autologous treatment useful? 0-050 Con' (2012) 27 *Human Reproduction* Supplement 2.

M Quigley, 'Property and the body: applying Honoré' (2007) 33 *Journal of Medical Ethics* 11, 631–634.

M Quigley, 'Property: the future of human tissue. *Jonathan Yearworth and Others v North Bristol NHS Trust* [2009] EWCA Civ 37' (2009) 17 *Medical Law Review* 457–466.

H Rabe and others, 'Long term follow-up of placental transfusion in full term infants' (2015) 169 *JAMA Pediatrics* 7, 623–624.

J Rachels, 'When philosophers shoot from the hip' (1991) 5 *Bioethics* 66.

A Rahmatian, 'Intellectual property and the concept of dematerialised property' in: S Bright (ed), *Modern Studies in Property Law* Vol. 6 (Oxford: Hart Publishing, 2011) pp 361–383.

M Rajnik and others, 'Early cytokine expression induced by hemorrhagic shock in a non-resuscitated rat model' (2001) 49 *Pediatric Research*, 4S and 44A.

N M Reboredo, 'Collection, processing and cryopreservation of umbilical cord blood for unrelated transplantation' (2000) 26 *Bone Marrow Transplant* 1263–1270.

M Redfern, 'The Royal Liverpool Children's Inquiry Report' (2001) www.gov.uk/government/uploads/system/uploads/attachment_data/file/250934/0012_ii.pdf

W Rei, 'Toward a governance structure beyond informed consent: a critical analysis of the popularity of private cord blood banking in Taiwan' (2009) 4 *East Asian Science, Technology and Society: An International Journal* 53–75.

M Roberts, 'A third of NHS contracts awarded to private firms – report' *BBC News Online* (London 10 December 2014) www.bbc.co.uk/news/health-30397329

S Robinson and others, 'Ex-vivo expansion of umbilical cord blood' (2005) 7 *Cytotherapy* 3, 243.

V Rocha and others, 'Graft-versus-host disease in children who have received a cord blood or bone marrow transplant from an HLA-identical sibling' (2000) 342 *The New England Journal of Medicine* 25.

V Rocha and others, 'Double cord blood transplantation: extending the use of unrelated umbilical cord blood cells for patients with hematological diseases' (2010) 23 *Best Practice Research Clinical Haematology* 2, 223–229.

Royal College of General Practitioners, 'Good medical practice for general practitioners' (July 2008) www.rcgp.org.uk/~/media/Files/Revalidation-and CPD/CPD%20Credits%20and%20Appraisal/GoodMedicalPracticeforGPsJuly 2008ashx.ashx

Royal College of Midwives (RCM), 'Position Statement 1: umbilical cord blood collection' (2002) www.rcm.org.uk/news-views-and-analysis/analysis/guidance-paper-1a-commercial-umbilical-cord-blood-collection

RCM, 'Routine commercial umbilical cord blood collection' (July 2006) *Midwives Magazine* www.rcm.org.uk/news-views-and-analysis/analysis/routine-commercial-umbilical-cord-blood-collection

RCM, 'Guidance paper 1a: commercial cord blood collection' (July 2008)

www.rcm.org.uk/news-views-and-analysis/analysis/guidance-paper-1a-commercial-umbilical-cord-blood-collection

Royal College of Obstetricians and Gynaecologists (RCOG), Scientific Impact Paper No. 2, 'Umbilical cord blood banking' (2006) www.rcog.org.uk/globalassets/documents/guidelines/scientific-impact-papers/sip_2.pdf

RCOG, 'Cord blood banking: information for parents' (August 2006) www.nhs.uk/ipgmedia/national/royal%20college%20of%20obstetricians%20and%20gynaecologists/assets/cordbloodbanking-informationforparents.pdf

RCOG, 'RCOG statement on the setting up of the Virgin Health Bank' (1 February 2007) www.rcog.org.uk/en/news/rcog-statement-on-the-setting-up-of-the-virgin-health-bank/

RCOG, 'RCOG statement on cord blood collection' (9 March 2010) www.rcog.org.uk/en/news/rcog-statement-on-cord-blood-collection/

RCOG, Clinical Governance Advice No. 6, 'Obtaining valid consent' (January 2015) www.rcog.org.uk/globalassets/documents/guidelines/clinical-governance-advice/cga6.pdf

RCOG, Scientific Impact Paper No. 14, 'Clamping of the umbilical cord and placental transfusion' (February 2015) www.rcog.org.uk/globalassets/documents/guidelines/scientific-impact-papers/sip-14.pdf

RCOG and Royal College of Midwives (RCM), 'RCOG/RCM statement on umbilical cord blood collection and banking' (2011) www.rcm.org.uk/sites/default/files/Joint%20Statement%20-%20UCB%20-%20aug%2011%20(6)%20v2.pdf

P Rubinstein and others, 'Outcomes among 562 recipients of placental-blood transplants from unrelated donors' (1998) 339 *New England Journal of Medicine* 22, 1565.

S Saigal and others, 'Placental transfusion and hyperbilirubinemia in the premature' (1972) 49 *Pediatrics* 3, 406.

E Salvaterra and others, 'The ethics of cord blood banking in light of ownership, informed consent, and solidarity' (2006) 4 *Cell Preservation Technology* 2, 91–96.

A Samanta and others, 'The role of clinical guidelines in medical negligence litigation: a shift from the Bolam Standard?' (2006) 14 *Medical Law Review* 3, 321.

I Sample, 'Row over cash for women donating eggs' *The Guardian Online* (London 21 February 2007) www.guardian.co.uk/society/2007/feb/21/health.genetics

P Sawyer, 'NHS hospital sells placentas for cosmetic use' *The Telegraph Online* (London 17 May 2008) www.telegraph.co.uk/news/1973229/NHS-hospital-sells-placentas-for-cosmetic-use.html

C Scarler, 'Trust the science and save a child' *The Guardian Online* (London 16 December 2001) www.theguardian.com/education/2001/dec/16/research.highereducation

B Schwartz, 'The social psychology of the gift' (1967) 73 *American Journal of Sociology* 1.

C T Scott, *Stem Cell Now – From the Experiment that Shook the World to the New Politics of Life* (New York: PI Press, 2006).

Scottish Government Health and Social Care Directorates, 'Independent Review Group on Retention of Organs at Post-Mortem: Final Report' (2001) www.sehd.scot.nhs.uk/scotorgrev/Final%20Report/ropm-01.htm

H Screzenmeier and others, 'Worse outcome and more chronic GVHD with peripheral blood progenitor cells than bone marrow in HLA-matched sibling donor transplants for young patients with severe acquired aplastic anemia' (2007) 110 *Blood* 1397–1400.

M Secco and others, 'Mesenchymal stem cells from umbilical cord: do not discard the cord!' (2008) 18 *Neuromuscular Disorders* 17–18.

N Shaikh, 'Fertility watchdog investigates serious IVF mix-ups at London hospital' (Progress Educational Trust, 3 May 2009) *Bionews* www.bionews.org.uk/page_13787.asp

S Sheldon, 'A responsible body of medical men skilled in that particular art: rethinking the Bolam Test', in S Sheldon and M Thomson (eds), *Feminist Perspectives on Health Care Law* (London: Cavendish Publishing, 1998) pp 15–32.

S Sheldon and M Thomson, *Feminist Perspectives on Health Care Law* (London: Cavendish Publishing, 1998)

S Sheldon and S Wilkinson, 'Should selecting saviour siblings be banned?' (2004) 30 *Journal of Medical Ethics* 6, 533–537.

Smart Cells International, 'Our customers' stories' www.smartcells.com/our-customers-and-their-stories/

Smart Cells, www.smartcells.com/blog/2010/11/08/sasha-3-is-infused-with-stem-cells-from-her-own-umbilical-cord-to-treat-cerebral-palsy/

Smart Cells, www.smartcells.com/our-clients-their-stories-kyle-carla-poppleton/

R Smith, 'Re-negotiating medicine's contract with patients' (1998) 316 *British Medical Journal* 7145, 1622.

P Solves and others, 'In-utero or ex-utero cord blood collection: an unresolved question' (2003) 43 *Transfusion* 8, 1174.

R L Sparrow and others, 'Influence of mode of birth and collection on WBC yields of umbilical cord blood units' (2002) 42 *Transfusion* 2, 210.

StemCyte, 'Why save cord blood?' www.stemcyte.com/why-save-cordblood-tissue/

C Stewart and others, 'Ethical and legal issues raised by cord blood banking – the challenges of the new bioeconomy' (2013) 199 *The Medical Journal of Australia* 4, 290–292.

C Stewart and others, 'Public umbilical cord blood banking and Charitable Trusts' in: I Goold and others (eds), *Persons, Parts and Property: How Should We Regulate Human Tissue in the 21st Century?* (Oxford: Hart Publishing, 2014) Chapter 5.

K Sugimoto and others, 'Clinical characteristics of chronic graft-versus-host-disease following umbilical cord blood transplantation for adults (2008) 41 *Bone Marrow Transplant* 729–736.

M Sullivan, P Browett and N Patton, 'Private umbilical cord blood banking: a biological insurance of future benefit' (2005) 118 *New Zealand Medical Journal* 1208.

M Sullivan, 'Banking on cord blood stem cells' (2008) 8 *Nature Reviews Cancer* 823.

B Sun and others, 'Mechanism study for hypoxia induced differentiation insulin-producing cells from umbilical-cord blood-derived mesenchymal stem cells' (2015) *Biomedical and Biophysical Research Communications* http://dx.doi.org/10.1016/j.bbrc.2015.09.047 (in press).

D V Surbeck and others, 'Optimizing cord blood mononuclear cell yield: a randomized comparison of collection before vs after placenta delivery' (1998) 22 *Bone Marrow Transplant* 3, 311.

D V Surbeck and others, 'Umbilical cord blood collection before placental delivery during Caesarean delivery increases cord blood volume and nucleated cell number available for transplantation' (2000) 183 *American Journal of Obstetricians & Gynecology* 1, 218.

G E Switzer and others, 'Understanding donors' motivations: a study of unrelated bone marrow donors' (1997) 45 *Social Science and Medicine* 137.

S Takahashi and others, 'Comparative single-institute analysis of cord blood transplantation from unrelated donors with bone marrow or peripheral blood stem-cell transplants from related donors in adult patients with hematologic malignancies after myeloablative conditioning regimen' (2007) 109 *Blood* 3, 1322.

A Taguchi and others, 'Administration of CD34 cells after stroke enhances neurogenesis via angiogenesis in a mouse model' (2004) 114 *Journal of Clinical Investigation* 3, 330.

M Taylor-Sands, 'Saviour siblings and collective family interests' (2010) 29 *Monash Bioethics Review* 2, 12.1–12.15.

Technopolis Group, 'Cord blood banking in the UK: an international comparison of policy and practice' (2009) www.hematos.com/docs/952_final_ 090114.pdf

S Templeman, 'Stem cell first for cerebral palsy girl' *The Sunday Times Online* (London 7 November 2010) www.thesundaytimes.co.uk/sto/news/article439988.ece

L M Terry, 'The child that might be born' (2002) 32 *Hastings Centre Report* 11.

The Bristol Royal Infirmary Inquiry, 'Learning from Bristol: the report of the public inquiry into children's heart surgery at the Bristol Royal Infirmary 1984–1995' (Cm 5207, 2001).

The Cord Blood Registry, www.cordblood.com/shared-stories

The Council of Europe, 'Umbilical cord blood banking: a guide for parents' (2015) *European Directorate for the Quality of Medicines and Healthcare* www.edqm.eu/sites/default/files/parents_guide_to_umbilical_cord_blood_banking_organ_transplantation_2015.pdf

The Family Planning Association, 'Teenage pregnancy factsheet' (August 2010) www.fpa.org.uk/sites/default/files/teenage-pregnancy-factsheet-august-2010.pdf

The King's Fund, 'Quarterly Monitoring Report' (July 2015) www.gov.uk/government/publications/nhs-foundation-trusts-quarterly-performance-report-quarter-3-201415

The Right Honourable Lord Woolf, 'Are the courts excessively deferential to the medical profession?' (2001) 9 *Medical Law Review* 1.

The Royal College of Surgeons, *Good Surgical Practice* (2014) www.rcseng.ac.uk/standards-and-research/gsp

The Scottish Government, 'Summary: ethnic group demographics, Scotland 2011' www.gov.scot/Topics/People/Equality/Equalities/DataGrid/Ethnicity/EthPopMig

The UK Stem Cell Initiative – Report and Recommendations (November 2005) http://webarchive.nationalarchives.gov.uk/20130107105354/www.dh.gov.uk/prod_consum_dh/groups/dh_digitalassets/@dh/@en/documents/digitalasset/dh_4124088.pdf

I Thornley and others, 'Private cord blood banking: experiences and views of pediatric hematopoietic cell transplantation physicians' (2009) 123 *Pediatrics* 1011–1017.

R Titmuss, *The Gift Relationship* (London: Allen & Unwin, 1971).

J N Tolosa and others, 'Mankind's first natural stem cell transplant' (2010) 14 *Journal of Cell Molecular Medicine* 488–495.

S Trotter, 'Cord blood banking and its implications for midwifery practice: time to review the evidence?' (2008) 18 *Midirs Midwifery Digest* 2, 159.

UK Government, 'Under 18 conception rate in England continues to fall' (24

February 2015) www.gov.uk/government/news/under-18-conception-rate-continues-to-fall-in-england

Umbilical Cord Blood (Donation) Bill 2008 [50] www.publications.parliament.uk/pa/cm200708/cmbills/050/08050.i-i.html

P Vanelli and others, 'Cardiac precursors in human bone marrow and cord blood: in vitro cell cardiogenesis' (2004) 5 *Italian Heart Journal* 5, 384.

P F Van Rheenan and B J Brabin, 'A practical approach to timing cord clamping in resource poor settings' (2006) 333 *British Medical Journal* 954.

T Verina and others, 'Pluripotent possibilities: human umbilical cord blood cell treatment after neonatal brain injury' (2013) 48 *Pediatric Neurology* 5, 346–354.

Y Verlinsky and others, 'Preimplantation diagnosis for Fanconi anemia combined with HLA matching' (2001) 285 *Journal of the American Medical Association* 3130.

ViaCord, 'Benefits of banking: current odds of use' www.viacord.com/healthcare-providers/benefits-of-banking/current-odds-of-use/

ViaCord, http://blog.viacord.com/lillians-story-cerebral-palsy-treated-with-cord-blood/

Virgin Health Bank (VHB), 'FAQs' www.virginhealthbank.com/find-out-more/faqs

VHB, 'Why Virgin Health Bank?' www.virginhealthbank.com/why-virgin-health-bank

R C Wadlow and D L Porter, 'Umbilical cord blood transplantation: where do we stand? (2002) 8 *Biology of Blood and Marrow Transplantation* 637–647.

J Wagner and others, 'Successful transplantation of HLA-matched and HLA-mismatched umbilical cord blood from unrelated donors: analysis of engraftment and acute graft-versus-host disease' (1996) 88 *Blood* 3, 795.

J E Wagner and others, 'Transplantation of unrelated donor umbilical cord blood in 102 patients with malignant and non-malignant diseases: influence of CD34 cell dose and HLA disparity on treatment-related mortality and survival' (2002) 100 *Blood* 1611.

J E Wagner Junior and others, 'One-unit versus two-unit cord-blood transplantation for hematologic cancers' (2014) 371 *New England Journal of Medicine* 18, 1685–1694.

F Walsh, 'The first successful saviour sibling treatment in the UK' *BBC News Online* (21 December 2010) www.bbc.co.uk/news/health-12055034

W Wiktor-Jedrzejczak and others, 'Simultaneous transplantation of three cord blood units in adults with high risk acute leukaemia' (2005) 106 *Blood American Society of Hematology Annual Meeting*, Abstract 5457.

I Wilmut and others, 'Viable offspring derived from fetal and adult mammalian cells' (27 February 1997) 385 *Nature* (Letters) 810–813.

C Witte, 'Cord blood storage, property and liability issues' (2005) 26 *Journal of Legal Medicine* 2, 275–292.

Wordstream, 'Top 20 most expensive keywords in Google AdWords Advertising' www.wordstream.com/articles/most-expensive-keywords

A Wong and others, 'Cord blood collection before and after placental delivery, levels of nucleated cells, haematopoietic progenitor cells, leukocyte subpopulations and macroscopic clots' (2001) 27 *Bone Marrow Transplant* 2, 133.

S Yamamoto and others, 'Quality of long-term cryopreserved umbilical cord blood units for hematopoietic cell transplantation' (2011) 93 *International Journal of Hematology* 1, 93–105.

M Young Choi, S Wong Yeo and K Ho Park, 'Hearing restoration in a deaf animal model with intravenous transplantation of mesenchymal stem cells derived from human umbilical cord blood' (2012) 427 *Biomedical and Biophysical Research Communications* 629–636.

T Ze-Zhong and others, 'Relationship between neonatal polycythemia and brain damage' (2006) 44 *Chinese Journal of Pediatrics* 11, 845–849.

Z J Zhang and others, 'Human umbilical cord blood stem cells and brain-derived neurotrophic factor for optic nerve injury: a biomechanical evaluation' (2015) 10 *Neural Regeneration Research* 7, 1134–1138.

Z Zhilai and others, 'A combination of taxol infusion and human umbilical cord mesenchymal stem cells transplantation for the treatment of rat spinal cord injury' (2012) 24 Brain Research 1481, 79–89.

J Zimmern, 'Consent and autonomy in the Human Tissue Act 2004' (2007) 18 *King's Law Journal* 2, 313.

Index

accreditation bodies 4
advertising *see* private banking
Alder Hey Hospital Inquiry 101
allogeneic transplants 14, 33, 65, 83
altruism motive for donation *see* donors
Antony Nolan (Organisation) 176
Antony Nolan Cell Therapy Centre 64, 65
Antony Nolan Cord Blood Bank 26, 27, 28, 64
Antony Nolan Registry 12
Antony Nolan Research Institute 42
Antony Nolan Trust 25, 64
'application of work and skill' 152
autologous cells: autologous transplants, definition 14; cost/benefit analysis 67; hybrid banking 65, 83; limitations on use 33, 36, 84, 88, 110; ownership rights over negligently damaged cells 174; private banking 32, 36, 128; reduced need 33, 83; risks disclosure 128; usage statistics 33
Ayala, Marissa 22

'Baby Mums' *see Gillick*-competency
bailment 150, 166
BBMR *see* British Bone Marrow Registry (BBMR)
Belfast Cord Blood Bank (BCBB) 29, 65
'best interests' of child 162
black, Asian and minority ethnic (BAME) donor shortage 12, 13
blood banking: accreditation 4; choice of 5; collection process *see* collection process; commercial banking *see* private banking; donors *see* donors; 'mixed banking' *see* hybrid banking; public banking *see* public banking; RCOG advice *see* Royal College of Obstetricians and Gynaecologists (RCOG)
blood banks: about 7, 63; conclusions as to 98; regulation 4
Bolam case 54, 120
Bolitho case 123
bone marrow: amount required for transplant 38; availability problems 12, 25, 35, 82; British Bone Marrow Registry (BBMR) 12; cord blood as alternative 15, 113; engraftment time 39; graft-versus-host disease (GVHD) 16; human leukocyte antigens (HLA) 11; matching requirements 11; multipotent (specialized) mesenchymal stem cells (MSCs) 18; problems with using 11; public banking 63; research 111; treatment by 11; UCB stem cells as alternative 6
Branson, Sir Richard 82
Bristol Royal Infirmary Inquiry 100
British Bone Marrow Registry (BBMR) 12

causation principles 132
Cells4Life 7, 33, 66, 69, 117
Chester case 9, 58, 128
children: 'best interests' of 162; *Gillick*-competency 116, 163; ownership rights of 153, 161, 162, 170
clamping *see* cord clamping
collection process: cell expansion 41; clinical need assessment 31; collecting hospitals, number of 27, 36; conclusions as to 35; cord clamping 43, 55; decision-making

pressures 87; delayed clamping 44, 55; early clamping 44, 55; ethics 21; ex-utero method 40, 49; facilitation of collection 8; formal and informal collectors, relationship 91; informal collectors 90; informed consent *see* informed consent; in-utero method 40, 49; methods 19; not routine 27, 36, 81; PGD technique 19, 23, 36; quality improvements prioritised 30, 36; RCOG advice 121, 140, 177; regulation 8, 20, 52, 87; risks *see* risks; storage methods *see* storage; TT technique 19, 23, 36
commercial storage *see* private banking
competency *see* informed consent
consent *see* informed consent
cord blood: advantages 15; author's premise 5; availability 3, 24, 30, 81; banking *see* blood banking; collection process *see* collection process; content of current study 6; controversies 5, 6; damaged blood *see* damaged cord blood; generation of 157; imported units 31; inventory 3, 30; limitations on use 38; longevity 34; natural killer cells 42; ownership *see* ownership; risks *see* risks; stem cells *see* stem cells; torts 5; transplants *see* transplants; use *see* use of cord blood
cord blood industry *see* blood banking; private banking; public banking
cord clamping: collection process 43; risks 55
cost/benefit analysis, private banking 67
costs: imported cord blood 31; private banking cost/benefit analysis 67; Quality Adjusted Life Years (QALYs) as cost effectiveness measure 30

damaged cord blood: negligence claims 51; ownership 166, 174
decision-making *see* informed consent
disclosure of risks *see* risks
disputed ownership *see* ownership
donors: altruism motive 8, 66, 73, 79, 80; bone marrow *see* donors (bone marrow); consent *see* informed consent; decision-making pressures 86; family reasons 76; motivations 8; 'non-identity principle' 22; self-interest motive 8, 72, 73, 79, 80; sibling donors 20
donors (bone marrow): black, Asian and minority ethnic (BAME) donor shortage 12, 13; database 110; *Gillick*-competency 117; mentally disabled 164; minimum age 117; sibling donors 21; waiting time 15
duty to warn *see* risks

engraftment time 39
European Group on Ethics in Science and New Technologies (EGE) 32
European Society for Blood and Marrow Transplantation (EBMT) 4
European Union Tissues and Cells Directive (EUTCD) 52, 61, 87, 89

Fairchild case 132
Farrow, Matthew 4, 14
foetal blood *see* cord blood
Foundation for the Accreditation of Cellular Therapy (FACT) 4

Gillick-competency 116, 163

haematopoietic stem cells (HSCs) 2
Hashmi family 21
Honoré, Anthony 9, 145, 147, 148, 158, 170
hospitals, cord blood collection *see* collection process
Human Fertilisation and Embryology Authority (HFEA) 20, 21, 73
human leukocyte antigens (HLA) 11
Human Tissue Act 2004, regulatory framework 3, 89
Human Tissue Authority (HTA), regulation by 3, 88
Human Tissue Regulations 2007 3, 8, 52, 61, 88
Human Tissue (Scotland) Act 2006 3
Hussain, Aneesa 13
hybrid banking: advertising 81, 83; allogeneic transplants 83; altruism motive for donation 82; autologous transplants 83; beginnings 81; controversies 83; forms of 65; outside UK 86; public/private collaboration 85; self-interest motive for donation 83; Virgin Health Bank 81

imported cord blood 31
informal collectors: midwives and 91;

qualification 90; third party liability 94; vicarious liability 97
informed consent: about 8, 100; Alder Hey Hospital Inquiry 101; Bristol Royal Infirmary Inquiry 100; competent minors 115; conclusions as to 118; effectiveness of written information 111; *Gillick*-competency 116, 163; guidelines 102; Human Tissue Act 2004 100, 104; information provision 8, 66, 108; knowledge 108; lack of consent 56; patient autonomy 9, 59, 125, 131, 132, 134, 139, 140; as pre-condition for donation 66; process of obtaining 113; regulation 100, 104; role of 103; Scotland 102, 104, 107; understanding 108; Wales 107
International Society for Cellular Therapy (ISCT) 4
inventory *see* storage

John Moore's spleen, case of 151
Joint Accreditation Committee of the International Society for Cellular Therapy (JACIE) 4

legal risks *see* risks
liability: potential 7, 8, 51, 62; third party 94; vicarious 97
'loss of chance' claims 168

marketing *see* private banking, advertising
Medical Research Council (MRC) 1
midwives: collection of cord blood 50, 87; and informal collectors 91; potential liability 7, 61; RCM *see* Royal College of Midwives (RCM); standard of care 54
mixed banking *see* hybrid banking
Montgomery case 9, 59, 134
Moore case *see* John Moore's spleen, case of

Nash, Adam 20
Nash, Molly 20
National Health Service (NHS): cord blood availability 24; facilitation of cord blood collection 8; midwives *see* midwives; NHS Blood and Transplant (NHSBT) services 26, 63, 64, 109, 117; NHS Cord Blood Bank (NHSCBB) 26, 29; potential liability 7, 8; public banking *see* public banking; UK Stem Cell Initiative 2
negligence: application to collection process 8; damaged cells 174; duty of care 54; lack of consent 56; legal harms 51; liability, potential 7, 8, 51, 62; mislabelled UCB units 51; standard of care *see* standard of care in negligence; time limits on claims 53
Netcord 4
NHS *see* National Health Service (NHS)
Nolan, Antony 25
'non-identity principle' 22
Northern Ireland, public banking 29, 65

ownership: about 9, 142; 'application of work and skill' 152; bailment 150, 166; 'best interests' of child 162; 'bundle of rights' 9, 143, 145, 147, 158, 170; child's rights 153, 161, 162, 170; conclusions as to 170; contract claims 166; damaged cord blood 166, 174; disputed rights 162, 174; 'loss of chance' claims 168; mother's rights 147, 148, 150, 153, 155, 160, 161, 168, 170; negligently damaged cells 174; 'no property' rule 143, 144, 153, 154; patient autonomy 142; possessory terms in relation to body 142; potential for legal claims 5; property law model 9, 143, 145, 173; RCOG advice 171, 172; 'right to use' 157

Parfit, Derek 22
patient autonomy *see* informed consent
personal injury claims 51
Pre-implantation genetic diagnosis (PGD) 19, 23, 36
private banking: about 63, 66; advertising 67, 76, 111; Advertising Standards Authority (ASA) regulation 68; autologous cells *see* autologous cells; choice to use 5, 72, 98; claims of benefits of 67; controversies 31, 36, 67, 77; cost/benefit analysis 67; ethics 36; exploitation claims 77; family reasons

76; first UK bank 7; growth of 31; information for clients 109; as insurance/investment 77; limitations on use 33; motivations for use 8, 66, 72, 73, 79, 80; potential need 32; regulation 7; UK banks 66; use of 4; worldwide stocks 66
property *see* ownership
public banking: about 63; Antony Nolan Cord Blood Bank 26, 27, 28, 64; availability problems 34, 36; beginnings 64; Belfast Cord Blood Bank (BCBB) 29, 65; choice to use 5, 72, 98; expansion 5; information for patients 109; motivations for use 8, 66, 72, 73, 80; NHS Cord Blood Bank (NHSCBB) 26, 29, 64; 'postcode lottery' 27; Scottish National Cord Blood Bank (SNCBB) 28; use of 4

Quality Adjusted Life Years (QALYs) 30

RCM *see* Royal College of Midwives (RCM)
RCOG *see* Royal College of Obstetricians and Gynaecologists (RCOG)
'right to use' 157
rights of ownership *see* ownership
risks: about 6, 37; causation 9; cord clamping 55; disclosure 9, 125; duty to warn 9; during labour 7, 8; legal risks 6, 7, 51; liability *see* liability; negligence *see* negligence; practical risks 6, 43; scientific risks 6, 38
Royal College of Midwives (RCM) 24, 33, 43, 55, 63, 92, 98, 121, 172, 178
Royal College of Obstetricians and Gynaecologists (RCOG): collection policy advice 121, 140, 177; cord blood collection statement 88, 98; cord blood information leaflet 109; ownership rights advice 171, 172; UCB banking report 24, 33, 38, 43, 48, 50, 55, 62, 63, 67, 89, 103, 110, 172; Virgin Health Bank statement 84

saviour siblings *see* sibling donors
scientific risks *see* risks
Scotland, informed consent 102, 104, 107
Scottish National Cord Blood Bank (SNCBB) 28
self-interest motive for donation *see* donors
sibling donors 20
Sidaway case 9, 57, 108, 124
standard of care in negligence: about 9, 120; '*Bolam* Test' 54, 121; causation 132; conclusions as to 140; definition of standard 54; risk disclosure 125
stem cells: bone marrow *see* bone marrow; collection *see* collection process; haematopoietic stem cells (HSCs) 2; increased use 2, 6, 35; location at birth of baby 13; longevity 34; multipotent mesenchymal stem cells (MSCs) 18; origins of use 6; pluripotent stem cells 16; regulation 104; regulatory framework 3; scientific and technical advances 1; storage *see* collection process; therapeutic value 17, 35; UCB stem cells *see* stem cells; UK Stem Cell Bank 1; UK Stem Cell Forum 30; UK Stem Cell Initiative 2; UK Stem Cell Strategic Forum 2, 24, 176; UK Stem Cell Strategic Oversight Committee 3, 14, 30
stocks *see* storage
storage: longevity of UCB 34; methods 34; private banking *see* private banking; public banking *see* public banking; Quality Adjusted Life Years (QALYs) as cost effectiveness measure 30; UCB inventory, optimum level 3, 30

Taylor-Sands, Michelle 23
third party liability *see* liability
Tissue Typing (TT) 19, 23, 36
torts: application to collection process 8; cord blood claims 5; negligence *see* negligence
tortuous liability *see* liability
transplants: accreditation 4; allogeneic 14, 33, 65, 83; autologous *see* autologous cells; cell expansion technique 41; engraftment time 39; first successful transplant 4, 14, 16; matching requirements 13; multiple

UCB units techniques 41; scientific and technical advances 35; successful usage 14
TT *see* Tissue Typing (TT)

UCB (umbilical cord blood) *see* cord blood
UCB stem cells *see* stem cells
UK Stem Cell Bank 1
UK Stem Cell Forum 30
UK Stem Cell Initiative 2
UK Stem Cell Strategic Forum 2, 24, 176
UK Stem Cell Strategic Oversight Committee 3, 14, 30
under 16s ('Baby Mums') *see Gillick*-competency
United States: bone marrow matching problems 12; collection risks 58; cord blood ownership 149, 164, 167; cord blood stem cell research 13; health care provision 80; informed consent 125; John Moore's spleen, case of 151; private banking, potential need 32
use of cord blood: about 11; 'application of work and skill' 152; 'right to use' 157

vicarious liability *see* liability
Virgin Health Bank 81

Wales, informed consent 107
warning of risks *see* risks
Whiston case 53

Yearworth case 9, 157, 165, 166

For Product Safety Concerns and Information please contact our EU representative GPSR@taylorandfrancis.com Taylor & Francis Verlag GmbH, Kaufingerstraße 24, 80331 München, Germany

Batch number: 10725973

Printed by Printforce, the Netherlands